How Was China?

Views and Vignettes from a Chinese Women's College

Dodie Johnston

Thanks for your comments, Ann.

Dodie Johnston
9/27/17

ISBN-13: 978-1523337521
ISBN-10: 1523337524

Paper cutting of old Hwa Nan College on front cover: Zhou Yan
Cover Design: Baxter Graphic Design
Book Design: Red Earth Writing

First Edition
PRINTED IN THE UNITED STATES OF AMERICA

You cannot open a book without learning something.

Confucius (551-479 BCE)

Knowing about others is intelligence;
knowing yourself is true wisdom.

Lao Tzu (601-531 BCE)

Thousands of candles can be lighted from a single candle,
and the life of the candle will not be shortened.
Happiness never decreases by being shared.

The Buddha (circa 500 BCE)

AUTHOR'S NOTE

That the Chinese language can possibly be translated and represented in alphabetic phonemes seems like a linguistic miracle to me and is far beyond my ability to explain here (or anywhere else, for that matter). It is the oldest continuous language in the world. The written language uses logographic script or characters, and the spoken language complicates things further by using four different tones to convey four different meanings to a character. Individual characters do not necessarily represent a syllable or a word in English and there are hundreds of different dialects.

What I *can* explain is why I spell the name of China's most famous leader Mao Tse-tung in the early chapters and Mao Zedong in the later chapters. The same goes for place names like Foochow (later Fuzhou) and Fukien (Fujian) and dynasties like Ch'ing (later Qing). Here's my rationale:

Many different systems were attempted in the effort to "Romanize" or convert the sounds and characters of Mandarin Chinese or Putonghua into alphabetical phonemes. When the story of Hwa Nan College begins, the Wade-Giles system of Romanization was commonly used to spell place and family names. The Wade-Giles system (developed by a British diplomat and his colleague, probably trying to avoid an international incident due to incorrect pronunciation) required the use of a confusing number of pronunciation marks per word. The Yale system, using more familiar English phonetic spelling, followed in the early 1940s. Both were associated with Western intrusion into Chinese business. Therefore, soon after taking power in 1949, Mao charged a committee with the task of developing a Chinese-generated system of Romanization for written translations. After prolonged consideration of multiple issues, the State Council officially adopted the Hanyu Pinyin system in the late 1970s.

To keep the flavor of the period of history being described I chose to use the old spellings of place and family names in the early chapters, shifting to Pinyin in the later chapters. I apologize for any confusion this causes to the reader.

I created names for many of the individuals in this book to protect their identity. Even though I tried to choose suitable names, my choices may still cause some displeasure, as Chinese names convey subtle status implications and often change with the maturity of the person to whom they are given. Surnames are always placed first but after that there is disagreement about whether a given name of two syllables should be one word, separated by a hyphen, or separated and capitalized. More apologies. I am sure to go wrong somewhere. The nuances of the Chinese language, its contextual variations and idiomatic mysteries have been pitfalls to countless westerners over the years. I am just another individual in that unrefined mob.

Contents

How Was China?

*Views and Vignettes from a
Chinese Women's College*

Prologue – Overview

*A good traveler has no fixed plans, and is not intent on
arriving.*
Lao Tzu

"How was China?" This frequently heard query bumped
and fluttered around me like a moth around a candle each
time I returned from Asia during the first decade of the 21st
century. Only three words, but what a huge question! The
scope of possibilities from which I could draw my answer
was vast. Furthermore, I knew that most of my curious
friends only wanted two or three sentences that summed up
the experience simply and neatly. I knew that social
convention dictated that the answer to that question be brief,
not too self-disclosing and preferably upbeat, similar to the
ubiquitous "How are you?". If anyone answered those kinds
of questions honestly and in depth, they were in danger of
demonstrating a lack of boundaries, a poor understanding of
social conventions or worse yet: being a bore.

So how to reply with an honest, inclusive answer that
summarized the breadth and intensity of my experience
teaching and traveling in China? Wasn't it my responsibility
to paint an accurate and vivid picture of the charm of my
students, the complexity of their history, and the astonishing
changes I'd witnessed during my five alternating years there?
Experimenting with different responses often left me feeling
my answers were too weighty or too glib, too pithy or too
frivolous. Long letters written to friends at home each year I
spent in the People's Republic gave the recipients a wider
view, but I yearned to share more of what I had learned living

and teaching in China with a wider audience. Most Americans wore clothes made in China, read about Chinese high-level economics and politics in the news media and marveled at their stunning performance in the 2008 Olympic Games. Overseas travelers joined tours that took them to the Great Wall, the terracotta soldiers in Xian, the towering stone spires of Guilin. But what did Americans know about ordinary Chinese people living everyday lives in a rapidly changing society?

Eventually, I decided to write a book. How else could I answer the question "How was China?" with integrity? This collection of stories, histories, and viewpoints is the result. It is drawn from explorations and observations made during my ten years in and out of China, 2000 to 2011. It weaves together the changes I witnessed during that decade, with a broader view of how that change is played out in the lives of friends and colleagues.

The views I offer are drawn from my experience as a teacher at a small vocational college for women in the mid-sized city of Fuzhou on the eastern coast. The history of that school forms another thread of the narrative, projecting an even longer view of events in China over the last century. Men may be partners in these stories, but women are the heroines, villains, successes, and failures. And in the process of weaving this narrative from history, my views of daily life, and a closer look at the personal stories of Chinese students and friends, I discovered how being in China changed my view of myself.

The stories are composed of rambles through the street life of my neighborhood as well as wider travels in the countryside. It includes a picture of the historical context that led to the birth, death and later resurrection of this unique women's college. Some chapters feature close-up views of the lives of my young adult students and Chinese teaching colleagues. My continuing correspondence with graduates and young faculty, who now balance work, husbands, and children, provides a look into the evolution of working professional women in Chinese society. Mostly, it chronicles events observed over a thin slice of history by an ordinary person from one culture meeting ordinary people from another. Perhaps it is in these acts of daily life we can best recognize our mutual humanity, and come to a deeper understanding of each other and ourselves.

My adventure began auspiciously.

"Please accept this small gift of 50 yuan," said the well-dressed Chinese gentleman in the San Francisco airport check-in line as he gave me a stiff pink bill. He had overheard the anxious farewell conversation I imposed on my son every single time I took off on a long flight to a strange country: *Why am I doing this? I don't know the language, don't have much emergency money, don't know a soul there, I'm going to miss my family and friends terribly.*

"This will get you through the first day," the man assured me as I gazed at him in amazement. If this was an example of Chinese hospitality, I could leave my anxiety at the gate.

In Chinese currency, officially named *renminbi* (People's Money), and often referred to as *yuan*, 50 Y equals about $8 US. His gift was of good use to me when a wing-rattling flight through the edge of a typhoon forced my plane to remain grounded for 24 hours in Shanghai. In the year 2000, very little English was spoken in China, even by flight staff. I had no choice but to trustingly follow my babbling Chinese seatmates into a bus, to a hotel, down to breakfast the next morning, and back to the airport, guided mostly by their gestures and goodwill. Another short flight south took me to my destination: the ancient city of Fuzhou, a few miles up the Min River from the East China Sea. Behind the grim faces of the stamp-happy customs officers, I was relieved to spot a small banner proclaiming "Welcome You Dodie to Hwa Nan" held by several smiling Asian women and one Westerner.

Without the benefit of teaching credentials or ESL certification, I had come to join the faculty at Hwa Nan College for Women in the People's Republic of China. My fascination with China began in 1962, when I met an Army Security Agency recruit and later hopped a freighter on its way to the Orient where I married him. He and his buddies had been steeped in things Chinese at the Monterey Language School and sent overseas to eavesdrop on radio broadcasts from the secretive People's Republic. After Mike's discharge we made friends in Taiwan and I spent a summer on the edges of their conversations in Putonghua[1] and English about the intriguing changes being made to the whole structure of society on the mysterious Chinese mainland under Communist rule. The conversations continued when two of those friends immigrated to the US and moved in with us in our garret apartment in San Francisco. Each word made me more curious about the new culture being built across the Pacific.

Forty years later, the husband had become a friend instead of a spouse, our children had grown, and China had

---

[1] Putonghua is the official language of the People's Republic of China. Mandarin is the word the early Western traders used for the language spoken by northern Chinese officials and is still in common use today. There are subtle differences but they can be used interchangeably.

gone through several transformations. Slowly its foreign policy gates were swinging open wider and wider. Opportunities abounded. An article about teaching in China in a professional journal ignited the embers that had been smoldering in me since the 60s, and I applied for a position in a rare educational setting, a private vocational college for women.

Now here I was, being bundled into the old white college van by the welcoming committee. I searched in vain for a seat belt as we careened through villages full of half-built brick and concrete houses toward Fuzhou, a port city of over three million people. Fuzhou is located in the mountainous province of Fujian, halfway between Shanghai and Hong Kong. And here I would live for the next nine months in a dorm with twelve other teachers from America, England, and Australia. The neighborhood would delight my senses with its markets and street life; the students would delight my heart with their youthful openness and bright dreams.

I was eager, optimistic—and completely unprepared for teaching two groups of 35 students in classes meeting three times a week. I was also assigned to lead smaller conversation groups once a week in which the object was to practice the English we'd covered in class by chatting together. Like the other "foreign experts," I was expected to make my own materials, borrow old textbooks left behind by former teachers, and tap Internet resources to build my own unique curriculum. At that time, there was little intra-department consistency, no collaborative planning toward a uniform goal. Incoming students had been instructed in basic English vocabulary through high school using the Chinese educational style of "memorize-and-repeat," but they could not answer unscripted questions nor carry on a conversation. My challenge was to get them talking.

At the core of the challenge was the students' terror of speaking to a teacher, conversing with a foreigner, or interacting with non-family members. In September 2000, foreign visitors to Fuzhou were few, access to the Internet was limited, and families were insular. Most large universities had one or two foreign teachers; little Hwa Nan College had twelve. We were viewed as exotic creatures, envoys from a world of consumer goods and glamour the students glimpsed only in movies and TV. My background as a school psychologist meant I had spent a lot of time *in* schools, but never actually taught a class. It was a toss-up as to who would be more ill-at-ease as the semester began, the teacher or the students.

Once we all relaxed, talk they did! I heard folktales and family histories, tales of romance and ruin, of dreams and disappointments. The Chinese faculty had their own stories of recent marriages and new babies and the difficulties of working with foreigners who didn't understand the subtle play of relational hierarchies within a Chinese culture. At first there was distance, but as the months went on, we became close. Some frightened students from the countryside wept nervously during the first classes when their blue-eyed foreign teacher walked around the room and addressed each of them personally, requiring interaction. By June 2001 as my train chugged out of the Fuzhou rail station, they wept tears of genuine grief born of the bonds we had forged together.

Years passed. We corresponded; they encouraged my return. I did return in 2002, then in 2004, 2008, and 2011. Each time, I found the students had changed, the school had changed, and Fuzhou had changed, reflecting a nationwide acceleration. "You cannot step into the same river twice," cautioned the Greek philosopher Heraclitus. True in 500 BC Greece; true in China today.

My time there spanned only a decade, but the upheavals in the college, the neighborhood, and most of all, the students, were seismic. In 2000, pony-tailed girls came to class in clothes that looked ordered from a 1950s Montgomery Ward catalog. In 2011, their counterparts might arrive in shorts and boots with dyed hair and makeup. During that decade, wrecking crews worked day and night in the old neighborhood, smashing the ancient walls and tiled roofs of labyrinthine compounds, replacing them with high-rise apartment buildings of concrete and steel. The college itself has moved to a huge 'university village' 45 minutes out of town, part of a countrywide effort to contain the energy of higher education in a centralized, easy-to-manage location.

Today's media sources are peppered with opinions and speculations about China, mostly related to economic growth or government policies, often tinged with amazement, and sometimes with alarm. Once a recipient of foreign aid, China's economic miracle has caused its benefactors to reevaluate and reduce contributions. When I was a child, American boys and girls found dawdling over their dinners were admonished to "think of the starving Chinese children." In the 21st century, these grown children might now partner prosperous joint ventures with Chinese peers. Charities that sent money and volunteers a decade ago have departed for more destitute destinations. "The Chinese" are often referred to as if they were a billion-person mass, multiplying like guppies, thriving like crab grass, and changing shape as one, like a flock of starlings. But even though the majority of its citizens are ethnic Han descendants, there are as many economic and geographic differences in China as exist between New York City and Nome, Alaska.

This book is about some of those people. It is not a political commentary, economic analysis, nor academic tome. It is an opportunity for the reader to accompany me as I become acquainted with daily life in China, as I look around my neighborhood, hear about the lives of my colleagues, ponder what delighted and appalled me about the place. There are personal stories from the lives of friends I made in China that illuminate some of the challenges of its citizens, particularly women. Some chapters are memoir while others are essays, combining research and observation. I have included four short chapters of history, so that the reader will have some knowledge of the social and political framework from which these stories evolved.

Most of the characters' names have been changed except those of the "Old Ladies" and other important figures in history. An unfulfilled desire to be an anthropologist infused my daily observations with speculations about cultural context. My own prejudices and perspectives have colored the details but these are true tales, filtered through my decisions about what to include and what to leave out. Sometimes the stories were heard secondhand. Some are presented in a composite that mixes and blurs the identities of specific incidents or individuals. Although I have tried to be accurate in my coverage of historical events, I have been inventive with the characters, imagining internal conversations, putting words in their mouths that I think they might have said, changing identifying attributes. It is a work of creative nonfiction.

Carrying the history of China's last century on her back is the Grande Dame herself, Hwa Nan College for Women. From 1908 until the late 1940s the College offered previously unheard of opportunities to aspiring females of Fujian Province, not to mention a sense of adventure to the American women who came to teach there. Shut down after the Communists took power in 1949, the college lived only in the memory of its graduates through the famine years following Mao's "Liberation," and through the howling fury of the Great Proletarian Cultural Revolution (1966-76). When damaged schools were finally reopened and disgraced teachers were reinstated, those memories revived (more about all of this in the history chapters). Cautiously, former classmates of old Hwa Nan College arranged a reunion. As fond memories were rekindled, a new flame began to burn: what if they could recreate their unique experience as students of a women's college to meet the emerging needs of a new China in the1980s? What about a more modest and completely secular Hwa Nan College for Women than the one inaugurated in 1908? Eventually, on inspiration and a shoestring, they *did* reinvent the college, in the old foreign trade sector of Fuzhou, not far from where the original campus still stands in stony grandeur.

Hwa Nan College provides the historical backdrop, the observational platform, and the launching pad for the people in this book. A radical institution at her birth when the notion of female education was revolutionary, she has ascended and gone extinct, been resurrected, shape-shifted, and relocated. She now hangs out with a snazzy new crowd of colleges in

9

University Village, following a central government decision to group all institutions of higher learning on the outskirts of urban centers. I don't like her as well, but she must assume the cultural markings of the time in which she finds herself in order to survive. When I left there were rumors that boys might be admitted to the exclusively feminine campus for financial reasons.

Whether you read for pleasure, enlightenment, or escape, I hope this collection of historical vignettes, on-site observations and personal stories gives a closer look at how the flux in China has affected the everyday life of individuals in a particular time and place. Yes, names have been changed, background information consolidated, exact wording of conversations have been imagined, but the core stories are authentic.

Being on a Chinese campus in a growing city, even for a blink of its history, allowed me to observe eye-popping changes; writing about it helped me understand more deeply the effect of these cultural shifts on individuals, including myself. Knowing these people, sharing their lives, observing their

losses and gains, changed me as well. "Change is inevitable. Change is constant," declared the British statesman Benjamin Disraeli, in the 1800s. There is no place change is more inevitable or constant than China in the 21st century, both for those who are born there and for people from afar who stay awhile.

I invite you to accept a traditional welcome, complete with a string of lit firecrackers, held by one of my village hosts in the picture (previous page). Come along with me and watch as the stories unfold.

Chapter 1: Looking Around – Views from the Neighborhood

*"Every wakeful step, every mindful act,
is the direct path to awakening."*
The Buddha

It's 5:30 a.m. and I am enjoying a rare Chinese experience: silence. Even in September the humidity settles around me like a damp blanket. I toss aside the crumpled sheet and hurry down the hall to perform a hasty toilette in the dingy shared bathroom of the old merchant's house that has become Hwa Nan College's foreign teachers' dorm. I tiptoe past the rooms of my still-sleeping colleagues, and down two flights of stairs before quietly sliding the bolt on the black iron gate and slipping into the empty street.

I've only been in Fuzhou a week and these early morning rambles give me an opportunity to become familiar with my new neighborhood as it awakes. Soon the bamboo brooms of street sweepers who push their wooden carts up and down the hills of Nan Tai Island will begin scritching–scritching against the cobblestones. The sound of Chinese throats hawking and spitting will follow, then neighbors emerging from ancient wooden doors will call to each other in their quacky Fuzhou dialect. Putonghua is the official spoken language of the People's Republic but local dialects are still used to fuse village loyalties and strengthen the bonds of family origins.

I skirt the high white washed walls of the current campus located on a hilltop of the tiny Island. Across Liberation Bridge over the Min River lies the modern business center of Fuzhou gleaming in the morning sun. The city lies within the Coastal Development Area established in the mid-80s to attract foreign capital with export-oriented products and special tax incentives. Here on the island, it is cooler because of the shade of overhanging banyan trees and the up-river winds. I can understand why this breezy location had attracted western merchants and missionaries who flocked to China in the late 1800's after the Opium Wars.

The Chinese waged their own war against narcotics more than a century before Richard Nixon issued his declaration of the "War on Drugs" in 1971. The so-called Opium Wars (1839-42 and 1856-60) had originally erupted in protest to the introduction of large quantities of opium into China by British merchants eager to acquire the teas and silks of China. Grown in the poppy fields of British India, it was cheap to pick up sailing east and easy to sell to Chinese trapped and miserable in the oppressive Ch'ing dynasty social structure. When concerned Chinese leaders spoke out against the practice, British guns spoke louder. The antiquarian Chinese navy was no match for the British fleet and the importing of opium expanded under the victors' new dominance. China was defeated again in 1860 by allied European forces, all wanting to increase their imports of silks, porcelain and teas, as well as to create a demand for some sort of export to China. More and broader concessions were demanded by France, Germany, the U.S. and England, including unrestricted access and territorial rights to several key Chinese port cities. Foochow (now Fuzhou) was one. Missionaries followed merchants to engage in their own form of commerce, converting heathen souls to Christianity, often through medical centers and schools.

Hwa Nan College for Women was such a school. Originally constructed in 1908, the elegantly designed college thrived for over 40 years as a well-funded version of the campus on which I had come to teach and live. Because of its taint of western missionary origins, the college was closed, all foreign teachers expelled and all assets frozen after the establishment of the People's Republic of China. Its demise was presumed final but presumptions are sometimes incorrect. One should never underestimate the strength of feminine determination, as this unfolding story will reveal.

As I walk, the morning sun begins to illuminate grand European-style buildings that had once sprung up beside mud-walled hovels in the early 1900s, reflecting a new community of both wealth and poverty, Chinese and Europeans. Today the architecture crumbles in neglected splendor. Tiles dangle from curved rooftops, balconies sag ominously but most structures still house generations of oldsters, younger adults and children that make up the traditional Chinese family.

Modern Fuzhou, with its skyscrapers and neon lighting, occupies mainland on the north side of the Min River, leaving the buildings of Nan Ti Island slumping and crumbling like an old person asleep on a broken down bench. I will live in this ancient neighborhood for this 2000-2001 school year, and eventually several more, watching with awe the seismic changes that shake the scene from year to year. I miss my family and friends most deeply in the mornings before my busy days begin, and exploring the neighborhood at dawn is a distracting cure for homesickness. My route is full of intriguing sounds and sights and smells—come on along!

At 6:00 a.m. sharp, music from the nearby dance pavilion is added to the sensory mix. Early risers waltz to "Mocking Bird Hill" or "It Came upon a Midnight Clear" before going off to work in office cubicles or downtown shops. The pavilion is dark and subterranean, lit only by twinkle lights. Cubbyholes full of street shoes line the entry way and a hostess beckons us to join the twirling couples.

Dance music is soon drowned out by patriotic march music from rooftop loudspeakers awaken sleepy students, and the counting for calisthenics saturates the remaining air space: *"yi! er! san! si!"* A few minutes later, men and women of all ages begin to gather in the neighborhood park for tai qi and other exercises of rhythm and concentration, waving red fans or thrusting plastic swords.

Early morning is the time when China is the most Chinese. Later these folks may don suits for the office or school uniforms or hospital scrubs, but 6:00 in the morning is the time when ancient habits and behaviors become visible as part of the awakening street life. There is little concern for privacy in the old neighborhood, so we are free to peek into arched courtyards and crooked alleyways. And we do, politely greeting people we meet with *Zao sheng hao!* Good morning!

Men hang bamboo birdcages on tree limbs or hooks in a rock wall. Owning caged magpies or mockingbirds is a guy thing in China; near the campus is a grassy area where the

 men congregate weekend mornings to compare their feathered pets' plumages and songs. Women burn paper money to insure their ancestors' financial

well-being in the hereafter or to request a special favor of the gods. Pushcarts and makeshift kitchens begin to arrive, filling the air with the smell of frying onion-and-oyster omelets (previous page). Squatting women call "*Yao, bu yao*", urging us to buy clutches of frogs with feet bound in raffia or live chickens they hold upside down by scaly yellow legs. Others preside over mountains of cabbage and bok choy grown in plots of land on the city's edge, and sea creatures kept alive in aerated plastic buckets.

Many street markets are being banned as motor vehicles gain dominance of the city streets, so carts and stalls can appear and disappear like magician's props. Every mango peddler and flower vendor has a cell phone in his or her basket to let colleagues know from blocks away when the market police are on the prowl. When that call comes, street sellers spring into action: crones roll up mats of pungent herbs and duck into nearby shops, men hoist baskets of cabbages onto their shoulders and trot around the corner.

We stop to listen to an old man play eerie melodies on his *erhu*, a two-stringed instrument with python skin covering the sound box. His favored spot is a low stone wall between a grove of graceful bamboo and a smelly public lavatory. Many of the ancient buildings have no indoor plumbing; water is hauled from the communal spigot, and lidded plastic buckets suffice as toilets. Avoid walking the same street at the end of the day when the "honey bucket" collectors pull their reeking carts from door-to-door to collect the day's waste and deliver it to outlying vegetable gardens to be used as fertilizer! This is one of the reasons raw foods are taboo and veggies are stir-fried quickly at high temperatures.

We are out early today so we have time to head downhill under the draping air roots of ancient banyan trees overhanging narrow lanes, originally footpaths, bounded by high rock walls and grilled gates. Time also to admire a dilapidated stone church built by missionaries in the early 1900s, and

peek in at an elegant, but abandoned, former embassy building. The twisting lane leads us through a tunnel and past a red brick Buddhist temple until we get a glimpse of the Min River and the hills upstream. See how the skyscrapers of modern Fuzhou catch the sunlight while the mountains behind are still dark. Don't look too closely at the tidal river's muddy flow, though. The current carries garbage and occasional grisly cargo such as animal carcasses when the river flushes out to the East China Sea several miles downstream.

But look up! This is what we've come to see! Our gaze drifts up a quarried stone embankment to the sweeping roofs and arched promenades of the original Hwa Nan College built in 1908 (see front cover). It had been funded with Methodist money when European influence was at its peak, and graduated hundreds of girls who went on to leadership positions both at home and abroad. After a triumphant Mao Tse-tung[2] established the People's Republic of China in 1950, missionary-educators were no longer welcome in the new Communist social order. Hwa Nan's student body was dispersed, all foreign teachers expelled and its stately granite facilities fell silent.

As we marvel at the quarried arches and mullioned windows, we try to imagine the rooms alive with the lilt of female voices reciting poetry, a group working out a chemistry experiment, or a calligraphy teacher demonstrating the proper way to hold a brush. Possibly hymns were wafting from the windows; its students were taught religion as well as science. High on a wooded hill, these graceful granite buildings have survived a century of revolution, reform, and reconstruction. A powerful vision is evident in the architecture, conceived at the turn of the century when Chinese emperors were bowing to European demands. Later, when the buildings were viewed as symbols of Western degradation (but deemed too lovely to be destroyed), they were incorporated into a nearby Communist-approved university in the early 1950s.

Difficult years followed. Famine due to Mao's botched Great Leap Forward killed millions; purges, torture and incarcerations added more millions to the grim statistics. But as sprouts of green inevitably poke up through blankets of asphalt, the memory of a women's college refused to die in

---

[2] The rationale for differing translations of place and family names is in the Author's Note. Don't miss it for an explanation of why Mao Tse-tung is now Mao Zedong, Foochow is Fuzhou, Fukien is Fujian.

the minds of Hwa Nan alumni. After the howling fury of the Great Proletarian Cultural Revolution subsided in the mid-1970s, ideas of resurrecting the college began to spring up in the conversations of hardy graduates who survived those devastating decades.

They were a small band of retired women who had attended Hwa Nan College as girls in the early 1900s. They had big dreams but little money. They organized a reunion and support began to grow like air roots on a Fujian banyan tree. Finally, in 1986, with the help of overseas alums and affiliations in the U.S., these determined women, many in their 7th decade, reopened a modest, vocational, secular version of their old *alma mater* with full government approval. This morning on our walk, we have connected the 20th and 21st centuries, beginning at "new" Hwa Nan, shabby but proud of its resurrection, to "old" Hwa Nan in all its colonial glory, now mostly empty or used for the administrative offices or meetings held by a nearby university.

Tell me more, you say? Who had the original vision for a women's college at a time when women in China were hardly more than chattel? Who had the dreams, who provided the dollars? What kind of inspiration and commitment funded and maintained this stunning architecture, built to last forever?

The source was, in fact, the unshakable determination of another woman who walked these streets at dawn in the late 1800s. An American middle-aged spinster, straight of spine, direct of gaze, this woman was ablaze with a sense of purpose. Her name was Miss Lydia Trimble.

19

Chapter 2: Looking back – 1890 to 1908

"Study the past if you would define the future."
Confucius

If you had awakened near dawn in a small village on the southeast coast of China in the humid summer of 1890, you might have heard the crisp, resolute footfalls of Miss Lydia Trimble, Methodist Missionary-at-Large, as she strode forth on the cobblestones for her morning walk. Armed with strong convictions and a few weeks of language training, she had taken rooms in a Fukien province village where she intended to establish a school—for girls!

Many schools had been established for boys in hopes of reaching the sons of officials and persons of influence through their desire to learn English. Lydia yearned to bring spiritual comfort and education to the rural women of the region as well, women who stood up to their knees in mud during rice planting season, women who gave birth almost every year of their childbearing lives, women who were often sold to other families who needed more workers, or to replace barren wives.

Miss Lydia's rooms were furnished with a wooden bed and thin rush matting on which she threw her quilts, a few hooks on the wall for her clothes, a desk and a chair. Each morning she drew cold water from the courtyard well for a quick sponge bath, laced up her sensible shoes, and visited the communal toilet, a fetid hole in the ground with a balance board for squatting. Even though the morning was already becoming warm and humid, Lydia gathered inner strength on these solitary dawn walks for the challenges of the day ahead.

Oh, to usher in the Kingdom of God to South China! Lydia's eyes blazed with determination behind her metal-rimmed spectacles. Soon the arrival of three new missionaries would free up the tireless Miss Trimble to make evangelistic tours into the mountains and fertile valleys of Fukien Province. To her own mother she wrote, "You cannot imagine the apathy, the dullness, and ignorance that has to be overcome. It takes every bit of one's life blood...."[3]

Indeed, blood had risen to the cheeks of the Ladies' China Missionary Society of Baltimore in 1859 when they resolved to challenge tradition by providing education for girls as well as boys. This was considered an outrageous idea to the Chinese at the time of bound feet and a view of women as slaves, while in America it was concurrent with the establishment of many colleges exclusively for women, notably Vassar, Wellesley, and Smith.

---

[3] Wallace, E. (1956). *Hwa Nan College: The Women's College of South China.* New York, NY: United Board for Christian Colleges in China.

One outrageous idea led to another, as ideas often do, and the rising of blood to cheeks led to the raising of money, with the expanded dream of having four women's colleges in China: south, north, east, and west. But how could church ladies sipping tea in the New World put such a lofty ambition into actual practice? Typical of many Christian accomplishments, war paved the way, war based on economic interests—and opium.

Tensions between China and the West had begun as early as 1793 when the Ch'ing dynasty Emperor Qianlong famously snubbed the British Ambassador[4]. Lord George Macartney had been sent to the imperial palace bearing royal gifts from King George III of England who proposed trade between the two countries. Qianlong looked down his imperial nose at this "humble desire to partake of the benefits of our civilization" and replied in a letter to the King: "As your Ambassador can see for himself, we possess all things. I set no value on objects strange or ingenious and have no use of your country's manufactures." The "objects strange and ingenious" brought by Ambassador Macartney were mechanical items like clocks and navigational globes, as well as English porcelain and other objects of European artistry. Qianlong continued, "I have but one aim in view, namely, to maintain a perfect governance and to fulfill the duties of the State: strange and costly objects do not interest me." In addition to being unimpressed with the lavish gifts, the

---

[4] The Ch'ing Dynasty (now spelled Qing) spanned the years 1644 to 1912. It is also referred to as the Manchu Dynasty because it was founded by Manchurian warriors who swept down from the north. The Manchus scaled the Great Wall with the help of a treacherous general and overthrew the Ming Dynasty when its emperor was believed to have lost the "Mandate of Heaven".

Emperor was insulted when Lord Macartney refused to kowtow (kneel and touch the ground with his forehead in an act of submission) to him. Enraged, the Emperor adamantly forbade any expansion of foreign trade.

Nevertheless, the potential profits to be made in a European market gone "gaga" over Chinese teas, silks, and jade were not to be foregone by the sea-going merchants of the time. The more exotic goods they brought back from the Far East, the more the demand increased. But how to surmount the fact that the Chinese only wanted to sell, not buy, and the silver flowed only one way...*into* the imperial Manchu coffers. What could be used to pry open the doors of those coffers and get the silver flowing both ways?

Opium! Grown cheaply in British-controlled India, opium could be easily procured for coppers on an eastward journey from England and sold for silver in China, if a market for the substance could be created. Why not load up opium in India, sell it cheaply in China, begin to raise the price as the demand increased? Dignified British and American businessmen of the 1800s saw nothing morally disturbing in their role as drug pushers. It was not lost on them that the common people were little more than serfs to the ruling landholders. Furthermore, the landholders were physically and mentally drained from constantly defending their turf.

Population was on the rise, droughts due to deforestation created famines, and competition for power among the ruling elite was brutal. The extravagant Emperor rode heavily on the backs of his people and, after his death, so did his ruthless self-indulgent concubine, Cixi.[5] The misery

---

[5] For more about Cixi, read Jung Chang's *Empress Dowager Cixi*, published in 2013. Chang is also author of the international bestseller

of everyday life during the late Ch'ing dynasty created perfect conditions for the spread of opium addiction, and the good captains of industry knew a market when they smelled one.

Opium importing into China began in earnest. As the addiction spread from well-heeled men of the elite Mandarin class to lowly dockworkers and prostitutes, the alarmed Manchu rulers declared opium illegal and forbade its being unloaded on China's shores. Too late! Such a large number of government officials had already been corrupted by the trade, either by payoffs or becoming addicted themselves, that regulation was impossible.

Smuggling intensified, diplomacy failed, cannons were fired, and when the smoke of the Opium Wars finally cleared, the pitifully outdated Chinese naval fleet had been destroyed. The Middle Kingdom had lost face and confidence. The British had emerged as the victors and demanded the right to conduct two-way trade with China for themselves and their European and American allies. The resulting treaty of Nanjing conceded unlimited access to five port cities where commerce with Europeans and Americans could be carried out without restraint—Shanghai, Canton, Ningpo, Foochow and Amoy. These concessions created "treaty ports" where European and American troops could be stationed to protect the merchants sailing ships and the community of Westerners that it took to run the warehouses and oversee the exchange of goods. Zealous missionaries who had been cautiously spreading the Christian message since 1807, often at personal peril, now had the protection they needed to increase their influence under the comforting canopy of

---

Wild Swans. a three-generational memoir of 20th century China during the Great Proletarian Cultural Revolution.

European troops. Foochow was one of those original treaty ports, and Lydia Trimble was one of those missionaries.

As more businessmen from France, England, Germany and America established consulates and warehouses in the treaty ports, more European wives demanded inclusion in their husband's exotic experiences. Why should the men be the only ones living a life of Oriental comfort far from the dampening chill of a London (or Hamburg or Boston) winter and social structures? Curious and adventurous women began to pack linens and fine hats into trunks, loaded themselves and their possessions onto a three-masted Blackwell frigate or a newly designed American clipper ship and sailed off to join their men folk in China. Some settled in Foochow on the banks of the Min River. Along with this feminine presence came the establishment of opulent residences and dining clubs. As merchant ships tacked carefully up the Min River to fill their holds with silk and black tea leaves from the mountains of Fukien, the breezy island of Nan Tai across from the walled city of Foochow became populated with silk-clad Western ladies serving that very tea in porcelain teacups in an imitation of colonial society life.

Of this society, the primly-frocked Lydia was not a member. She had more pressing business than filling painted cups with tea. She had already established two schools for local girls in neighboring villages and was attracting eager students from liberal Chinese families affluent and progressive enough to liberate some of their daughters from the boredom of domestic duties. The girls boarded at the schools and were taught basic reading, writing, and math by Chinese-speaking instructors, closely supervised by Miss

Trimble. Bible studies and the singing of hymns also figured heavily in the curriculum as it was Miss Trimble's mission to spread the Christian messages of service and faith in which she so fervently believed.

In a few years, the surrounding Fukien countryside began welcoming graduates returning from Lydia's boarding schools. These women often assumed positions of local leadership, as they might be the most educated people in their villages. Many graduates became teachers, others provided their communities with guidance in matters of local governance in a quickly changing world. Lydia, during her morning rambles, now shared the streets with fedora-wearing Europeans as well as pig-tailed Chinese (obedience to Manchu dictates required all men to wear their hair in long plaited queues). She began to see the crest of her mountain: a college preparatory school for women in Foochow out of which would evolve Hwa Nan College itself.

Her previous successes helped her acquire substantial support from Methodist missionary societies in America. "Spreading the Word of God in China," she assured her stateside supporters, "will be accomplished by educating women." Her goal was to train committed leaders to guide rural women out of ignorance and poverty. Even rumors of the "Boxer Rebellion" that left hundreds of northern missionaries battered or dead did not deter her.[6] The Boxers attracted a following of impoverished countrymen, driven to desperation by drought, widespread famine, and the

---

[6] These independent warriors officially called themselves The Society of the Righteous and Harmonious Fists. They were a group of deeply spiritual Chinese men who believed their martial arts training and wooden weapons would protect them from bullets. They were wrong.

irritation of an increasingly haughty foreign presence. In their short violent rebellion, they employed hand-held cudgels accompanied by savage cries and chants to kill foreigners and Chinese Christians, as well as to destroy property. Their unshakeable belief in their righteousness and invincibility proved a poor defense against European firepower and the Rebellion lasted a mere two years (1900-1902).

By 1906, the Foochow College Preparatory School for Girls was established and Miss Lydia became its head. The new school made do with crowded rented quarters, a very small staff and considerable local opposition to the concept of higher education for girls, but Lydia embraced the challenge like a rock climber preparing for an ascent. What was needed, she declared to the missionary societies in America, was an impressive edifice, visible evidence of the sacred pursuit of knowledge within a Christian framework. Lydia selected a plot of land overlooking the Min River and the Methodists employed distinguished architect Wilford Beech to design the buildings.

The land chosen for the campus was atop a rise of land separated from the walled city of Foochow by a channel of the river and looking out toward the steep forested mountains in the distance. Much effort and expense was respectfully devoted to removing the earthly remains of those buried in the piedmont graves. Here, great family tombs shaped like resting turtles contained tall urns that held the bones of ancestors. The success of the entire building project depended on the careful relocation of the honored dead, just as the success of the college depended on clearing away ancient attitudes about gender and feminine intelligence.

Funds raised in America needed to be sent by ship's packet and communications between the two countries was slow. Even employing Lydia's best efforts at clarity and diplomacy, progress on the building project was hampered by the realities of time and distance. Securing foundations for the stately stone buildings on a hill that had previously been a Chinese cemetery required a combination of sensitivity and dynamite, concessions and concrete. Lydia's Preparatory School students, experienced in the practice of patience, were also aflame with eagerness to begin college life. As the tomb-clearing process dragged on into the fall, the girls decided to hurry things along. They arrived at the site with baskets slung on bamboo poles and shovels at the ready to begin the dirty work of building their college.

Slowly the turtleback tombs were replaced with quarried stone classrooms and dormitory buildings boasting soaring tile roofs and Grecian pillars—a visually astonishing combination of Chinese and European architectural tradition. Sweating coolies moved like ants across the hillside, hauling sand and mortar in baskets suspended from bony shoulders by bamboo carrying poles. Others rolled blocks of grey stones into place with the help of logs and pulleys. By 1908 Hwa Nan College for Women at last had a location, a cluster of fine buildings and a student body ready to fill the buildings with youthful energy. Providing the compass, the human bedrock, and the single-minded energy from start to finish was Miss Lydia, who righteously claimed the title of President Trimble for the next 14 years.

Chapter 3: Looking Around – Views of the College

"When the student is ready, the teacher will appear."
The Buddha

The hill atop Nan Ti Island buzzes like a beehive in September 2000, as the "first year" or freshmen girls arrive to begin their scholastic endeavors at Hwa Nan College.[7] The tiny cobbled lanes squeezed on both sides by towering stone walls reverberate with the sound of taxis, minivans, and motorbikes, laden with parents nervously counting registration money, daughters clutching the belongings they'll need for their first year away from home, and all carrying the hopes and dreams of many generations. Engines whine, straining up the steep narrow streets; horns blare to warn competing drivers of their dominance on the one-lane passages. Whole families arrive on motorcycles, balancing a tower of bedding, plastic buckets and basins, and other personal belongings on the luggage rack.

This swirl of excitement and activity I am watching is accompanied by the tonal soundtrack of several different dialects from the arriving girls' villages spilling out of flung-open taxi doors. In China it seems like everyone is talking at once, all the time, at high volume. The chorus of raised voices gives the occasion a sense of importance and urgency. I'm curious about the one student who arrives alone, at the hilltop campus, in a chauffeur-driven car. This student would sit in the back of the classroom, scowling and forlorn for the entire school year, an anomaly in a culture that strives for

---

[7] The use of the term "girls" throughout this book to refer to females age 18-22 follows common Chinese usage. It is how the girls refer to themselves; they will become "women" when they marry.

group cohesion and harmony. When I presented a list of English names from which they could choose their class name, she chose "Teddy", the name of one of my best friends at home, but it did not suit her and did nothing to bring out her hidden personality.

Although many of the students' families live in or near Fuzhou, today most students are seeing the campus for the first time. And, in spite of the flapping red banners of welcome, an aura of disappointment trails them though the concrete entryway. No longer located in the impressive stone architecture of the earlier campus, this new version of Hwa Nan has been built on a shoestring, and a threadbare one at that. When the aging alumni of the original Hwa Nan held their reunion to reminisce, China was still poor and had been made poorer by the Great Proletarian Cultural Revolution (1966-76). This revolutionary brainstorm of Chairman Mao's had blacked out education in China. Academics, professional people and the "Four Olds" (old customs, old culture, old habits and old ideas) were the target of the Cultural Revolution's destructive chaos. Old Hwa Nan fell empty and quiet.

During the Cultural Revolution educators were humiliated and beaten, often by students. Several distinguished Hwa Nan graduates had been banished to the countryside to work menial or degrading jobs in order to be "re-educated." Their crime was having once been educated by American missionaries and thus infected with poisonous Western influences. Many had gone on to become teachers and school administrators after graduation and for that they were physically abused and imprisoned, some held for months within their own classrooms. All lost their jobs when schools were universally closed, while their students, drunk with power and encouraged to violence, went on hysterical rampages as self-appointed Red Guards, waving Mao's *Little Red Book* of inspirational statements from selected speeches and writings of the so-called Great Helmsman.

After the havoc of the Cultural Revolution subsided and schools reopened, those Hwa Nan graduates who survived the abuse returned to teaching or administration, and in time, a well-earned retirement. But instead of relaxing into shopping or mahjong playing, or reliving their grueling ordeals on a therapist's couch, these gritty women re-created a life-changing educational opportunity for another generation. Now fondly referred to as the "Old Ladies" in honor of their wisdom and status (and age...most are in their 80s), these former students of old Hwa Nan, wrote proposals, raised money and badgered other alums for involvement. They conscripted faculty wherever they could find former teachers who were available. The motto of Hwa Nan was "Having Received, I Ought to Give." And give those women did! Against all odds, in 1986 the Old Ladies reopened Hwa Nan College for Women as a private three-year vocational school with full approval of the Chinese bureaucracy.

Communist Party officials permitted some oversight and financial support from the United Board of Christian Education in China in the U.S., but the deep collection plates of the overseas missionary community were no longer available. There would be endorsements but little money. Although the campus is located on a breezy hill dotted with the ruins of foreign consulates and elegant residences from the former Trade Agreement days, this 1986 version of Hwa Nan College is a plain white-washed concrete quadrangle of buildings, four stories high, with outside staircases and one communal squat-over-trough toilet. Several Norfolk Island pines huddle around a gazebo in the center, making a valiant attempt at arboreal beauty.

The picture below is of the main classroom building where I will spend my days, climbing its concrete stairs, pacing its concrete classroom floors. The English department office is on the top floor and provides a spectacular view of the Min River, modern Fuzhou on its opposite banks and the rugged green mountains that cover 80% of Fujian Province beyond.

Today, registration day for the fall term, "second year" girls act as greeters to help lift spirits of the incoming students as they leave families and enter their new world. The older students can remember their own experience of seeing this version of Hwa Nan College for the first time and try to banish the shadows of disappointment with their sunny smiles. We foreign teachers were asked to join in the arrival festivities to help boost morale.

College recruiters, campus visitations, and glossy application brochures published to attract students to a particular school have no place in the life of a Chinese senior school student. Instead, students must choose from a small handful of college options based on their scores on the annual National Exam (called *gaokao*), taken the summer of their senior year. It's a grueling ritual; futures rise and fall on that score. Most of the girls arriving in the fall of 2000 had received a lower score than one required for attendance at a four-year national university. Perhaps they were top students in their village school, but in a nationwide competition they placed only high enough for this three-year vocational college. Adding to their gloom was the absence of boys.

After the National Exam scores are made public, parents largely take over the process of sorting out information about the level of higher education for which their child has qualified. Even a young person's choice of majors may be influenced by his or her score on the National Exam, combined with parental preference. College attendance is an investment made by the extended family with an eye to future monetary returns for the whole family. Many of my students were not talented in language acquisition nor interested in business, but their parents were convinced that learning English at a vocational school was a good economic move.

The absence of boys in the student body also appealed to vigilant fathers and mothers. This meant their carefully protected daughters, who had been forbidden to have boyfriends in high school, would continue to be buffered against the distractions of a romance. Crushes and flirtations had not been tolerated by families or senior high school staff; public sanction or even expulsion could be the price paid for rebellion. Because there would be less oversight at college, parents favored fewer temptations.

In traditional Chinese schools, boys typically get more teacher attention and are more aggressive class participants. Being in an all-female setting would give their girls a chance to shine. I later heard the girls congratulate themselves on becoming more independent in an all-female setting. "We learned we can do things for ourselves," they declared, as if it hadn't occurred to them before.

Not all the students are disappointed to be attending Hwa Nan. The college is known for attracting many foreign teachers and graduating competent English speakers who could then find jobs in local foreign trade businesses. To add a note of exotica on this arrival day, we Western teachers of fair skin and varying eye color were encouraged to swim through the sea of short black-haired people, introducing ourselves in English and letting our pictures be taken with the newcomers. The girls stared with amazement at Amy's blond curly hair, and giggled with shyness when Jason, a young man from the United Kingdom on his "gap year" assignment, spoke with a Liverpool accent.

Latisha, black and voluptuous, with cornrows and tongue piercings, got the most attention—in fact, more attention than she wanted. A walk into town with Latisha was like being with the Pied Piper: people stopped and stared, followed and chattered, making comments to their companions and taking a close interest in what she was buying or where she cast her attention. Chinese have a very different concept of personal space than that of Westerners. I often had people in bank lines press against me, looking at my passport or the money being exchanged, curious about the foreigner's business. It was too much for Latisha. She was relieved to leave when family matters called her home after the first semester.

Although Fujian province is fairly cosmopolitan due to its port cities of Fuzhou and Xiaman, its inhabitants are largely Han Chinese.[8] Foreigners were few in 2000 and black foreigners extremely rare. Dark skin is associated with being a peasant, oafish and backward, something to be avoided by using umbrellas and long-sleeved arm coverings. These beliefs were prevalent with students from town and from the countryside where their relatives kept pigs and tilled the paddies with oxen. As their exposure broadened, they learned to appreciate teachers with funny accents, dark skin, or blond, curly hair. Many were both excited and terrified about a new life in the "Big City," away from the dirt and stifling intimacy of a village childhood. Most had few personal belongings and brought little with them. Each girl carried a rolled bamboo mat on which she would sleep in her bunk, a plastic bucket for washing clothes, a basin for washing her body, and a duffle bag filled with clothes, toiletries and personal belongings.

Ni hao! Hello! Are you a new girl? Ni jiao shema ming zi? What's your name? Let's take a tour of your new home! Sure, your parents can come, too, but you'll have to learn to live

---

[8] This dominate ethnic group (about 92% of all people in China) takes its name from the Han dynasty, a rich and fertile period of cultural development in Chinese history.

without them here. First we'll take a quick peek at the communal squat toilet cubicle where water is occasionally flushed through a trough, then walk slowly past the row of concrete tubs and spigots of cold water where you will bathe and wash your clothes. We'll climb 108 steps (think how strong your legs will get!) to the 4th floor dorm. You'll get to share your living space with seven girls you haven't even met yet. What an opportunity for togetherness and cooperation! The room is simplicity itself: 4 bunk beds, 7 desks and a dim light bulb dangling at the end of a cord. The extra bed is where you will all keep your bags and belongings; there are no closets or dressers. Clothes can be washed in your tubs (cold water's on the first floor, remember) and hung to dry on lines up another flight of stairs from here on the roof. Really, you'll be happy for the exercise because the dorm isn't heated in winter. Showers? Oh, yes, you can buy a bucket of warm water once a day in which to bathe. Now, let's say zai jian—goodbye—to Mama and Baba and get on with the exciting business of transforming your half of the bunk bed to your very own personal space for the year!

I thought back to my own dorm when I entered college in the late 1950s. At that time the Chinese were suffering the privations of post-war recovery and starving in the wake of flamboyant but disastrous social experiments envisioned by Chairman Mao, a great revolutionary but a hapless and headstrong political leader. As a freshman at Whitman College I shared a well-appointed heated room with one other girl. We each had our own desk, chair, lamp, bed, closet and built-in dresser. The bathroom down the hall was communal, but had private stalls for toilets and showers, hot water on demand, and a row of sinks. The luxury I accepted

36

as normal would have been inconceivable to the average Chinese in 1958. It was still a fantasy to these incoming freshmen in 2000 who shared their unheated dorm room with seven others.

Practical majors for women in several areas were offered at Hwa Nan: Food and Nutrition, Clothing and Design, Early Childhood Education, and Applied English, the major to which most of the foreign teachers would be assigned. Most students studying English aspired to work in the office of some sort of foreign trade company. They had little interest in what the company was producing or selling, as long as it provided a paying job. A new Tourism and Travel major had been added that year.

A student was assigned her major upon entering, based on family preference, test scores, or department enrollment needs. She would also be given a number by which she would be officially known, would be assigned to class A, B, C, or D and would stay with that class unit through the full three years in the college. There were no provisions for changing classes nor did I ever hear of a change being requested. The students would also remain in their assigned classroom all day long; only the teachers moved from room to room. I gradually came to appreciate that these shy giggly girls, who I first viewed as immature, were so much more skilled in maintaining social harmony and adapting to uncomfortable situations than their more sophisticated Western counterparts.

The final semester of their third year would be partly instruction, partly an internship in a business setting. A Hwa Nan grad could expect to find jobs in local companies with a history of successful connections with the school. In 2000, teachers of third year girls had trouble keeping their students' attention after the Chinese New Year vacation in February or March. When I left in 2011, third year girls were scrambling for employment by the end of fall semester in order to stay ahead of the increasing number of college grads pouring into the workplace from schools all over Fuzhou.

But now I was teaching first year girls for two full semesters and after the fever of arrival day I was prepared to plunge into the cold pool of my new profession. My previous training and experience was in school psychology, not teaching. I might have had to deal with the most troubled students in the classroom, but only one at a time, not in gangs of thirty-five. Being a school psychologist called for a cool head in crisis mode; teaching required the opposite--bringing razzle-dazzle to humdrum lessons. My lesson plans were planned to the split second. I was terrified of dead air space. But my tight planning was often for naught; scheduling surprises were the only constant.

For instance, a few days after the semester began, my students disappeared from the grounds to take care of their military training obligation, leaving me like a bride at the altar. Nobody seemed to be given much advance notice of events occurring on campus and there was no semester calendar. Both students and Chinese staff were used to doing what they were told to do without prior explanation. It was news to me that before beginning classes, all entering students must leave the campus to participate in two weeks of military training (p. 39). While they drilled with wooden rifles and did sweaty calisthenics in red tee shirts on an open field, I paced my classrooms in an agony of anticipation.

The rooms were a dismal sight compared to the visually stimulating classrooms common in  stateside schools. Floor, walls and ceilings were unadorned whitewashed concrete that bounced and amplified each sound. Overhead fans managed only to move the humid late summer air of south China; there was no air conditioning and no heat in the winter. Tall windows, many of them cracked, could be opened or shut to regulate the temperature, although open windows invited flying insects and competing racket from the street. Thirty-five straight wooden chairs, each with a writing surface on the arm, were arranged in precise rows. In front of the student chairs stood a fragile wooden table and chair for the teacher (I would never use that chair—I never sat). Behind these the chalkboard loomed black and empty, its tray stocked with chalk that seemed to snap with the slightest pressure. It was traditional for Chinese teachers to sit behind the desk, intoning their knowledge to a passively listening class, hour after hour, subject after subject. This was not my intent.

Like classes anywhere, the students represented a wide range of abilities, backgrounds, and exposure to the English language. Very few had been taught by a native English speaker. Their English instruction had consisted of oral repetition and memorization of a vocabulary presented by teachers who themselves were a product of the Cultural

Revolution when schools were shut down and foreign influence was seen as a scourge. These students now aspired to go forth into the world of business, armed with the ability to sell products, fill orders, and negotiate problems in the primary international language of trade (English), quite a different process than uttering badly pronounced, memorized phrases.

As I rearranged the chairs into two semi-circles so that it felt more like a big conversation group, I wondered how I could hold the attention of seventy-plus girls in two separate classes, communicating only in English for two hours each class, three times a week. Teaching English as Foreign Language (EFL) in the students' home country is different than teaching English as a Second Language (ESL) in the U.S. where students must use on the street whatever they learn in the classroom. ESL students have no choice but to practice; EFL students return to their native tongue the minute there's a break in the classroom action. Furthermore, my Mandarin went as far as the greeting, *ni hao ma* (literally "you good?"), *xie xie ni* ("thank you"), and the universal *cesuo zai nar* ("Where's the bathroom?"). Thank goodness their understanding of English was greater than their ability to speak it! At least they could follow a little of what I said if I spoke slowly and clearly.

In order to get these kids to actually converse in English, I was going to have to wrench them away from the safety of repetition and memorization. Could I get them to loosen up enough to engage in play-acting and imagining and creativity? I would have to learn to pronounce my words very precisely and use simple grammatical structures without many idiomatic references. (I eventually did this so well that when I returned home to the U.S. and chatted with friends, they accused me of losing several IQ points.) Could I mold these strangers into a group that trusted one another enough to take linguistic risks, where each could unfold and bloom at her own speed, and would they trust *me* to lead them to these goals? I was called a "foreign expert" on my work permit and sometimes the old pejorative term "foreign devil" by passersby on the street...neither title encouraged bonding.

I entered the classroom with a thudding heart on the first day of actual student attendance. All I saw were seventy coal black eyes, set in thirty-five heads framed with glossy black hair, staring at me shyly, expectantly. In 2000, current fashion trends had not hit the student population and many were dressed in ruffles, hair bows, pom-pom fasteners and bobby socks like kids out of a 50s film. Nevertheless, their individuality began to leak through the impression of dark-haired, black-eyed sameness. Granted, we had to get past the first shy days when the fact that I didn't sit behind my desk and lecture made them wary. I wandered among them, asked simple questions I thought they could answer, trying to shake limply offered hands. The formality of the Chinese classroom often requires students to stand when answering a teacher's query; I discouraged this. When I required that they ask some questions of me, the whole class fell silent. I let the silence stretch as I strolled among them, given them time to put together a query. The bolder ones spoke. Most remained silent. Even my appearance made some of them anxious; a few shy girls wept and turned away when my blue alien eyes held theirs for the first time.

After a few weeks the collective clump of faces I called "the class" morphed into a clearer knowledge of each student

41

with her own weave of history and dreams. When I began to see them as individuals, my worries flew straight out those cracked windows. I presented topics I hoped would be irresistible to them: our families, our hometowns, our favorite activities. We made up adventure stories with romantic plots using newly acquired adjectives and verb tenses. I brought in some architectural drawings from an old Sunset magazine and we designed dream houses and described them to each other. We learned rounds, Beatles songs, and re-wrote "This Land Is Your Land" with Chinese place names.

Using a questionnaire I found in a college prep magazine, we talked about qualities they valued in a teacher and compared their preference with those of American kids. Americans college students wanted their teachers well informed, passionate about their subjects, and funny. My Chinese students wanted teachers who were kind, encouraging, and not too punitive. Many of my students told stories of harsh punishment at the hands of their teachers, both physical and emotional. In their experience, it was acceptable for teachers to hit misbehaving students. Poorly performing students were berated in class, their grades were posted publicly, and parent-teacher conferences were held collectively with all the parents present. No wonder these kids were wary of me and my unpredictable ways!

Cheerios got us over the final bonding barrier. Each class was divided into four small "Free Conversation" groups of nine students. The girls would come to my room in the foreign teachers' dorm for more intimate or playful gatherings, designed to stimulate actual conversations. The items in my room that excited them the most were my retractable walking sticks, the throw rugs I'd made out of the bamboo mats they used to sleep on, and the pictures of my handsome son. Giggles and squirming accompanied any reference to boys or romantic interests. The absence of both in their lives kept them on high alert for those very subjects.

Eventually the talk turned to food and typical meals eaten by Americans. Food is deeply important to Chinese relationships. Mothers often feed their children by hand until they are five or six. When Americans greet each other we might say "Hi, what's up?" The traditional Chinese greeting is, "(Ni) chi le ma?" or "Have you eaten yet?" This was an essential question in the lean years of war and famine and also implied the possibility of being fed by the asker. Their incredulity at my description of the boxes of flakes, Krispies, and Chex that graced the average breakfast table at home led me to troop us all down to the foreign teachers' kitchen, pour small bowls of the Cheerios the Americans kept on hand for comfort food, slosh in some milk, pass out spoons and let everyone have a taste. Waaah....delicious! After I shared my own exotic food in a few communal bowls, they were mine.[9]

Because it was too hard for the foreign teachers to remember names like Wang Xiulan or Zhang Lijing, each Applied English student was required to pick an English name. Some students came with a name from high school. One was Cassie, the second daughter born to a peasant family that elected to try again for a boy. The One Child Policy permits two children to peasant families if the first child is a

---

[9] By 2008, there were two Walmarts as well as German and French supermarkets in Fuzhou and packaged cereal is no longer a strange food, although its sugary presence has never become common on the Chinese breakfast table.

girl. To make way for another attempt, the infant Cassie was given to a maiden aunt living nearby to bring up and to eventually care for the unmarried relative in her dotage, thereby taking both burdens off other family members. The complex and enduring nature of the Chinese kinship group permits children to be passed around when there is a need for an heir or a caregiver. Cassie's parents got their boy on the third try and she spent her youth watching her older sister and younger brother be loved and cared for by her parents while she grew up under the grudging weight of her aunt's bitterness.

A class favorite was Gryphon, full of sparkle and zest, whose well-heeled relatives would later obtain her a residency permit in a more prosperous port city where moneymaking prospects were brighter. Ginger made her mark by being loud and assertive and fearless--opposite traits to the ideal of Chinese womanhood. Ginger's willingness to push the envelope would be sorely exploited by a male foreign teacher in her senior year, but later in our story we'll see how those traits served her in good stead.

Beth worried about a cousin who was selected by the family to be the first of its members to go to America, thus paving the way for the others. Her cousin's method of immigration was to become the mail-order bride of a Laotian man who had become a naturalized U.S. citizen. The arrangements were made through a local "snakehead," an outlaw who made his living smuggling Chinese into America, sometimes using false documents, sometimes by nailing several of his clients up in wooden packing crates to be shipped over in the hold of a freighter. It had cost the family about $10,000, and the cousin had to divorce her Chinese husband before the new marriage would be legal. Beth brought all the documents to me to verify their authenticity, assuming I was experienced in these matters. I was not, but I was dazzled by the determination of this family and the lengths they would go to get a relative established in America.

Golden Penny was my dependable technician, cheerfully coaxing the ancient video equipment to life, Tulip the class artist, and Grace the peacemaker. Fanny dropped the F and became Anny when I explained to her how the word "fanny" was sometimes used. Victoria represented the transcendent and romantic element in the classroom, bringing me lute recordings with meticulously written descriptions of the musical themes, and translations of Tang dynasty poems. Victoria was the child of revolutionary parents, trained in engineering and the Russian language when China was a political bedfellow with the U.S.S.R. Her mother and father desperately wanted a mathematician; they got an artist.

But it was Shelley who stood out like a bean in a rice bowl.

Chapter 4: Looking Closer – A View of One Girl's Life
Shelley's Story

Shelley's eyes crackled with curiosity at the sight of me, her first foreign teacher. Short, black-haired, and dark-eyed like every other student in the class, she proclaimed her individuality by her eagerness. When I asked for volunteers to act out a dialogue or explain a scene from one of the teaching videos, she was quick to raise her hand. Chinese students are taught to sit quietly in class with their hands folded on their desks, and to raise their forearms only at the elbow. When I encouraged my class to participate more vigorously, Shelley easily adopted the Western style of raising her whole arm and waving. She began a campus-wide broadcast of amplified pop music during the long mid-morning break and DJ'd it herself. Her English, if not fluent, was understandable. In a student competition for the title of "Miss Hwa Nan," most girls sang patriotic songs or performed repetitive traditional dances; Shelley rented a sparkling blue drum set and banged out an exuberant solo. She was NOT voted "Miss Hwa Nan" by the astonished judges.

How did a bright, eager student like Shelley end up in a three-year vocational college, I wondered? To find the answer, I had to look closer at the Chinese educational system and found it a grim sight.

By law, education is supposed to be free and compulsory for nine years, from primary school at six years of age to the end of junior secondary school around age 15. The quality of that education varies widely from rural to urban schools, with Beijing schools receiving the biggest chunk of the educational budget. The teacher and the four walls may be provided without cost but families usually have to pay for books, heating, food, or dorm fees if the family lives far from the school (common in rural areas). Uniforms are required in middle and senior school and must be purchased by the family. Some poorer schools in the countryside even ask the students to bring their own desks. Teachers are poorly paid and not immune to the temptation of earning a little more. In fact, with classes often as large as 50 to 75 pupils, affluent parents have been known to pay to have their child's desk located in close proximity to the teacher's mostly stationary position at the front of the classroom.

After junior secondary school (also known as 'middle school'), the road to the future forks decisively and the tyranny of the qualifying test kicks in. To be admitted to *senior* secondary school (similar to U.S. high school), a student must take an examination (*zhongkao*). The more scholastically able students qualify for three more years in senior school, a necessary stepping-stone to higher education. Although senior schools are also supposed to be free, parents are often encouraged to make "voluntary donations," and some parents pay thousands of dollars to middlemen in order to get their children enrolled in select high schools.

Academically disadvantaged children who do poorly on the *zhongkao* may try to find a state-supported vocational school to attend after middle school, However, these schools have not been popular because they are historically under-funded, widely scattered geographically, and often not in sync with current or local job opportunities. Enrollment in vocational training programs has been sparse and the dropout rate high. Young people who do not score high

47

enough on the *zhongkao* to move up to senior school, or whose families cannot continue to support them in vocational school, take up hoes and hammers, or seek positions as workers in mega-factories supplying the Western world with everything from cheap underwear to Mardi Gras beads.

What's a slower learner to do? Or a visual learner in classrooms taught by lecture and repetition? There are no special education classes, no modifications and accommodations, no speech and language therapy for the learning disabled student. There's only the ubiquitous "backdoor". Students with a low score on an admission test may slip through a school's "backdoor" by paying extra fees to institutions that are willing to lower their standards in exchange for money. Attempts have been made to control the practice of bribing high school and college administrations to admit underachieving students but in China, money always talks louder than erratically enforced laws. It is thought foolish not to pay for privilege whenever possible. The institutions look at this practice as merely another income source.

Once students have qualified for senior school by achieving an acceptable score on the *zhongkao*, they have two years to enjoy learning from a wide range of academic classes. Then the pressure is cranked up again. During their third year, the students focus all their energy on preparation for the mother of all Chinese academic achievement tests called the *gaokao*. This is the National College Entrance Examination that determines whether the student can go on to higher education and at which institution. Now the tyranny of the test intensifies. Parents who have been supportive and encouraging, involving themselves in their kids' primary school days to the point of taking notes in class when their children are ill, become hoarse with harangues about the necessity of constant study. Entrepreneurs have seized this lucrative opportunity by providing individual tutoring and weekend classes for pupils from ambitious families who demand that their children excel. No weekend slumber parties or TV marathons for these teenagers, just more schoolwork. I was lured in to teaching a few of these weekend classes and found teaching them very frustrating because the majority of the students just wanted to horse around or sleep through the lessons. I can't say that I blamed them.

After constant drilling on the probable contents of the test, high school students take the multi-subject *gaokao* over a period of a few days the summer of their senior year. This one score ranks their eligibility for particular universities and colleges nationwide. A few decades ago, it determined the students' major also. In the case of Shelley's parents, both scored high in science and were routed to medical universities. No matter how well a student performs academically in senior school (and there is no other way to perform since electives and special interest classes are not part of the curriculum), this is the one score that counts in China. Seventeen and eighteen-year-olds who sit in class all day often sit in private classes all weekend. Recreational sports and extracurricular activities are out of the question. Futures of whole families depend on the outcome of this defining examination, as entrance to college promises status and potentially higher earnings. The whole family may contribute to sending their young person to college; in return, all members of the family expect to benefit from this achievement in the future.

Bad luck visited the Jiang family during the week National Exams were given. Shelley's father had suffered a life-threatening cardiac event and was under diagnostic observation. As are all doctors in China, Father Jiang was employed by the government health care system, and was now a patient in the same local hospital where he provided professional services. Shelley knew he would get the best care available, but she adored her father and was sick with worry. Her mother, a doctor as well in a nearby OB-GYN hospital, was busy bringing food for her husband and tending to his bedside needs, as most Chinese hospitals don't offer the luxuries of attendant care to their patients. Nurses are employed to assist doctors and run units, not to plump pillows or bring trays well-balanced meals to bedsides. These duties are up to the patient's relatives and most wards are noisily crowded with family members providing comfort and care to their ailing loved ones.

The female Dr. Jiang's own work with pregnant women and their babies, plus the hours of bedside attention now needed by her husband, left young Shelley alone and uneasy in the family's dreary concrete apartment during the most important week of her life. As employees of the Chinese health care system, the Jiangs, like most doctors, qualified for government-sponsored housing and modest salaries, sometimes augmented by contributions from grateful patients. It is considered a profession of service, not one of great remuneration. Shelley had been raised to be independent but had been used to a routine that involved her one of her parents' daily presence.

As the days of the *gaokao* approached, Shelley felt forlorn and nervous. All by herself within the comfortless grey walls of her home, with no rowdy siblings nor pets to distract her (the former being illegal and the latter not yet in vogue), she wandered from room to room anxiously nibbling on *baozi*, a doughy meat-filled bun. In addition to having to temporarily fend for herself, she was anticipating her month menses, an event that weighs heavily against adolescent girls in this pivotal academic contest. Some families go so far as to provide daughters with contraceptive drugs to prevent onset of a menstrual cycle during the exam. Shelley's back ached; she felt nauseous. She just wanted to crawl back into bed and hug her stuffed bunny, but she knew she had to get to the examination center on time, ready to compete.

Then it was time. Shelley had slept fitfully the night before and try as she might, she could not keep focused. She had no appetite for her own cooking the morning she left to begin her tests, so, with no one there to insist that she eat, she skipped breakfast. She mounted the crowded bus without her usual brio and hurtled through the moist morning air with a sense of dread. As she claimed her wooden desk in the stuffy hall, her head ached, her abdomen cramped in waves, and she felt near tears. The air in the huge examination hall was hot and heavy with humidity and adolescent perspiration. When the testing session began, three hundred glossy black heads bent over their booklets; three hundred pens scratched out memorized answers in subjects of math, Chinese, a foreign language, science, and civics. Answers swam before Shelley's eyes, but not the right ones. Instead, images of her father in his hospital bed crowded out algebra formulae and vocabulary words.

51

In the end, Shelley's scores had not been high enough to qualify her for a four-year university. She had the choice of trying again the next year or choosing a local vocational college. However, even the phrase "Shelley had the choice" suggests more freedom than actually exists for a young person in a culture where decision-making rests with elder family members. Enrolling in her former high school as a repeating student and taking the exam again was neither psychologically nor financially appealing. Because Hwa Nan College for Women had a reputation for progressive English instruction by native speakers, admitted only women, and was in town where they could keep a close eye on her, the Jiangs favored this venue as a fallback position. In murmured consultation with her weakened but recovering husband, Shelley's mother garnered his support for her decision to enroll their daughter there, whether she liked it or not.

But the closer Mother Jiang looked, the less she liked what she saw. When she dropped her daughter off at the gate of the Hwa Nan campus in September of 2000, she had to cross the arched and ancient Liberation Bridge to the old part of town, now fallen out of fashion with the rising business stars of greater Fuzhou. Many of the buildings from the turn-of-the-century "trade agreement days" had been a graceful combination of European and Chinese design, but now the masonry was crumbling, windows were cracked, and roof tiles were sliding to the ground.

Across from the entrance to the campus, the graceful moon gate of the former British consulate now led to a home for aging People's Liberation Army soldiers and their families. Next door stood the stately proportions of the former Foochow Merchants' Club, now noisily inhabited by

35 or 40 squatters, who sold soft drinks and cigarettes in the once-elegant entryway. Laundry hung drying on bamboo tripods and flapped in the Min River breeze. Old men played cards between the stone pillars framing the doorway. To Dr. Jiang it did not look like a place that could provide an education that would guarantee the prosperous future she envisioned for her daughter.

As mother and child entered the campus grounds, their hearts sunk further. Though the welcome was warm, the college buildings peeled flakes of whitewash, the dorms were crowded and the library musty and out-of-date.

"No hot water in the dorms?" Shelley repeated incredulously after the campus tour. "Warm water must be purchased by the bucketful?"

The toilet was a metal chamber pot under the bed provided by the student or an enclosed trough on the ground floor shared by the whole campus. Shelley was used to squatting, as most Chinese toilets consisted of a porcelain floor fixture with a hole in the middle and two strategically placed footpads. But this central latrine served a row of squatters. Water was flushed through the trough by the users with a bucket of water from a nearby spigot.

"It is the education you are here for, not the comforts of accommodation," declared Mother Jiang, setting her shoulders. Chinese students were used to the hardships of unheated classrooms where 50 or more students sat at desks nailed to the floor, and had long since learned the art of harmonious coexistence so vital to Chinese society.

"The faculty seems alert and the college has a good reputation in the business community. You can improve your

53

English quickly to get ahead of the competition," she continued.

The sight of me and the other foreign teachers soothed Dr. Jiang, and her worried face became collaborative and respectful as we shook hands. "My daughter is very capable," she declared. "I hope you will demand a lot of her."

However, as the months wore on, and Shelley's mother learned more about the pace of the lessons and the conditions of the dorms, she began to make other plans for her only daughter. She loved this child very much and wanted the very best future for her. In February 2001, after the Spring Festival holiday (the Chinese lunar New Year) and after her father had safely returned home, Shelley was enrolled in an English-language transitional program in Birmingham, England and put on a plane alone for the United Kingdom. She was 18 years old.

This young girl, so confident and outgoing in my classroom, found herself terrified and alone in the cold, soggy English winter. Through Chinese connections, she found a room in a student boarding house. She got a job in a Chinese restaurant. She learned better English and how to compete in schools where speaking out, challenging the teachers, and sharing one's opinions were expected behaviors, not disrespectful acts as they would have been in China. Even asking the teacher a question was forbidden in her former school, for if the teacher didn't know the answer, he or she would lose face and this would be intolerable. The loss of face in Chinese society goes far deeper than simple embarrassment or a temporary dip in confidence.

By day Shelley was often exhilarated with these new freedoms, but by night her tears fell, wetting the plushy ears

54

of the stuffed rabbits and teddy bears she hugged alone in her room. She ate British fast food. She grew fat.

The lonely girl called her mother frequently and, for broader comfort, she began to e-mail me, her first foreign teacher, telling me of her fears and accomplishments. She also wrote her drumming instructor who had helped her with her unsuccessful Miss Hwa Nan bid. He was a bright, full-hearted man with a wide bohemian streak—a musician, an artist, and an entrepreneur who owned a small shop near a teeming teacher's university. A decade older than Shelley and a deep thinker, he was uneasy about trends in Chinese civic life and cautiously viewed the rising economic spiral so celebrated by economists and the popular press. He spoke of the need for individual identity, for free speech, for living a life fueled by passion rather than acquisition. He adopted the English name "Freeman."

Their long-distance letters and e-mails permitted more self-disclosure than a weekly drum lesson might have done. With the sharing of fears and the sharing of dreams, their relationship flourished. By the time Shelley went home for the summer, she felt she knew him well. By the end of that long holiday, they were in love.

This was not at all what Mother Jiang had in mind! No. Her daughter was adorable, intelligent, and now cosmopolitan. Such an agreeable combination should attract a husband who was rich, well educated, and enjoyed a high standing in Chinese society, even Fuzhou society. "There will be no drummers or small shop owners in this family," muttered Shelley's mother when she began to suspect the source of her daughter's lightheartedness. She wanted the best for her daughter and was clear in her mind that the choice of an appropriate mate had absolutely nothing to do with romantic love.

As Shelley continued her British education with a double major in business (for her mother) and art (for her new-found sense of personal fulfillment), Dr. Jiang became increasingly uneasy. Adding to her disquietude was the fact that her husband, whose initial recovery had foolishly driven him to smoke even more heavily and to work even longer hours, suffered a second and more severe heart event. He was now slipping in and out of consciousness in his own former hospital; his recovery was uncertain. Mother Jiang, needed to know that her daughter was working hard, not only on her studies abroad, but also on seeking an appropriate match in order to support the aging and now somewhat ailing family.

One of the unintended consequences of sending children overseas to be educated is that they're apt to acquire a broader perspective than their parents are comfortable with. The content of Shelley's Western education was not all academic. She was learning about personal freedom, individual choices, and the possibility of having preferences outside the family unit at the same time as she was learning business math and English grammar. She was making friends with other girls her age who planned to be artists and lived with their boyfriends, sometimes in defiance of their families. She was wearing boots with short skirts, and fingernail polish. And she was convinced that her destiny and Freeman's were indelibly intertwined.

Their relationship deepened with each letter and each visit home to Fuzhou. Shelley kept her feelings for Freeman in a well-monitored chamber of her heart when she was with her mother, but let those feelings fly out when she was with him. During the day, they took trips, went to musical events, cooked together, and shared friends, but every night Shelley went home to her mother in the Jiang family apartment.

Eventually, Shelley began to spend the night at Freeman's apartment. The tension between old ways and new beliefs was building, even as mother and daughter practiced the familial charade of avoiding what therapists often call "the elephant in the living room". Pretending the situation didn't exist would postpone the collision for as long as possible.

Father Jiang, still useful to his wife as a valuable ally even as he remained in an unresponsive coma, was blissfully unaware of his role in the family drama or how he would be used as that drama played out. Even a husband in a coma was better than no husband at all when it came to applying parental pressure, and that is exactly what Mother Jiang intended to do. Would parental pressure have the traditional power over a new-age young woman who would soon be making more money than her parents, driving her own car, and living against the backdrop of a modern society? Would the Confucian directive of obedience to parents trump economic power and global cultural influence, or vice versa? These cultural shifts were influencing Shelley's judgment, just as they were raising questions asked by millions of Asian parents and adult children in the 21st century. We'll let this family drama evolve and look in on them later for answers.

Chapter 5: Looking Around – Views of Some Teaching Moments

"Real knowledge is to know the extent of one's ignorance."
Confucius

When second semester began in February 2001, my class seemed a little flat without Shelley's buoyancy to set the emotional tone. She had been the monitor, the student in each classroom who was responsible for delivering administrative announcements, taking attendance, and rallying enthusiasm for assigned tasks. Her successor, a dutiful but duller girl from the countryside, was gifted with neither enthusiasm nor imagination. She was hesitant to inspire her peers to participate in campus activities, or to hector them to clean up the room, a janitorial responsibility that fell to the students. Although Shelley's individuality had

won her no close friends, she had led her class-mates into games and group work with courage and glee.

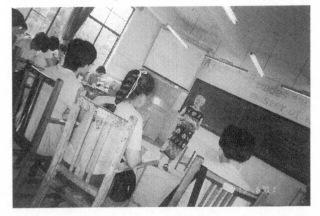

I tried to introduce a kaleidoscope of topics that might be of interest to these 18-year-olds who had some depth of knowledge but not much breadth. Their exposure to the history and geography of other countries was scanty while their acquaintance with the Middle Kingdom was heavy with dates and facts. Before the unification of the empire, the name

Middle Kingdom referred to a culturally distinct center of civilization along the Yellow River as opposed to the barbarian tribes on its geographic margins. The moniker stuck, and has since been used to suggest that China thought of itself as the center of the known world. China's not alone in ethnocentrism: the map of the world I brought from America had the USA front and center; the same map I bought in a Fujian Province bookstore featured China as its centerpiece.

Even so, I was surprised at the students' limited knowledge of global events and their settings. Any one of them could recite lists of emperors of ancient Chinese dynasties, quote from their classical poets, affirm the glorious leadership of Mao Zedong in convincing detail, but they'd never heard of Winston Churchill, couldn't locate Mexico on a map, and had only a vague idea of what the Holocaust entailed. In an effort to expand their worldview, I broke the class into seven groups of five students. Each group was to choose any country in the world that interested them, research, prepare and present a summary description of its geography, climate, and culture to the class orally, in a way that would make the rest of us yearn to live there. They consulted piles of ancient National Geographic magazines left by former teachers, flipped through dusty library books, shared information about family members who had gone abroad. It was a lively and successful enterprise.

"Now how would you describe China to a person from another country who wanted to live here?" I eventually asked at the end of their presentations.

"Nobody wants to immigrate to China," was the students' reaction.

I was taken aback, but then realized that there did not seem to be an overwhelming multitude tourists or visitors requesting asylum or taking out citizenship papers. China did not seem to have the civic and moral dilemmas European and North American countries were grappling with due to waves of people from other countries seeking a better education for their children or dreams of political freedom for themselves. I recalled a quip I'd read about a prominent European politician who suggested that to evaluate the soundness of a country's governance, ask this question: Are people trying to get into the country or out of it?

There were some breathtaking gaps in their recent Chinese history as well. One day in early 2001 we were practicing "ice-breaking" conversations and discussing subjects to avoid in a cross-cultural conversation. To illustrate, I mentioned some taboos when chatting with a new acquaintance. In the west, asking a person's age is considered nosy, even rude; in China it's a fact of universal public interest. One phrase I'd learned to recognize in Putonghua was "How many years are you?" because total strangers on the bus or merchants selling me their products would ask my age. Because it was so commonly asked, I learned to say the answer, in English and Mandarin, which would elicit bursts of conversation among the on-lookers. In China, there were always on-lookers.

Conversely, before coming to China in 2000, I'd been warned not to bring up the four "T's" in conversation because of strong and differing global opinions.

"What are the four T's?" my students wanted to know.

Uh-oh, maybe I was adding another T for trouble with this discussion. I hoped I could trust them not to be offended.

"Tibet, Taiwan, the World Trade Organization and Tiananmen Square," I numbered on my fingers, starting with my pinkie finger as my students would.

Mentally, they sifted through what they knew of these matters. Tentatively, hands went up and positions were stated in halting English. The gist of the discussion was that Tibet was part of China and soldiers sent there in 1950 conducted a "peaceful liberation," rescuing Tibetans from the scourges of superstition and poverty. What was damned in the West as a bloody and brutal takeover of independent Tibet was praised in China as the rescue of these hapless people from the iron grip of the stupid and evil Dalai Lama, who immediately fled to India.

In regards to Taiwan, they argued, all the Taiwanese people had been yearning to reunite with their Motherland since 1949 when Chiang Kai-shek and his illegitimate Nationalist Government set up a separate Republic of China there. Many families had residents in both the mainland and the island. Furthermore, now that China had become manufacturer to the world, it was only just, they maintained, that China should be admitted to the World Trade Organization (and it was, less than a year later, in December 2001).

"But what about Tiananmen Square?" they queried. "Why was that an offensive topic? Wasn't that just the huge central plaza in Beijing, next to the remains of the Forbidden City and overlooked by the huge painted gaze of 'The Great Helmsman,' Mao Zedong?"

Not one of them had heard of the 1989 student protests and massacre in that location, nor were they aware of the world's reaction to the military action resulting in the deaths of hundreds of Chinese young people. This event is a banned topic in China and any mention of the "incident" in the media, literature, or art is subject to censorship.

"Tell us!" they urged, but I easily resisted, knowing caution was the better part of my own protection.

"Nope. Ask your parents," I countered. In 2000, most of my students had little exposure to the Internet, and if they did, they used it only for social outreach. "Google it" would have meant nothing to them.

My silence did not prevent me from wondering if students then attending the newly opened Hwa Nan College in 1989 had known of the student protests in Beijing, and if there was a sense of solidarity with their protesting peers, some of whom may have traveled to the capital from local universities. During the demonstrations the students were assured by their protest leaders that the government would not retaliate with deadly ammunition. Besides, their leaders pointed out, the military police were just young people like themselves who openly sympathized with the movement. Even Communist Party officials were arguing among themselves as to how to react! But when serious fighting began and bullets began to fly, they were real, not rubber bullets. Survivors felt betrayed by both their government and the protest leaders, many of whom fled to America and prospered there, basking in their unearned reputations for rebellion and bravery.

This seemed a good time to introduce a tiny exercise in democracy into my class curriculum. It was an election year in the U.S., and I had gotten a lot of questions about possible outcomes during English Corner, a once-a-week informal gathering on designated street corners throughout most major cities for people who want to practice English. Every college had one, and Hwa Nan was no exception. Older adult community members sometimes came and were curious about the inefficient and destabilizing American process of choosing a new leader every four years. My students understood little of the process and saw no point of all the hoopla surrounding elections.

In fact, most people I encountered, young and old, seemed only mildly interested in the whole business. They had never voted for anything in their lives and the responsibility of making such weighty choices seemed unappealing. They knew their voices were not important and that was fine with them; such was the price of stability. The messy and disruptive system of democracy seemed too risky to people from a culture historically consumed in civil strife. As far as they were concerned, only a dominant and consistent central government could prevent the bloody struggles by powerful warlords for territory and political control that ground the citizenry to dust in the past.

An upcoming choral contest between Applied English Department classes provided me with the opportunity I sought to conduct an election. Each class was expected to sing two songs, one in Chinese, one in English.

"What shall we sing for the English song?" my competitive students implored. "Tell us what to sing so we will win!"

Believing they would be more apt to enjoy singing a song they chose themselves, and wanting them to experience that thrill of voting, I created a little song convention. Anyone who wanted to propose a favorite song could do so, pointing out its merits as a contest song, maybe providing a short demonstration. I suggested and demonstrated a few songs myself to model the spirit of the process. There was elaborate debate. Feelings were hurt, factions developed, secret resentments were brought to light. During the vote (a simple heads-down, hands-up affair) some voted twice, some not at all. An actual majority identified a winning song title, but the losers sulked because they saw no reason why they should have to yield to the rule of their peers, just because there were more of them. Preparation for the competition stalled and it seemed like we might suffer the disgrace of nonparticipation.

Finally, the dutiful monitor appealed to a Chinese teacher who sensibly assigned them a song: "Sing this one," she commanded.

Once they received the assignment from a higher authority, they settled right down to practice, putting the unsatisfying uproar of the democratic experience behind them. I lost serious face over the activity and my belief in the inherent value of democracy teetered. Clearly the concept could not just be slapped down on an ancient culture, like another layer of wallpaper.

When I grumbled about American politics or the current administration, the students stared back at me blankly, another sure sign I was losing face. Voicing disapproval of authority publicly is unthinkable to them. Furthermore, they were embarrassed by my discontent. The energy and excitement generated by western exercise of political argument and choice seemed a waste of time and simply not very interesting. Making money and spending it was.

When asked how they spent their weekends in 2001, I heard few variations on this answer: "Eating, sleeping, shopping, watching TV."

One bus route through town took me by a huge golden fist outside of a shopping mall, not raised in a gesture of revolutionary angst, but with its gold thumb up in the universal sign of approval for shopping and owning. In Wuyi Square, the main paved square for official ceremonies in Fuzhou, stands a huge inspirational statue of Communist leader Mao Zedong in flowing greatcoat, his arm outstretched in a protective salute to his people. At and under his feet now spreads a huge underground shopping mall.

In a writing assignment on life goals, one student wrote that her goal was to "work hard to get a good sock (she meant 'score;' the alphabet is very tricky for kids used to writing in characters), so I can get a good job and make many, many money. That's all." It was succinctly put and echoed by many of her colleagues.

In 1944, Mao declared, "Serve the People, Wholly and Entirely." But it is the famous slogan, often attributed to Deng Xiaoping, considered China's "Paramount Leader" in the 1980s, that holds the younger generation in thrall: "To Be Rich Is Glorious!" If that is the goal, then a strong, enduring government, interested in wealth itself and held firmly in place by the suppression of social interference, allows the most fortunate individuals to concentrate on making "many, many money."

Participatory politics also suffers from a deep belief in fate and destiny. I asked my students why most Chinese women don't take their husband's name when they marry and was told that the birth name is linked to the person's destiny and it might be dangerous to change it. This depth of belief in destiny also played out in staff attitudes. While I was there, the husband of a Chinese teaching colleague died of liver cancer at age 36, leaving a wife and a two-year-old son. Two years before his death a small tumor had been found growing on his liver. He took no action, partly because of the uncertainty of surgical outcomes in China, but partly because he believed his fate was already determined. Why vote, or for that matter, seek cancer treatment, when the outcome of life and death is already written in the stars?

Having badly botched the choral contest song selection, I tried to redeem myself in the speech contest preparation. I assigned a topic, issued a timeline, and cajoled staff members to listen to the speeches and help me make the first cut. From each oral English class of 35 girls, the three best speeches delivered in English would be chosen to compete in the final Applied English Department contest judged by a panel of foreign and Chinese teachers. In order to help pull their thoughts together on the topic, I spent class time demonstrating outlining and drafting, going over grammar, and practicing delivery styles. I knew that once we had the content expressed clearly on paper, memorizing the speech would be a cinch, as memorizing was their strong suit. The girls were reluctant speakers but were flowery and dramatic writers, often with help from small electronic dictionaries tucked inside their notebooks. In hopes of impressing the reader, or in this case, the speech contest judges, the students chose to use the most difficult and impressive words they could locate on their devices.

Electronic dictionaries are great for direct word-for-word translations but often fall short of expressing the actual meaning that the writer intends when translating from characters to alphabet. The device can't take into account syntax, context, or idiom. One girl assured me in a written assignment that she "had really grown up at Hwa Nan because of its moisting." I spent many evenings sitting in my poorly lit dorm room with a mug of green tea, trying to decipher sentences like "The unique style lingering lingering charm couldn't tear yourself away." The writer went on to declare, "The standards of the measure is the reaction," and ended her impassioned motivational speech with these inspirational words: "The very love will encourage you to try your best and arouse the latent power. This kind of love have truly the prompting upward process. Because you could realize your ideal at last and ever have a bright future!" Her passion shines through the grandiose verbiage, but it wasn't going to win a speech contest judged by native English speakers.

In case you are thinking these are backward and peculiar language learners, consider the many differences between English and Putonghua, the official spoken language based on the Beijing dialect (as opposed to the five or six other major regional languages and the countless regional dialects spoken in the home). First of all, English employs a twenty-six-letter alphabet to form words of one to several syllables, whereas each Chinese logographic symbol, known as a character, might represent part of a word or a whole idea. Each character sounds as one, occasionally two, syllables and can be combined to create complicated and beautiful visuals. However, each syllable can be voiced in four different tones, or pitches, each of which gives the character a different meaning. English speakers use pitch or tone to emphasize or express emotion; in Mandarin the tone can change the meaning of the word completely. Characters are most often written from the top to the bottom of the page. The average Chinese person will learn 3,500 characters in order to read and write, and more than twice that before he or she is considered well-educated.

The plot thickens. In Mandarin, there are no plurals (the suffix '-men' is added to plural nouns) no verb tenses, no articles (the, a, an), no possessive pronouns (his, her), and no phrasal verbs (back up, take after, get rid of). Tiny particle words are used to assign tense or indicate questions. Heavy-use idioms and cultural references are used to locate action in time and place. I had no idea how I took idioms and clichés for granted speaking to my American friends until I needed to simplify and clarify my language to communicate with people who had limited knowledge of informal English. Bridging the gap between our two languages and becoming fluent would take tremendous effort and talent. My struggles with learning Mandarin helped me empathize with the struggles of my students. Furthermore, to really walk over the language bridge, the learner must wrestle with differences between the artful Chinese characters and the alphabet.

The shock I experienced the first time I entered a Chinese bus station and realized I couldn't read, or even look up one piece of information plastered over ticket windows or arrival gates, must be the same shock for a Chinese person arriving in America. There is absolutely no correspondence between our alphabet and Chinese characters. No wonder I occasionally got 'sock' instead of 'score;' it was close enough for the writer. Sometimes the consequence of alphabet confusion is more dire. A traveling Welsh teacher was desperate for a train ticket back to Hwa Nan College from Sichuan Province, but the railway station was a teeming mass of people and the signs unreadable. A helpful young Chinese man muscled his way to the correct window and managed to procure a ticket for her but cautioned her there were "no tests."

"Okay," she thought. "Why would I want to take tests on a train anyway?"

But when she boarded for the 48-hour trip east, she found that there were, in fact, no *seats*. Tests/seats—approximate in the mind of the young man but not close enough for my friend's comfort.

Our speech contests were a staple of Chinese higher education and apparently there were some pretty standard topics, none of which would have been the choice of American teenagers. "How Much I Love My Mother and My Mother Loves Me" was the most common subject, followed by "Inspiration from My Grandmother/Grandfather/ Teacher," with the "Overcoming Obstacles" theme coming up in third place. The girls waxed poetic as they spoke before the audience of the English Department staff and students, trying to wrench hearts and jerk tears from the judges, a sure path to the prize. My class had three out of the four winners and we repaired to my dorm room for Magnum ice cream bars, a rare treat then.

Did this mean I was a spectacular teacher who had coached her students to dazzling oratory? No, it actually reflected a serious mistake Jeanne Phillips, a senior foreign teacher, and I had made at the beginning of that school year. Jeanne and I were both psychologists, intrigued with individual differences and assessment. Like teachers everywhere, we lamented the wide range of abilities in our classes and the difficulties of teaching the slow learners as well as challenging the more gifted in language acquisition.

We privately devised a short screening using an array of tasks, and administered it to all the first year girls. Then, based on the results, we divided the incoming students into a class of advanced learners (Class C, which I agreed to teach), 3 classes of students that scored in the middle ranges (we split these classes between us), and a class of slower learners (Class B, Jeanne's choice). What we didn't account for was that every competition and theater production and speech contest and pop rally was undertaken as a class and that class remained the same throughout their entire three years at Hwa Nan. As Class C, the high achievers, walked away with trophies, prizes and ribbons, even the students began to smell a rat. There was some grumbling...this was not the Chinese way...and we never attempted to influence the make-up of our classes again.

After so much time indoors working on speeches for the contest, I decided to get the whole class out of doors to learn how to give and receive geographical directions. We had done direction-giving-and-following exercises in class with simple textbook maps; now it was time to take our practice on the road. My plan was for the students to look at actual maps, discuss and choose ways to go, be able to orally share directional decisions with others. Nervously, the girls clustered around me as I passed out neighborhood maps. They held hands, doubting the wisdom of this venture. They weren't used to heading off to an unknown destination without a tour led by a knowledgeable guide with a flag on a stick. We shared the same destination, indicated by a red dot on the map, but there were several ways to get there, and I imagined a sort of treasure hunt, with splinter groups trying to beat the others to the destination.

Again, I was wrong. They stuck to me like Konrad Lorenz's goslings, not trusting the map, unpracticed in shifting from the abstraction of the printed route to actual city streets. Many of them had never ventured farther from the campus than Student Street, the grungy commercial strip supported by a big university campus nearby, teeming with adolescents, full of street food, cheap clothing stores, and CD shops. Raised to fear encounters with strangers and not wander, they were uncertain of their ability to find their way back. It was a hot, sticky afternoon walk and the girls were plainly wishing they were still sitting in their drab classroom in their hard wooden chairs. The printed maps wilted in sweaty hands and I had to feign being lost myself to engage them in referring to the maps and vocalizing the directions as we trudged farther away from their known world.

In all honesty, it *was* difficult to follow routes that involved winding stairways, tunnels, and tiny alleys, but we doggedly worked our way toward the red dot. I'd promised a surprise at our destination, and finally, there it was before us: the original Hwa Nan building complex, stately, elegant, surrounded by trees and wisteria vines (p. 72). Carved in the granite arches were the college name and names of the halls.

The girls had never seen the old campus before and there were ooh and aahs of appreciation. "What happened?" they wanted to know. "Why is this not *our* campus still?"

As we sank onto the stone stairs and benches in the shade of ancient trees to gratefully rest, I spun a story of the mother college, populated by students their age, the very same women who are now the "Old Ladies" they see glaring sternly at awards ceremonies.

"Were the Old Ladies really that young once?" they marveled.

Irrational as it seems, in my experience most young folk see the aged as having been forever old while the same  elders still perceive themselves as young. The students' curiosity was triggered: How had they come to be students at Hwa Nan so long ago? Had the college really been as impressive as it now looked? And what was life really like among the ruins of the Manchu dynasty just before the war with Japan?

Chapter 6: Looking Back – Late 1800s to 1937

"It doesn't matter how slowly you go as long as you don't stop."
Confucius

Unless you had the misfortune to be born into the large class of officially inferior people entitled "mean or ignoble commoners" (slaves, bondsmen, entertainers or low-level government officials), life could be good for a Qing dynasty resident in the early 1800s.[10] Rising above the "inferior people" were the born aristocracy, members of the imperial court, and men of learning. They enjoyed a long period of peace and stability under the Manchu emperors. The government encouraged geographic movement for these so-called "good commoners" (scholars, farmers, artisans or merchants). If a young man fell within this official definition by birth, was adequately fed and ambitious, he could seek his fortune beyond the boundaries of his village, sending money home to the elders as duty demanded.

And more people *were* adequately fed as a wider variety of food became available due to the import of new crops from the Americas and Southeast Asia. In spite of a general distaste for the mobs of foreigners with rude manners (according to Chinese standards of decorum) arriving in their country, urban dwellers enjoyed prosperity. A merchant class emerged and began to patronize literature, theater and the arts.

But later in that century unfortunate events seemed to take the reins out of imperial hands, even if those hands were believed to belong to the Son of Heaven, mandated to rule.

---

[10] See previous footnote, p. 22.

Unsuccessful military confrontations with foreign countries seeking access to trade in China during the 19th century were undermining the authority of the dynasty. While the Emperor was haughtily enjoying his throne at the center of the Middle Kingdom, European nations, viewed as barbarians by the Chinese rulers, were developing superior sailing vessels and weapons.

A sequence of trade wars, droughts, famines, and resulting rebellions further weakened the Emperor's mandate. Plotting servants close to the throne manipulated government officials and created ruthless power struggles within the court. Despite the efforts of the clever dowager Empress Cixi, who lavishly ruled the country in the name of her nephew and weak son in the last years of the 1800s, Manchu rule continued to crumble. After her death in 1908, the control of Puyi, the boy emperor (as seen in the Bertolucci film *The Last Emperor*) slipped into the hands of scheming eunuchs and warlords. Without a central authority or a sense of national unity, struggles for territorial dominance intensified. Powerful landowners commanded hired mercenaries to expand their territory and then to defend it. These armies swept violently across the land, trampling peasant populations in their path. Chaos and bloodshed began to replace the long period of peace, resulting in destitution for the commoners, both "good" and "ignoble."

The missionaries of the early 1900s were quick to assure nervous Manchu bureaucrats that they were not there to do business, take sides in political struggles nor to Westernize China. They wanted only to spread the word of their faith through schools and medical centers. Nevertheless, Lydia Trimble's spirit of determination and her belief in the necessity of taking action based on one's beliefs were rubbing off on this new generation of Chinese women, along with the conventional curriculum. Without intending to do so, the Mandarin merchants of the newly established "treaty ports" imported European traditions and social behavior along with opium, cotton, and wool.

Eager female students, the bright, inquiring daughters of progressive-minded fathers, began to yearn for an education beyond the family courtyard still dominated by beliefs of their elders. They yearned to peek beyond their mud brick and mortar residences with curving tiled roofs fuzzy with moss that were like tiny city-states ruled by the matriarchs and patriarchs of the family. Young students were hungry for other sources of wisdom in addition to that of their ancestors, who were honored on the family altar and consulted daily for guidance.

Thus the college was conceived, born, and blossomed against a background of events that marked both the apex and the decline of an increasingly frightened, insular and self-indulgent Manchu dynasty. Was dynastic collapse imminent? What fortunes might a new dynasty bring? Many Westerners heard the first chords of a new song for China coming out of the chaos.

Lydia, however, sang only one song, the song of her mission. Once her college for women was established firmly on the educational scene, she sought to improve its reputation by attracting local teachers of status to expand her staff of overseas volunteers. Her efforts frequently clashed with prevailing attitudes about the education of females. When an eminent male Chinese scholar agreed to establish a Chinese Language department at the college, his lofty colleagues teased, "Why use a cannon to shoot sparrows?" indicating his talents would be wasted on these twittering girls. But these young sparrows were sometimes more eager to learn than their brothers, and the scholar soon found *his* energies challenged by the intensity of his students' enthusiasm for their new opportunities.

In Boston and St. Louis, committed Christian women leaped up from the confines of their parlor chairs, willing to endure months of pitching seas and cramped quarters in order to educate young Asian girls in the name of leadership, competence, and service. These were not frail, pitifully pious females but strong-minded women of faith with an appetite for adventure. They welcomed the thrill of the open sea and the exotic Orient, as well as the opportunity to share modern educational practices with their Chinese sisters. Few knew, and those who did, ignored the violent history of missionary resentment in many Chinese cities and the current atmosphere of civil unrest in the northern countryside.

In the midst of this instability, a handful of idealistic intellectuals dreamed about establishing a republic based on nationalism, democracy, and equal economic opportunities. Needless to say, this garnered little support from the landowners and warlords who were engaged in acquiring and defending territory. A sense of China as one unified nation was still decades off, but the first breezes of socialism were in the air, fanned by groups of optimistic thinkers hoping to create a utopian state. But when they tried to put their dreams into action, the young revolutionaries often found their efforts rewarded with assassination and exile. While the intellectuals struggled to define a new Chinese republic, those in power struggled for control and the peasantry struggled to survive.

The most famous of these hopeful intellectuals was Dr. Sun Yat-sen. A bright, romantic and international figure, he believed, as did his comrades, that the people of China should rule themselves. Following a series of minor urban rebellions, Sun Yat-sen became the provisional president of the hastily founded Republic of China in 1912, even as his unlucky supporters were being picked off by court assassins dedicated to the continuation of Manchu rule. The newborn republic, prematurely formed and weakened by a diminishing core of leaders, was eventually passed on to Chiang Kai-shek upon Sun's death in 1925. The warlords' armies took advantage of the failing republic and the frail political alternatives to continue rampaging across the northern countryside, burning crops, killing rival landlords' vassals and claiming territory for themselves. In an effort to subdue them Chiang slyly joined forces with members of the newly formed Chinese Communist Party. Once that campaign was successful, Chiang set about eliminating all the once-useful Communist allies he could round up in a brutal purge. He then established himself as head of the Kuomintang or Nationalist Party. Many young Communists fled south where they could plot their revenge in secret.

While the northern air resounded with clashes between Communists and Nationalists, the southern and coastal provinces, such as Fukien, remained relatively prosperous and peaceful. However, a growing number of citizens in all of these port cities, fed up with being overtaxed by their own rulers and abused by the invasion of haughty foreign traders, were cautiously beginning to push back. To add to the change, girls and women were beginning to think for themselves. "Just look at the possibilities for a new belief system to emerge from this chaos," Lydia might have mused. It no doubt seemed to her that the fall of the Emperor, viewed by his subjects as The Son of Heaven, would make it an expedient time to teach of a different sort of Heaven, presided over by more Biblical deities. Lydia was seldom wrong, but the political leaders of the time were inexperienced visionaries. She couldn't foresee the consequences of their utopian ideas as the country stumbled toward an uncertain future, rife with civil war, purges, changing allegiances, and broken promises.

Hwa Nan College leadership suffered no such internal struggles and ignored the storm brewing nationally. Lydia and her niece, Ethel Wallace, with guidance from their stateside missions, provided the structure and the goals. The early curriculum offered students two years of English, science, P. E., and home economics, all taught by a progressive force of western women and Chinese scholars. By 1917, Lydia had put together such a substantial staff that she could offer a four-year course of study. She fervently yearned for wider recognition of the college through gaining a provisional charter from a New York university. While working toward that achievement, Lydia nevertheless saw to it that academic subjects were laced with Christian traditions, ethics, and songs; her goal was to educate spiritually, as well as in earthly matters.

By the 1920s, an innovative kindergarten, whose curriculum encouraged creativity and exploration, was established for children of alumni and staff. "The development of young children is enhanced when they are given freedom to choose their activities, to explore possibilities and to let their individual talents bloom," the progressive western teachers Lydia hired assured skeptical parents. These women brought with them new beliefs in a child-centered approach to early childhood education.

With the help of missionary organizations in America, graduates went abroad for further study. These opportunities lent even more status to the academic enterprise. Enrollment increased, and when it approached 250 students a new dormitory was needed. With the arduous tomb-moving that had been required in 1908 already accomplished, the dorm was constructed without delay to match the administration and classroom buildings. In 1922, slightly more than 32 years after her unheralded arrival in China, Lydia Trimble saw her name chiseled into the façade of the new stone hall which still stands on the original campus in Fuzhou.

The college also increased its exposure to the public through rural programs of basic education for peasants. These programs were beginning to earn widespread respect and imitation by other colleges and would add a shine to Hwa Nan's reputation as a "server of the people" in the second half of the 1900s under Mao's Communist regime. Then the college's motto, "Having received, I ought to give" was changed slightly to "Having received, I ought to serve" in order to echo the words of the Great Helmsman, as Mao liked to be called.

Whatever the exact wording, the sentiment reflected Lydia's belief that the privilege of higher education brings with it an inescapable obligation to give back to one's fellow men and women. From this belief sprung the idea of selected

Hwa Nan students offering lively Sunday afternoon programs in a dozen villages surrounding Foochow. Armed with songs and stories to attract the village children, the girls also taught hygiene, basic first aid, handiwork, and games designed to instill Christian principles. Lydia heard from her charges that one little girl so loved the games that she "forgot all about her bound feet and later suffered much pain. Still later the girl tore off her little shoes and threw them up on a roof."[11] Foot binding had been banned unsuccessfully before, first by the Manchus, then later in 1912 by Sun Yat-sen's shaky Republic. But the Manchus had been seen as invaders, the new Republic as too new to influence such an ancient tradition. Families deeply faithful to cultural beliefs were often slow to adopt such a radical idea as letting their daughters' feet grow normally, without the bone-breaking binding process. "The mountains are tall and the Emperor is far away," declares an old folk saying, referring to the difficulty of enforcing edicts from the central capital. After he took power, Mao Tse-tung banned the practice with more success by creating the slogan, "Women Hold Up Half the Sky" and granting women more status and freedom.

The movement to abolish the crippling belief in foot binding was not the only change in the Chinese air. The young republic was wobbling on its ideological foundations, warlords were fighting for dominance, and anti-foreign feeling was running high. Flames of resentment toward European enterprises on Chinese soil were sparking real fires in the structures of some of the Foochow missionary schools, and the chill of protectionism began to affect the sunny

---

[11] Wallace, p. 59.

confidence heretofore felt on some campuses. As the people of China struggled to develop a proud national identity, schools and hospitals built by foreign missionaries became tempting targets for vandalism and arson and some fared badly. However, the girls of Hwa Nan seemed immune to attempts to enlist them in either Communist Party rebellion or Nationalist Party support. They continued their studies, sporting events, and community outreach without catching the fever of the spreading ideological unrest.

Pleased with her accomplishments and a keen observer of the political climate change, Lydia wisely felt the time was right to retire from administrative responsibilities. In 1925, Dr. Ida Belle Lewis succeeded her as president. Ida Belle's charm, her doctoral degree from Columbia, and her fluency in Mandarin provided all the ingredients deemed necessary for a long and successful tenure. In addition, Lydia intended to give frequent counsel. The indomitable founder could not bear to leave and remained in residence on campus to oversee the transition. Both hoped this change would invigorate the position of Hwa Nan during this time of social upheaval.

But by 1927, Nationalist troops had taken possession of Foochow and it was decreed that all Christian institutions must be administrated solely by Chinese leaders. In addition to millions of dollars in financial support from the United States (which was deeply invested in keeping a communist system from prevailing in Asia), Chiang Kai-shek understood that popular support for his Nationalist Party depended on the ability to take back China for the Chinese. Dr. Lewis' presidency was over in just short of two years, as was the American domination and leadership of Hwa Nan College.

Both Lucy Wang and Carol Chen, graduates of Hwa Nan who had completed post-graduate degrees in the U.S., were considered qualified to head the college under the new protectionist ruling. However, direct action towards a quick appointment is not the way of Chinese culture, in which subtle patterns of acquiescence and refusal must be observed.

"Carol Chen is an intelligent and hard-working woman," Lucy pointed out, "and would be perfect for the job as first Chinese president of Hwa Nan!"

"No, no," countered Carol. "Only Lucy has the leadership qualities and personal stamina to be the first Chinese president of Hwa Nan!"

Finally the correct number of protestations and counter-protestations had been offered, and Lucy Wang was appointed president. That Lucy was described as "lovely as a lotus above water," with a feminine demeanor and charming manners, helped quiet the masculine murmurs that these educated women were getting a bit too big for their

britches. In fact, they weren't supposed to be wearing britches at all! Lucy's command of diplomatic Mandarin worked to her advantage in deflecting the suspicion of provincial Ministry officials regarding Hwa Nan's scope and influence. And in a province where every region spoke its own dialect and power still remained in the hands of puffed-up local officials, her fluency in the local dialects was useful in creating a sense of community with her geographic neighbors.

President Wang also kept her lovely dark eyes on the barometer of change in China and saw it falling rapidly in south China. She knew that Hwa Nan needed to comply and compete with other schools in new regulations regarding salaries for teachers and breadth of academic curriculum in order to stay viable. Christian content would need to be minimized, and proselytizing discouraged. She also knew the school needed to retain the support from abroad.

"We (who have graduated from Hwa Nan) cannot help but be grateful to our American friends of the Women's Foreign Missionary Society," Lucy wrote. "I myself am a product of the institution and words cannot express my gratitude."[12] She challenged other graduates who had gone on to earn degrees at universities and colleges such as Columbia, Michigan, Morningside and Mills College to join her in turning all their energy into making this possible for other women in South China.

In order to strengthen ties to educational interests abroad, she made connections with seven sister colleges in America to help secure endowments and forge ongoing

---

[12] Wallace, p. 54.

loyalties. With a combination of charm, intelligence, and support from outside sources, Lucy was able to secure approval from Chinese government leaders, as well as a charter from the Board of Regents of the University of the State of New York by 1934. The degree-granting capacity of Hwa Nan seemed secure.

Chinese politics, however, were becoming less secure and more unstable. Chiang Kai-shek vacillated between promoting friendship with the Communists in order to halt the escalating Japanese aggression, and ruthlessly competing with the same Communists to rule and represent China. Chiang's leadership was rife with corruption and began to look to global on-lookers like another dynasty in the disguise of a republic. The Generalissimo, as Chiang was addressed, enjoyed considerable support for his campaign against the communists from the U.S. under President Roosevelt (some say because of efforts of the beautiful Soong Mei-ling, Chiang's charming wife who had been educated at Wesleyan College). Later President Truman was more reluctant to become deeply involved in the on-going civil war.

Young Mao Tse-tung demonstrated his skill as an inspired revolutionary leader at a time when the Red Army was on the run from Chiang's ambitions. Mao's philosophy of extending support and assistance to the people who worked the fields on which the battles were being fought was new and very welcome to the Chinese people. The 4,000-mile Long March, which began in the southeastern province of Jiangxi as a retreat from the Kuomintang in 1934 and ended in a triumph of endurance in 1935, confirmed Mao Tse-tung as the undisputed leader of the Chinese Communist Party. Under his leadership 85,000 poorly equipped and heavily burdened young men, devoted to the cause of liberation for their people, set out at night to escape from the encirclement by Chiang's army. The March took them over 24 rivers and 18 mountain ranges, including the 18,000-foot Snowy Mountains and the swampy marshes of the northern grasslands. More than 70,000 of these men perished due to cold, exhaustion and poor nutrition, but they befriended thousands of villagers on their journey to Shaanxi Province in the northeast and earned Mao loyal support for his Communist cause.

Meanwhile, Lucy Wang juggled her duties as a Barbour fellow at the University of Michigan with her role as President of Hwa Nan College for Women. She boarded steam ships and railroad cars in China and America, represented the school at important government conferences, and promoted interest in (and sought money for) the college by speaking engagements and soirees. Fund-raising was becoming increasingly difficult as the dark clouds of the Great Depression began to cast deeper shadows in America. Cuts in the college's budget meant lowering teachers' salaries, and questions arose whether the underpaid staff could gain approval of the newly formed Ministry of Education. Government officials were casting suspicious eyes at Christian schools previously staffed by volunteer Western missionaries and demanding the recruitment of Chinese staff at competitive salaries.

More clouds had gathered over Fukien skies by the summer of 1937 when the long struggle between China and Japan over territory became open warfare. The Japanese brought the deposed child emperor, Puyi, out of exile and converted him to a shadow puppet in his young adulthood, allowing the Japanese to lay claim to Manchuria and lands in the northeast. Japan's superior air force had recently bombed Peking and Shanghai; both eventually fell under Japanese control. There was reason to believe that Foochow and its environs would be the next target. The area was prosperous and the Min River was a major transportation route. Japan's global ambitions included conquering and possessing China's resource-rich lands, while within China itself the struggle for dominance continued between the Communist and the Nationalist armies.

"Prepare to defend the Motherland!" shrieked loudspeakers on public buildings. Foochow students were bombarded by slogans of propaganda and patriotism that summer. They willingly attended lectures on wartime knowledge where they learned about air raid precautions, wartime communications, and control of food distribution. Hwa Nan girls were trained in first aid every Saturday by local medical professionals and were required to prepare and carry a bag that contained all necessary medical materials in case of Japanese attack. They sewed padded jackets for brothers and childhood playmates who had been conscripted to fight and embroidered the characters for "Wishing You Victory" on the lapels. The soldiers carried with them a kind of rice flour bagel called *guan bing* that could be strung on twine threaded through the center hole. The girls packed the *guan bing* with personal messages of encouragement and good cheer. As the war dragged on, the winter was cold and the troops poorly equipped; these notes from home warmed the spirits of more than one soldier in his frosty encampment.

In 1938, the still-dominant Nationalist government required all high school and college students to engage in mass education programs in order to alert communities in the countryside against the growing danger of Japanese attack. Schools were closed for the first three months of that year so the students could carry on this vastly important role in the war effort. All students were expected to travel by foot and ox cart to assigned mountain and riverside villages, to live in hastily built huts, eat basic local food and help organize these communities against possible occupation. Because of the superiority of Japanese military equipment, resistance could only take the form of subtly undermining the invader's authority.

Many Hwa Nan girls were urban daughters of merchant families raised with cosmopolitan perspectives and privilege through their families' trade with Western firms. They were shocked at conditions in the rural villages to which they were sent.

"I hated having to do mass education," one of the Old Ladies, who had been a student at that time, later confessed to me. "The villages were dirty and backward and nothing in my upbringing had prepared me for the discomfort of being among ignorant strangers."

Nevertheless, they undertook the task with grace and kindness. "If every woman in China were like you," declared one peasant woman, "our country would be strong."[13]

"The Motherland" was a noble concept, but the notion of the entire population as a group of people united under the flag of a modern Chinese nation, with shared concerns, privileges, and responsibilities, was still new and lightly grasped. The family was the fundamental unit of solidarity,

---

[13] Wallace, p. 80.

society was deeply stratified in regards to financial and social position, and many young people had never ventured far from their tiny comfort zones of home and school before.

Young Ma Xiufa, a sophomore at Hwa Nan, found herself caught up in the excitement of collecting food and clothing for refugees from the conflict, learning how to dig a bomb

shelter or how to treat a burn. Xiufa[14] and her best friend, Xu Daofeng, had been raised in well-to-do households where indentured servants waited on their large extended families. They initially loved the sense of urgency and the satisfaction of doing real work. Music lessons and hymn singing were replaced by preparing lessons in wartime survival for country strangers with no family connections to the Ma or Xu clans. But living temporarily and teaching in

[14] Chinese surnames are stated first, their given names stated second. For example, this student's family name is Ma, and the name she would be called by friends is Xiufa.

88

the discomfort and grime of mud huts and dirt roads, with no running water and with only rice and field greens into which they could plunge their chopsticks after a hard day's work was another matter.

Clad in the pajama-like suits and straw hats of rural people (p. 88), Xiufa and Daofeng traveled with their classmates to villages near Foochow, teaching first aid, resource conservation, what to do in case of attack, and rudimentary reading skills. None of the villages had the capacity for radio communication, so a simply written newspaper informing the peasants of the rapidly changing situation was developed and circulated.

Xu Daofeng was especially good at math and taught simple calculations while a literature-loving student, Chen Zhongying, taught basic reading skills. The three girls grew closer as they lived out the Hwa Nan motto on a daily basis. There was plenty of giggling too, at the quaint ways of the peasant youth and the stares the urban girls initially drew. They were too young to know that they were establishing lifelong bonds during these times, bonds that would support them through periods of elation and despair and provide a resilient springboard for the resurrection of their *alma mater* almost fifty years later.

Chapter 7: Looking Around – The Students Compare Generations

"To see things in the seed, that is the genius".
Lao Tze

After hearing some of the old Hwa Nan stories, I was hoping the students could view the Old Ladies from a new perspective. They now had information that might allow them to see these women, who carried so much history on their rounded shoulders, through different lenses. Chen Zhongying, square and severe in hairstyle, demeanor and dress, was the current president of the college. Xu Daofeng, still full of spirit and energy, was head of Foreign Affairs, and Ma Xiufa served beside them on the governing board. The students respected them, but I found they still had trouble imagining these severely-dressed women, now well into their 80s, as graceful frolicsome girls. The Old Ladies could mostly be seen sitting impassively on contest-judging panels, shuffling to weekly planning meetings or being escorted to awards dinners. Try as they might, many of the students confided it was impossible to picture the octogenarians playing hide-and-seek among the columns in the old Hwa Nan buildings, writing sentimental messages to tuck into soldiers' packages, or giggling in peasant villages. So I proposed an imaginary time travel game with my classes one morning to get us talking about generational change.

"Shut your eyes and think of your grandmother or your great auntie, the way she looks now, what her voice sounds like, the kind of things she says, her outlook on life. Next try to imagine her when she was the age you are now. What kind of clothes did she wear? How many people were in her primary family and how did they live? What skills did her education include? Who educated her? Did she have a love interest? On what consideration was her marriage based? Who had the power in the family?" The students jotted down notes as I asked questions. I gave plenty of time for them to generate images, to brainstorm in small groups..."*in English!*" I had to constantly remind them. This was an oral English class, after all.

Family stories were sometimes kept under wraps because no one wanted to admit having the slightest connection with a land-owning background. Landlords were seen as enemies of the people, an attitude leftover from both the Communist revolution culminating in the establishment of the People's Republic in 1949 and the more recent Cultural Revolution of the 1960-70s. For that reason, I didn't know how much honest sharing I would get.

Grandparents (or great aunts if there were no surviving grandparents) had been many of the girls' primary caregivers when they were infants in order to free up their parents to work long days in community paddies, or to leave home for better jobs in urban areas. My students' memories of that time in their ancestral villages was bittersweet. Many girls told fond tales of simple rural life, but also remembered missing their parents sorely.

Cousins Abby and Margaret recalled that they only saw their parents once a year at Spring Festival when they were toddlers. Most had to wait to join Mama and Baba in the city until they were school age and could be cared for there. Sometimes grandparents reluctantly joined a young family in a town apartment, but felt crowded and disoriented by the urban uproar. In a country setting with little media to distract them as toddlers, these young people became imprinted with the lives and habits of their grandparents, listening to their old stories, sharing the old ways. *The Analects* of Confucius still informed the character development of individuals, prescribed the structure within a family and influenced the governance of the larger community.[15] A strict order of respect and power, and their unavoidable responsibilities, was fundamental to Confucian beliefs.

After we had recorded and charted on the blackboard what life was like in Grandmother's day regarding education, dress, domestic life, and the source of family power, we moved on to visualizing what their mothers' lives were like as young women, using the same questions. What a range of experiences they reported! And what striking differences depending on whether the family was rural or urban, well off or poor, intact or scattered! After we recorded this episode of our time travel on the dusty chalkboard, I asked them to describe their own lives using the same guidelines. We added that information to the now-crowded board, and came up with an intriguing comparison chart of living history. The changes in lifestyle were so vivid that I was able to use it later to help orient visiting U.S. students to the width of the generation gap in the families of their student "buddies."

Here's what we saw: In the 1950s, when most of their grandmothers or great aunts were teenagers (as was I), much of life in China was transitioning from a feudal state to a Communist form of government patterned loosely after the

---

[15] Confucius (551-479 BCE) was an influential social philosopher whose models of familial and social order have been revered for generations. He advocated education, self-discipline, compassion, and strong leadership from elders who fostered these characteristics in themselves, their families, and the community.

Russian model. The chairman of the Communist Party, Mao Tse-tung, was trying everything possible to level the playing field between previously powerful landowners and powerless peasants. Most Chinese in those days lived in large extended family compounds, with a strictly prescribed social order based on seniority. There might be eight or ten siblings, many without names other than First Elder Brother or Third Sister. Girls were undervalued and could be sold or traded as wives or extra pairs of hands when times got hard. When a girl married, she completely left her family of origin anyway, and became a member of the groom's family forevermore, so why get sentimentally attached? Marriages were arranged by the elders, based on the family's reproductive needs and the monetary advantage acquired by such a union. Status and financial recompense were primary considerations.

My students thought the clothes Grandmother and Great Auntie wore as girls were mainly functional and very few. Pictures they had seen showed serious people in durable, plain, homemade pajama suits, sometimes homespun. Clothes were worn until they were worn out and handed from girl to girl. No one confessed to having grandparents dressed in silks or having servants as youngsters. A barrette or hair ribbon might be added to her wardrobe if the girl were favored by her family, but if the family were poor, the clothes would be patched and sometimes ragged. If she lived in the countryside, she probably didn't go to school, but would be taught domestic chores by older sisters and women. Even boys could not be spared from the paddies for more than four to six years of schooling. If Grandmother had been a city girl, more educational opportunities might have existed, but it was up to her elders to decide if it was to the family's benefit to allow her to attend school. In Grandmother's day, the students recounted, power rested in the hands of the older generation; long-deceased ancestors were gravely consulted. Senior members of the family were the unquestioned authorities. The care of these elderly relatives, when they became infirm, was the primary duty of the eldest son or the next son in seniority and to shirk this duty was unthinkable.

I tried to reconcile these lives with memories of my teenage years in the Pacific Northwest during that timeframe. The Korean War had ended and war hero Dwight Eisenhower was presiding over an America enjoying expansive economic growth. There was a surge in manufacturing as the country produced airplanes, automobiles, and appliances. Brown vs. the Board of Education opened doors of equal education to all, "regardless of race, color or creed," and the Civil Rights movement was gathering energy. The Vietnamese had just defeated the French at Diem Bien Phu, an event that was to pull the U.S. deeper and deeper into a disastrous war. But my friends and I, giggling schoolgirls in poodle skirts and flipped up hairdos, cared for none of this. Well-raised young ladies, but now obsessed with clothes and boys, we ate hamburgers at drive-ins, and jitterbugged to doo-wop at the Community Center dances. We stomped and clapped madly when the high school band segued from a Souza march into "Rock Around the Clock" and swooned over the angst-ridden films of James Dean. While I was wondering if I'd get invited to the prom, my students' grandmothers were wondering if they'd have any meat with their rice and field greens this week or whether their commune would meet the production quota set by Chairman Mao.

What about their mothers' lives when they were in their late teens and early twenties? The students were tentative. Most of them had heard more about their grandmothers' early lives than that of their parents. The students' mothers had been young in the 1960s or 70s and had been in their teens when the country was churning with paranoia and persecution during the Great Proletarian Cultural Revolution. Memories from that brutal era were seldom bandied about and were not part of family or community anniversaries. Talking about the dark times was considered pointless, a waste of energy, and venturing dangerously close to governmental criticism.

"Let's not talk about sad times that have passed," my Chinese friends would say  whenever I tried to get them to tell me about their experience in the Cultural Revolution. "We should leave those memories behind us."

Few pictures or songs sentimentalized the notion of the "good ole days." Occasionally a performer could be seen on the deafening TVs mounted inside long distance buses, singing of the beauty and happiness forfeited when people left their ancestral villages to seek their fortunes in urban areas, but no one was fooled; the village was a cold dirty place filled with hard work and few amusements. Parents rarely spoke fondly of "the old country" or became misty-eyed about the rough life they had lived there. Therefore, most of the girls only spoke of their mother's generation in terms of the general history of the period.

After liberating China from its feudal past in the late 1940s, Mao Tse-tung embarked on a series of sweeping reforms and poorly conceived social programs that had resulted in the death of millions through starvation, forced labor, and executions. During the 1950s until the mid-60s, he elevated the status of women through new laws and propaganda campaigns to popularize their new status. Education for women under Communist rule was provided primarily in the realm of the practical skills. Some of my students' mothers had been educated as "barefoot doctors," serving the residents of rural areas as visiting health consultants, some as factory workers, some as leaders of a commune. Several of the girls' more academically-talented parents had received mathematics or engineering instruction while some trained as teachers. One student shared a story about her mother being sold to a wealthier family to pay off the debts of her desperate family. Many only knew that their mother's people had been shattered and scattered during the Cultural Revolution as either Red Guards or persecuted professionals.

Almost all formal education was suspended during the Cultural Revolution in order to free up young people to form cadres of Red Guards and purge society of the "Four Olds"(old customs, old culture, old habits, and old ideas). Red Guards were given free access to public transportation, and millions of peasant youth surged into cities to assert their dominance. Schools were emptied out as privileged urban youth and their teachers were assigned to remote villages in the name of "re-education." Academics and professionals were banished to the countryside to experience manual labor. Western music and instruments were burned, and doctors were sent to communes to work in the fields while students took over hospitals. Even a person who wore spectacles could be suspected of academic accomplishment and persecuted. Survival depended on conformity to the new order and a verifiable peasant background. Young people of both sexes wore loose drab pantsuits, possibly adding a red neckerchief, and young women sported no decoration to call attention to themselves, in the name of sameness and simplicity.

When my students' mothers neared marital age, their parents continued to be very influential in choosing the husband, but a daughter now had more voice in a parent's choice of mates than Grandmother had. Nevertheless, marriage was still seen as a practical matter to strengthen the family and increase its wealth, not as a romantic venture. Not until 1980 did the Marriage Law officially establish the rights of women to choose partners, as well as to divorce them. Even though families were already getting smaller due to economic pressures, a new official policy *required* the use of birth control. The policy made it clear the government frowned on infanticide, previously a common strategy to ensure an abundance of boys and limit family size. Abortion was viewed as just one of many acceptable forms of birth control. In spite of this trend, female infanticide continued to be common. After bearing a child, most of my students' mothers handed over their babies to *their* mothers to raise, while the middle generation did the hard work of making a living for the whole family. This often involved combining farm and factory work, and negotiating the tricky footwork required of them by a swiftly changing culture and economy.

Age still conferred respect in the 1970s, but the Cultural Revolution had reduced the older generation's power. Schools began to reopen in 1977, but most of my students' mothers were too old to return to the lockstep Chinese system that required college attendance directly from high school. Besides, a two-parent income was increasingly necessary to provide the family with the new consumer goods slowly becoming available in the marketplace. Many of their mothers went to work in factories. Care of the elderly was still a family responsibility but, as more and more members of the middle generation left villages to replace subsistence farming with a salaried job in cities, the actual care often fell to older children left behind, and sometimes to the community of oldsters left behind themselves.

As we built our comparison chart on the blackboard, we noted gigantic differences between the three generations of women. They had memorized the official history of their country, but were still impressed to see summarized before them how much had changed within the lifespan of close family members. It also helped the girls to see the Old Ladies in a broader perspective. They were not just women who had always been old. These women had survived two revolutions with their optimism intact. They were giving back energy from what they had learned over the course of hard lives that might have exhausted lesser women. The Old Ladies became more like heroines—maybe not the lithesome beauties of fairy tales, but models of intelligence, endurance, and large measures of good luck.

Over the next few days my students discussed our chart and talked about how their own rights to be educated, to choose whom to marry, to wear bright, fanciful clothes, and anticipate careers in business evolved from the lives of women before them. The most vivid recollection of the old days that had been passed down from their elders were that there were "a lot more people and a lot less food."

"Who holds the power in the family now?" I asked.

"The person who makes the most money!" they unanimously answered.

Mostly born in the early 80s, they all recognized their own measure of good luck in being conceived by parents who welcomed a girl as their only child. China's famous One Child Policy, introduced in 1978 as a temporary measure to limit population growth, resulted in the frequent abortion or abandonment of female babies. Even though they were declared illegal except in cases of suspected disability, ultrasound procedures were frequently used to determine the sex of the child *in utero*. If the fetus was a girl, the couple might choose to abort and try again for a boy. Many a female newborn had been abandoned on doorsteps or in public markets because of the importance in Chinese culture of a boy to carry on the family name and to care for elderly parents.

There are virility issues involved, too. One of my teaching colleagues proudly showed me pictures of her naked baby in which all the frames focused on the boy's genitalia. Men are physically stronger, still have better moneymaking potential, and thus are believed to be able to provide a better life for the elders who would be dependent on them. The One Child Policy was primarily directed to urban Han Chinese; country folk and ethnic minorities could try again for a boy if their first child were a girl. However, whether the policy was enforced by a steep fine, pressure to abort, or forced sterilization, it varied with the vigilance and diligence of the local authorities and their flunkies.

One of my colleagues retained vivid memories of such diligence. Linda's mother, a woman from a large family in the countryside, had a girl first, and on the second attempt, bore my colleague. There was no question of infanticide in this family, but when the two girls were eight and ten, the couple decided to try again for a boy.

Word leaked out, as word always does in close communities long on gossip and short on excitement. The pregnant mother was warned to abort by the local authorities, and when she refused, the little white abortion van pulled up to the gates of the family compound in mid-morning, while most of the able-bodied adults were at work in the fields. Linda remembers her mother's struggles to resist the medical personnel who restrained her, aborted the child, and sterilized her. A few years after the deed was done, the family adopted a boy from another arm of the family to take the place of the lost son. Such is the strength of family commitment and the desire for a male heir.

My students were well aware of their parents' progressive thinking in cherishing them, their one-baby girl. As unintended consequences of the One Child Policy became more visible, such as the much-publicized higher number of males in the general population, many parents have begun to reconsider the wisdom of the traditional position. Adult males often desert the ancestral village in search of better job opportunities in more prosperous locations, leaving elders to fend for themselves. "Girls are more filial, more caring," some parents suggest, "even if they move away."

Also, modern women are no longer required to leave their birth family completely. Decisions are usually made in partnership by the new couple, according to their needs and preferences. The authoritarian patriarchal family structure is being replaced by one in which the middle generation of wage earners, many of them stylishly dressed women, are ready to take on the traditional role of the first-born son, and to treat their elders with deference and respect.

Another unintended consequence of the One Child Policy has been the booming adoption market for Chinese babies that surged in 2003. The legitimate commerce in girl babies has subsided due to stringent new rules that have sharply restricted who can adopt children: no one obese, with a facial deformity, single, over 50, or on anti-depressants for a serious mental disorder. The new rules also sought to curb a less legal, more lucrative baby-selling market. The $20,000 to $25,000 Caucasian couples from Europe and America paid to adopt Chinese babies was an irresistible temptation to those willing to traffic in adorable dark-eyed infants. I once encountered a couple from the Netherlands in Zhou Hai Park taking their newly adopted 3-year-old for a walk. The Chinese child stood listless and unresponsive as they spoke lovingly to her in Dutch. My Chinese companion, Linda, squatted down and said a few kind words of Chinese to the child, whose face lit up with joy. In the ensuing conversation, we gleaned that the Dutch couple believed they had gone through proper channels to adopt the child, but the toddler had vivid memories of her former family. Could she be feeling kidnapped? Linda did what she could to soothe her, but we were left with a sense of unease about the child's origins.

While my students and I were charting the differences between three generations of Chinese women and discussing the new world of choices available to them in terms of education, mates, clothes, and careers, one of my off-campus friends was quietly making choices of her own. A married woman of intelligence and heart, she enjoyed her existing family, purposeful employment and a law-abiding life. But in spite of severe financial reprisals and social stigma, a few Chinese parents are courageous and self-determining enough to dream of having *both* a boy and a girl, defying a policy that limits them to one child. Meiling was such a parent.

Chapter 8: Looking Closer at One Woman's Life
Meiling's Story

Meiling wanted a daughter. Such a simple wish, and yet it was only occasionally she allowed herself to toy with the forbidden possibility. Since the 1980s when China's population reached 980 million and the One Child Policy went into effect, it was dangerous to even think about having a second child, especially if you lived in a city. Thinking might lead to doing, and doing in this case, would lead to heavy fines and certain punishment. If the fines were not paid, the child would be "unregistered" and not eligible for public school, hospital health care, or a residency permit. No, such a wish was not simple for urban government employees such as Meiling and her husband, Wenji.

Nevertheless, Meiling sometimes indulged in dreaming about what it would be like to make such a decision freely, without fear of government retribution. She already had her boy child to carry on the family name, care for her and Wenji in their old age, and burn paper money for their comfort in the afterlife. Meiling had fulfilled the deepest duty of an honorable wife and given her husband a son, but she, herself, felt unfulfilled. Being the mother of a son, even a strong-willed, big-eared son like her own, was a source of pride in her family and in her community. She could feel the envious eyes of childless women on her as she lifted her heavily-bundled toddler onto a bus seat or fed him the choicest morsels in a noisy restaurant. But when she looked into his eyes, she saw unfamiliar masculine elements in his nature, elements no woman could understand.

Meiling yearned for a daughter to be her mirror, her

youthful twin, a little girl for whom she could provide the pink dresses and piano lessons not available to children of the 60s and 70s when the Great Proletarian Cultural Revolution ripped childhoods to shreds. During that time, her teacher-parents had been accused of embracing Western ideas and were sent to the countryside for "re-education." Meiling was shipped off to a reluctant relative who met the approval of the Red Guards, and spent her young years unwelcome in her foster home and scorned in the village. Now shops were filled with ruffled anklets, hair bows and tiny plastic purses printed with Hello Kitty images. These she longed to possess for her daughter—and maybe also for the young, abandoned Meiling, clad in hand-me-down clothes that she still carried indelibly in the arms of her memory.

Discussions with her husband about her fantasies were short and unfruitful. Wenji would only frown and shake his head. As an employee of a municipal regulator agency, there was no question of having a second child. Wenji must demonstrate, at all times, obedience to government policy. Meiling's employment in the office of a state-run university yielded the idea doubly unthinkable. True, peasant families in the countryside were allowed to have a second child if their firstborn were a girl. After all, what was the use of raising a girl when, upon marriage, she became the exclusive property of the husband's family? Rural parents could try again for the essential male child, with full government approval and the resulting civic recognition that included health care and education. Also true was the fact that money bought anything in China and families with more than one child could buy their additional children citizenship with the payment of substantial fees. But penalties for city dwellers who claimed their livelihood from government coffers were severe, and often resulted in the doors to those coffers closing with a resolute clang.

Nevertheless, like so many women before her, Meiling found Mother Nature a hard woman to ignore. She secretly envied her friends with daughters, no matter how much they despaired over their son-less situations. To admit to jealousy was to lose face, and yet the sight of her friend, Jiaolian, braiding her daughter's glossy hair made her weak with yearning. Going shopping with her cousin Yan intensified the yearning. While Meiling bought cartoon-printed tee shirts and sturdy pants for her son, her cousin selected small frilly dresses and flowered undies for her daughter. Most weekends, contests were held in the crowded shopping malls in which tiny over-dressed children performed acts of entertainment to the encouragement of parental applause. As the two women watched these exhibitions, the clouds of Meiling's imagination swirled around her, creating images of her graceful daughter accepting the prize for her well-performed song or dance. At night, embracing her husband in the family bed, she flirted with the fantasy of a failed condom, an incautious coupling.

In fact, Chinese-made products sold in China are not subject to rigorous quality control as are exports to foreign countries. As many reproductive health NGOs focusing on Asia have discovered, locally-made condoms are generally smaller and often undependably-made, due to substandard materials. There is even a small industry devoted to their re-use. The couple had for many years imposed on the goodwill of an American teacher at Meiling's university to bring them condoms made in the USA, when she arrived to teach each year. They were small, light and essential; the teacher did not mind adding them to her luggage. In fact, she often chuckled at the expression on the face of the customs officer who inspected her suitcase. It would make good gossip around the official's tea break room!

One summer the teacher became unexpectedly ill and did not return for fall semester. The condoms did not return, either. By October, Meiling was pregnant.

When Meiling discovered her pregnancy, the conversation she had with her husband was different from those she had attempted in the past. Possibility had become reality. The couple was Christian in perspective, but one has to eat and pay rent no matter what one believes. In spite of his recent conversion to the faith, Wenji was a rational man and reason dictated the pregnancy be terminated. While China might be on a rising curve of economic advancement, it is still not the land of opportunity for many. Residency regulations attempted to restrict the movement of a current population of 1.3 billion without much success. Greedy provincial officials put their own prices on work permits. Office workers were graduating from college by the millions. Financial support for the unemployed was not a government responsibility but a family responsibility. Without jobs, he and Meiing would have to depend on their family and friends, resulting in great loss of face. Steady legal jobs, such as they had, were hard to find, and not to be jeopardized by one woman's longing.

An abortion was scheduled. Because atheism is the official religious position of the Chinese Communist Party, there are no zealous "Right to Life" groups, nor public conversations about the souls of unborn babies. Abortion is considered just another method of birth control. Repeated abortions are recognized as hard on a woman's body, but it bears no personal or social stigma. As a Chinese citizen, Meiling agreed with the government's position and methods. She understood that forces strict and powerful were needed to contain her country's population growth. She knew that local officials were often rewarded for detecting an illegal pregnancy and that they, in turn, rewarded informants. As a dutiful wife, she knew she should obey her husband. But as a pregnant woman, Meiling heard the whisper of a higher authority.

As the time neared for her abortion, she became distraught. Meiling saw the little fish now swimming in the amniotic pond of her womb as a new soul, a Christian soul, possibly a female soul. She desperately wanted an ultrasound reading to verify the gender of the child before she returned it to the karmic cycle. But hospitals in China are government agencies; all doctors are government employees sworn to uphold government policy. Meiling's medical records, which must be presented for treatment of any kind at any hospital, would contain information about the birth of a previous child. When the second pregnancy was revealed, it could be brought to an end for the good of society, never mind the mother's protests. The welfare of the group has always been valued over individual choice in Chinese culture. Government policy trumps personal preference as far as the Communist Party is concerned, unless one is very rich or very powerful.

Making matters even more complicated, routine ultrasound procedures had recently been declared illegal, because too often their main purpose was to detect the sex of the fetus in order to decide whether to continue the pregnancy. In the past, if the child were a boy it would be allowed to develop full term; if the child were a girl, often the family would decide to abort the fetus in order to try again for a boy. The government's smile of approval for this particular approach to birth control was changing to a frown, as the demographics began to show an alarming increase in the ratio of males to females in the general population. People with money and connections could still obtain an ultrasound test from doctors willing to justify the test with medical suspicions of abnormality, but Meiling had neither money nor influence. However, she had a hunch she could find some of both on Flower Lane.

Not one flower grows on Flower Lane these days, but when the old stone Methodist Episcopal church was built there in the late 1800s by American missionaries, Foochow was laced with flowery footpaths and leafy trees. The city's densest population clustered nearby along the banks of the Min River. Beyond the tile-roofed family compounds, housing generations of lively Chinese families from birth to death, were the orchards, fields, and lanes that buffered the port city from the lawless countryside. It was on this blooming edge of town that the missionaries erected their sturdy Gothic structure, a church they hoped would survive the country's regional wars and political instability. In fact, it survived battles and revolutions with seemingly greater ease than the current threat of urban renewal in a sprawling city of 7 million. It stands today on a gritty dead-end alley, no longer surrounded by flowers but tucked in the shadow of shining skyscrapers and specialty shops crammed with consumer goods, like a pious old aunt peering out with a granite stare at the excesses of a younger generation.

The congregation of Flower Lane Church is now 99% Chinese. Some of the faithful are descendants of the original converts; many more are newcomers to the religious experience seeking a deeper satisfaction than non-stop shopping gives them. The church is a lively center of Bible study, religious ceremony, and quiet comfort in a cacophonous urban center. Cranes building a new subway system swing overhead. Across busy Avenue Bai Yiqi, teeming with cars, buses, and bicycles, McDonald's dispenses Happy Meals to new fast food converts. Once a month, the Flower Lane congregation gathers to "make a joyful noise unto the Lord" at Grace Night. It is an astonishing musical experience complete with a five-piece band, a full choir, and the waving hands of Chinese worshipers gathering qi energy from a gospel tradition. It is to this congregation that Meiling turned for direction and means.

Members of the congregation rallied! "You can hide the pregnancy," they advised, "under the layers of warm clothing you will wear as the weather gets colder. Don't go to a doctor or a hospital. We'll find a way to obtain an unofficial ultrasound."

People with connections to the medical profession promised to use the "back door" to obtain medical assistance if Meiling decided to keep the baby. They would face the financial and social consequences as a unit. Funds would be raised; she would be supported. Meiling was elated. The story she told herself was, "This baby must be a gift from God and surely such a gift (as well as Gift's parents) will be protected."

A few weeks later she visited a female cousin in the countryside who was experiencing some difficulties with her pregnancy and had scheduled an ultrasound investigation.

109

Meiling went with her and when her cousin's test was completed, she slipped the technician a handful of yuan to quickly research the sex of the child with the magical diagnostic wand. "I had no idea I'd be in a clinic this weekend," she declared, "or I'd have brought my medical records." Government dictates in the countryside are often softened by human sympathy. The technician yielded; the undocumented test was hastily conducted.

It was a girl! The baby growing inside her was the duplication of herself she longed for! "How can we deny God's gift?" she implored her reluctant husband. They climbed the 500 stone steps to the temple atop Gushan near Fuzhou to ask the guidance of Guan Yin, the female goddess of mercy and compassion. Incense was lit, offerings made to gold-plated statues, and cashew-shaped divination blocks were thrown. The signs were auspicious. Tendrils of excitement began to cling to Wenji as the breezes of approval from both the Buddhist goddess and the Christian community began to blow, and he began to waver. Perhaps the fetus should be allowed to grow and see what fate would bring.

Meiling bought jackets cut to flare and jumpers gathered above the waist. During his rule, Mao conservatively declared there would be no coal burned for heating buildings south of the Yangtze River and the bone-chilling tradition survives today. Fresh air is thought to be an important source of health, blowing away flu viruses and cold germs. In spite of a bitter wind off the East China Sea, windows are propped open, doors left ajar. People in Meiling's office wore coats as they shuffled government forms, teachers paced their classrooms in down jackets, students sat bundled in hats and gloves. Prenatal secrets can easily be hidden in winter wraps.

But as the hopeful warmth of spring began to yield to the humid heat of summer, Meiling began to lose courage with every pound she gained. The southern Chinese are strong believers in bundling up until summer on the lunar calendar, never mind the weather. How long could she hide her swollen belly under a winter jacket? Would she be reported to the One Child Policy authorities by some self-righteous citizen? Where was she going to find a hospital that would deliver her baby instead of performing an abortion? She had heard of such things happening; she began to imagine it happening to her.

She awoke from frightening dreams. In one, she walked in the front door of the downtown Hospital for Mothers and Infants and was grabbed by white-shrouded interns who hauled her to surgery. In China, white is the color of death and mourning. There were white lights, white sheets, white faces staring down at her. She'd awaken, sweaty and shaken, running her hands over her taut belly to make sure the child was still there. She prayed to her departed ancestors for protection, lighting sticks of incense and offering choice foods on the altar of their images. She prayed to her Christian God, too. This was a time to cover all the bases.

If the front door of the hospital was for nightmares, the "back door," through which so many transactions in China pass, was the door Meiling needed to enter any hospital. And to open that "back door" she needed to activate her *guanxi*, the ancient and complicated network of reciprocal favors and obligations. For centuries the use of *guanxi* was an essential survival strategy in a society where laws were enforced according to the whim of petty bureaucrats, where official channels were corrupt and relationships more real than rules. Guanxi and using the "back door" are practices that have flowed through 2,000 years of brutal war-torn feudal history, so much so that one scholar suggested the worst enemy of the Chinese people has been the Chinese people themselves.

To open a back door into the hospital system was a subtle and delicate process. Guanxi could not be exercised by direct request. Possibilities had to be mentioned, contingencies suggested, repayment described with discretion. Meiling began to make some tentative inquiries. And as she begins her search for the key, our presence in the story will end. The trajectory through this maze of relationships is personal and clandestine; to make the process transparent would be a betrayal. Did she find her harrowing way through the back door? Yes, she did. Did she and her husband lose their jobs? Yes, they did. Were they penalized financially? Yes, and their workplaces were fined as well. But when Meiling walked out of the *front* door of the obscure hospital where her child was born, she was carrying a baby girl in her arms, a girl she named Qiwang. In English, her name means Hope.

Chapter 9: Looking Around -- Views of the Neighborhood and Beyond

"Wheresoever you go, go with all your heart."
Confucius

Later in the fall of 2000, the temperatures were cooling as the calendar turned toward winter. Welcome winds swept up the Min River from the sea, clearing away the stifling humidity of the previous month; late afternoon walking became a pleasure again. Let's go for another stroll around the neighborhood, as early evening brings on a resurgence of family life in the street. We've seen the neighborhood in the early morning when it's stretching and greeting the day. Now let's take a look at how it winds down.

Small tables are set out on the cobbled lanes so children can do their homework while adults wash veggies at the community spigot and prepare to cook dinner on charcoal braziers nearby. Sweet potatoes roasting on an improvised barbeque sends sugary perfume into the air, erasing odors that might have been left by the evening "honey bucket" cart pulled by a man collecting "night soil" to fertilize urban gardens. A manual laborer rinses off the day's sweat with water in a bucket from the community spigot. Storefronts selling cloth, rice, gold jewelry and bamboo furniture will stay open indefinitely but will gradually morph into their vendors' homes as evening falls. Cots are set up on customer floor space or in lofts, small TV sets begin to glow from behind merchandise. Old ladies play mahjong on the sidewalk in front of the shop selling multicolored paper and bamboo orbs to be displayed at funerals. A man, who earlier hung his laundry to dry on plastic hangers hooked directly on the electrical wires outside his door, uses a notched bamboo stick to retrieve his clothes.

Earlier in the day, agile men carrying long bamboo ladders swarmed through the neighborhood clearing branches from those very same wires. Their method was to scramble up the ladders laid directly against the power lines, keep one foot on the ladder, support the other foot on the line itself as they swiped at the vegetation with their machetes. No orange cones suggested danger, no cautionary warnings were posted. Pedestrians and bicyclists dodged falling

branches as they passed under-neath the oper-ation. We now tread on the smaller leftover debris, all the while keeping vigilant for the gaping holes and loose cobbles that pock the local streets.

Listen to that commotion! Let's follow the blast of whining horns and clang-ing gongs down towards the Min River. An outdoor opera performance is beginning and we sink down onto tiny low bamboo stools provided for the audience to watch. A wooden stage has been loosely constructed and hung with a red velvet curtain that separates the audience from the handful of actors constantly changing costumes behind the scenes. The band consists of some wind instruments made of brass and bamboo, a couple of *erhus* (the two-stringed bowed instrument we heard on our morning walk in Chapter 1), and some bronze cymbals and gongs. Chinese music is not harmonic like Western music, but heterophonic, with all the musicians playing different versions of the same melodic line at the same time. It is also pentatonic, which is like having a scale of only the black keys on a piano. The din is terrible to my ears and yet the folks in the audience, mostly old people, sit enthralled. After a polite interval, we depart, heading back toward to our rooms and our supply of pirated Western music CDs that can be purchased on the street for the equivalent of about 75 cents.

One student assured me that Chinese ears were constructed differently and that's what accounted for the difference in musical taste. In adult education classes I taught one semester to prepare enrollees for immigration to Canada, I received a similar explanation for the constant hawking and spitting done on the streets, in buses, even sometimes in the classroom. "Chinese throats are different," my adult students maintained, "and they need to be cleared more frequently."

An evening or two earlier, my American ears perked up as I explored a narrow cobbled alleyway down the hill, past tinkers' repair carts and a school ringing with children's voices. Could that possibly be "Rose of San Antone" wafting from one of the gloomy rooms where people both worked and slept? I peeked into courtyards until I found three

115

grizzled Chinese duffers in a greasy machine shop, pickin' and grinnin' on banjo and guitars, one hooked up to an ancient Fender amplifier. They sounded like hillbilly angels to my Western ears, and I pulled up a dirty stool while they continued through a repertoire of "country music with Chinese characteristics".'[16]Although it is considered bad manners to weep in public, a few nostalgic tears escaped my eyes as they segued into "Eleanor Rigby" and then ricocheted back to "Streets of Laredo." Several years later when I returned to teach again, they had vanished, their building torn down and replaced with condos.

There was little need for any of us foreigners to watch TV in China. All we had to do to be entertained was to go out the dorm gate and head down the street-- entertainment un- folded in the form of street life and people doing what they ordinarily did every day. If we walked over Liberation Bridge we could watch old men fishing optim- istically with bam- boo poles and lines

---

[16] The Chinese economic system has been officially referred to as "socialism with Chinese characteristics" by the ruling Communist Party. However, its energetic mix of public and private enterprise appears more capitalistic than communistic to some observers.

that reached from bridge to current. On the street leading down to the river, little altars, smoky with candles and incense, were tucked into adobe wall niches. Offerings of fruit or Coke stood hopefully beside small golden Buddhas and plastic lotus lamps. Barbers set out their chairs on cobbled streets, enticing shaggy passersby into haircuts or shaves. A man soaked and folded and looped thinly cut bamboo into intricate renditions of insects. Another drizzled melted sorghum into fanciful animal shapes, affixed each creation to a stick and sold them to delighted youngsters as lollipops (p 116).

Many evenings I watched men standing on their rooftops waving brightly colored flags to attract a flock of pigeons back to their cages. Each flag was quite different. Apparently pigeons have excellent visual memories and were trained to pair the flag with food. They were allowed to fly free all day but were called back to their rookery at night by their owners sweeping flags at the end of long bamboo sticks in a long arc across the sky. It was like watching a ballet for bird and banner and, when the dance, was over the pigeons produced lovely little speckled eggs for the family to eat. In another display of aviary wisdom, certain kinds of sparrow could be hired from a vendor to tell your fortune. You picked out a bird, held it in your hands a few minutes to let it absorb your essence, then set it down to peck in a bowl holding printed predictions of the future. The one your bird picked out and held in his beak revealed your fate.

Do your eyes need a rest from all this looking around? Let's get a massage! It won't take us long to find a massage provider as they're everywhere, especially in hospitals, because massage is considered a healthful necessity and not just a luxury. We climb the dingy stairs to my favorite blind massage parlor and choose our masseur by a number under his picture on the wall. In China, where everyone must earn his or her keep, people afflicted with low vision or blindness were traditionally steered toward the masseuse trade. In the late 90s, training programs patterned after the one in the Beijing School for the Blind began to pop up all over China. Now we are the beneficiaries, getting ready to lie face down on a sheet-covered table in a room full of tables, while our masseuses put out their cigarettes and prepare to press their thumbs along our acupressure points. Were you expecting perfumed oils and soft music? Not here. And wait! Don't peel off your shirt or wiggle out of your pants! This massage is done while you are fully clothed. The masseur will also cover the part of your body being worked on with a light towel. The masseuses chuckle and chat with each other, no doubt commenting on the peculiarities of the well-padded *laowai* (old foreigner) physique. Who cares? It costs about $5 and you'll float like a cloud all the way home.

Each of the foreign teachers approached living in China differently, depending on his or her motivation for being there. Some still came to quietly advance the Christian message, not during teaching time, but perhaps through their friendships with students and colleagues after hours. Some came to perk up a humdrum life or to make themselves useful. The younger staff members wanted to party and ferreted out the bars and nightlife that afforded them groovier, flashier companionship than campus life. They would often go off together on weekend evenings and return very late, very happy, and sometimes quite drunk, to the irritation of the gate man who had locked the rest of us in by then.

A few teachers made humbling attempts to become students of the complex culture and language. Others spent their free time shopping for incredible bargains in silk scarves and pirated DVDs. A few dedicated churchgoers sought and found government-approved congregations to join for Sunday services. Some preferred sybaritic rather than spiritual pleasures and spent weekends sampling both a range of Chinese cuisine from Mongolian hot pot to seafood specialties of Fujian Province, along with a range of massage parlors. We were an inclusive group, keen to share our enthusiasms with the rest, and I could go bar-hopping with the 20-year-olds one night and cruising markets with the bargain-hunters the next day.

No matter where we went, there was always a spectacle. A multi-storied indoor showplace filled with provincial specialties drew the serious shoppers. On the ground floor, delicate carvings in rust-red Shoshan stone in the shape of lychee nuts, bouquets of flowers, or writhing dragons were arranged to amaze the viewers. On the next floor up, women crouched over silk stretched on rotating frames. Using multicolored thread, they embroidered landscapes, goldfish in ponds, cranes feeding, and moon bridges crossing streams. The third floor housed jewelers and jade sellers. Out on the sidewalk, hawkers sold fake antiques and soapstone "jade."

In West Lake Park, jugglers spun plates or balanced stacks of dishes on their heads. One day, while passing through a park on my way to a friend's condo, I watched a family of three—mother, father, and daughter—set up two 30-foot-high poles secured by guy wires that held a taut horizontal wire between them. The father rode a bicycle back and forth across the wire to test it before placing his daughter on his shoulders. She balanced, arms out, standing on his shoulders while mother followed the bicycle on foot holding a parasol.

Once the foreign teachers got to know the central city a bit, we were ready to expand our range from the confines of the neighborhood to outings in the countryside around Fuzhou. "Outing" may call up scenes of bucolic meadows or picnics by streams, but in China it often meant climbing a mountain by way of hundreds and hundreds of steep rock steps, as most available flatland has been cultivated. Meandering switchbacks, so familiar to me in the Sierra Nevada of northern California did not exist here. No. The angle of ascent matched the mountainside and often seemed straight up. Visiting a famous shrine required climbing wide slabs of granite stairs. Going to see a waterfall required climbing slippery moss-covered stairs. On one particularly steep ascent on Wuyi Mountain, it was possible to hire bearers with a bamboo chair mounted on poles they carried on their boney shoulders. I never stooped to this shameful luxury, but saw others who did.

Xu Daofeng, head of the Foreign Affairs Office (FAO), was our handler, our dorm mother and our entertainment director. When she hadn't scheduled a banquet at which we were feted, she was arranging college-sponsored field trips for all the foreign staff during which we piled into the campus van and hurtled through town or countryside for a cultural treat. Guo Ping, driver and commander of the college's white, bread-shaped van, was a man of compelling adrenalin needs and steely nerves. Whether we were going to a concert, a multi-course dinner to be held across town, or a nearby village, he approached the task with aggression and élan. As if time were of the most vital essence, he passed on curves honking savagely, drove on sidewalks, went down one-way streets all under the pretense of getting us there on time, even if it didn't matter because nothing began on schedule anyway. It must have tickled Guo Ping to hear the gasps and giggles of his passengers. If the road is better than the inn, as Cervantes claimed, then the real attraction was often the trip there and back, no matter what spectacle we went to see.

Some outings sent us ducking into manmade caves built of porous rock, climbing stairs around ancient tombs shaped like the backs of turtles, and scaling more stairs to tiny temples atop stone precipices where incense and paper money were burned to ensure the dead were fiscally sound. The colorful money has more recently been joined by bigger sheets of paper printed with hairdryers, button-down shirts, and TV sets, all to be burned in hopes that the ancestors could enjoy the new consumer pleasures of the modern world. One weekend, we climbed 834 shallow granite stairs up the side of a rock face with only lengths of draped chain anchored with bolts to the rock to steady us until we arrived at a teahouse.

There we drank gallons of green tea and descended the 834 stairs with full bladders. Public toilets were almost nonexistent, often grubby, and required strong knees for squatting. We rated bus station toilets as the worst; toilets in MacDonald's and Pizza Hut received gold stars because those businesses attempted to maintain Western standards of cleanliness, even though the stalls barely contained a Western-sized body.

A favorite Fuzhou stair-climbing activity was to ascend Mount Gushan, or Drum Mountain. One of my students reported, to the amazement of all, that her father made the climb every day before work! Tourist pamphlets boast there are "160 sceneries on Drum Mountain and 180 inscriptions." That may be, but exact numbers became blurred after an ascent of 3,000 feet up stone stairs, past looming rocks carved with poems and philosophic statements, crowned by a series of temples, tea houses, and a hazy view of  the city below. Along the way, vendors sold small crabapples glazed with sugar and sweet green tea in bottles. We enjoyed a recognizable vegetarian meal (no beaks or tentacles) made by the monks of Gushing Spring Temple and then mini-bused it back down in deference to our creaking knees.

In spite of the much-ballyhooed scenery, the sight I enjoyed most was the sign at the entrance of the mountain stairway admonishing the visitors to:

1. Stress civilization and courtesy. Joint observe the social ethic.
2. Cherish every tree and blade of grass. Strictly forbid pick the flowers.
3. The stud may not at random toss. It is everybody's duty to protect a forest fire prevention.
4. Mountaineering good for one's health. Respect the old and the young. Find it a pleasure to help others.

5. Raise one's awake to safety. Observe discipline and be law abiding, ready to take up the cudgel for a just cause.

During my first year in China, my favorite outing was a visit to a Chinese country home for some special occasion. As I made more friends, more opportunities presented themselves—a wedding, a birthday party for Buddha and, in later years, an opportunity to admire a newly-acquired suburban condo. At first I accepted every invitation eagerly, because the visits could be uniquely endearing experiences. I gradually learned that they could be also fraught with physical discomforts and a sense of being on display. The huge sofas and chairs, popular in living rooms of Chinese homes and offered to honored visitors, were either made of shellacked wood, or modern plastic, cold and uncomfortable. The local or seasonal specialties generously prepared for a guest was often so "special" as to be somewhat horrifying to Western tastes, and conversation around the dinner table was in the local dialect.

Older brick and concrete dwellings were not heated and the indoor climate was much like that outdoors. Chinese put great faith in the healthful value of "fresh" air blowing through open windows, summer or winter. Most families wore their coats inside as well as out, using specially made sleeve covers to keep their sleeves from getting stained by domestic chores. If the visit were deep into the countryside, the youngster and old people stared at me with amazement, usually because they had never seen a walking, talking foreigner before. As a visitor to a wealthy suburban family, I was trotted around the neighborhood so that they would all know what cosmopolitan people my hosts were. By my last year teaching there, I politely declined invitations to Chinese homes for longer than an afternoon.

But in May 2001, I was still enthusiastic. As in much of the world, spring is a time for weddings, and a Chinese colleague, Dong Meihua, offered to take me to her childhood friend's country wedding in a neighboring county. We could stay in the Dong family farmhouse, only if I "wouldn't do too much complaining." The previous year, she'd taken a different teacher who wasn't quite up to the challenges, and the result had been abrasive for both. I agreed to the "no complaint" clause.

At one of Fuzhou's four directional bus stations, we boarded an ancient bus with a population of hardy farmers in straw hats and housewives in aprons. Our bus rattled noisily along country roads, through a landscape of neon green rice shoots anchored by clusters of huts in which mushrooms were cultivated. When we arrived in the village where the wedding would take place, we needed to walk like runway models along the narrow, raised-mud levies that bounded the soggy rice paddies, swinging one foot directly ahead of the other in a mincing trot. Pungent smells of earth and barnyard fertilizer billowed up at every step further into the field, and my resolve not to misstep and fall into it increased as we moved farther from the road. Meihua floated gracefully ahead of me, and I could see how a young girls of the paddies learned balance and fluid movement.

The groom had already arrived at the bride's mud-and-brick house, accompanied by an odd number of family members, and was demanding his bride be handed over. Tradition dictates that the groom be assertive in his claims

124

and the bride's family feign reluctance. Finally, with much parental lamenting, the bride, dressed in a traditional red *qipao* (a long slim satin dress with Mandarin collar and side slits, also called a *cheongsam*), departed her childhood home with the groom's family, thus making the man's wedding party an even number. Even numbers insure good fortune for the couple, as does the color red.

The bride's now fully recovered family set out bowls of steaming longevity noodles (endless lengths of glutinous noodles to symbolize long life) with red pigeon eggs on top for fertility. We slurped up the noodles with the remaining guests in the bride's family compound while the happy couple hopped on a motorbike to join the groom's extended family. *Dao la!* Let's go! We want to watch them seal their intentions by bowing to all the elder relatives and ancestors pictured over the groom's family altar.

Motorbikes waiting on the road and driven by the groom's cousins sped us to his family's compound. As we walked through the courtyard chickens, ducks, and pigs that had escaped being part of the wedding feast scattered, squawking and oinking. Two, round, brick fire towers had been assembled and filled with wood on which bamboo steamers were stacked. Some cooks wielded cleavers with lightning speed, while others sweated over enormous woks as they stir-fried, steamed, and simmered a 21-dish banquet for both families and their guests. I was comforted by the familiarity of the dishes; only the segmented coiled eel looked too daunting.

When weariness overcame us, we hired a motorcycle to carry us to Meihua's family home, a two-story mud-walled house with swooping tiles roofs and a new brick addition.

The surrounding rice paddies were soggy in preparation for spring planting. Dampness arose from them like steam from a warm bath. Mama and Baba Dong met us at the arched doorway and extended a warm, but incomprehensible (to me), welcome. They were happy as parents anywhere to have their daughter home.

"You have your own bed," Meihua proudly declared, showing me a wooden structure surrounded by mosquito netting, its boards covered with well-used cotton quilts. Mattresses as we know them are thought to be hot and unsanitary by countryside dwellers, and sheets, which we use to keep heavier bedding clean, are not used. Without washing machines, bedding is refreshed by occasionally hanging it in the sun. Not knowing who or how many I deposed to sleep in such unshared luxury, I crawled gingerly between the clammy covers to sleep.

Mother Dong cooked our breakfast of rice soup and vegetables over a fire, burning the pressed sawdust logs on which mushrooms had been grown in the huts that lined the road and rice paddies. Once the logs are spent as growing mediums, they are dried and used as fuel. Sunday dawned drizzly, but farmers in rain capes made of palm fiber slogged in mud up to their knees behind recalcitrant water buffalos pulling ancient plows. Women of the village stayed indoors and wrapped long stalks of wire with colored paper, to which they attached clusters of plastic berries and fake seed pods. A second group of women then dusted the stalks with red and gold spray paint, and popped the finished product inside a cellophane wrapper. The stalks were collected weekly by an export company representative, who paid the women by the piece.

126

"What could these possibly be used for?" they asked me. I recognized the array of fake dried pods, artificial evergreens and decorative stalks sold by the stem in American craft shops for use in floral displays, but how to describe this nonsense to the wives of subsistence farmers? After unsuccessful attempts to explain the stalks to women whose only home décor might be the small ancestral altar, an out-of-date calendar, and a painting of Mao, I promised to send them a picture, through Meihua, when I returned home. A few years later when affluence increased and home decorating became more popular with the new urbanites, these impostors of nature began to appear in Chinese malls as well.

We were enthusiastically offered tea and sticky rice or sweet potatoes in every home we visited. All the villagers were curious about the foreigner in their midst. They clearly admired Meihua for having such an exotic friend, even though I was a pretty ordinary American. I nibbled and sipped, but the thought of having to visit one of the public outhouses, hanging perilously over the paddies, limited my consumption. Because human waste is still used for fertilizer

in the countryside, building latrines that drained directly into the fields made sense to them, but made for a high-risk experience for me. By Sunday evening we were back on the bus again, rattling towards Fuzhou, bearing a whole plucked chicken with its scaly legs sticking out of our plastic carryall, a farm gift for a pregnant colleague.

In spite of whatever embarrassment or discomfort either guest or host might have suffered, I am grateful to my Chinese friends who took me home to meet their family or arranged my outings. Without their generosity I never would have chugged up the oily slough that is what's left of the 1,200-mile-long Grand Canal between Hangzhou and Suzhou, nor toasted brides with tiny cups of *baijiu* (a strong liquor made from grain, usually 40-60% alcohol), nor watched workmen pound buffalo horn into combs, reputed to beautify the users' hair. Without their hospitality, I never would have seen the rooftop farm that a police official and his doctor wife had established on the top floor of their elegant suburban condo. They were proud of their new affluence, but missed the countryside of their childhoods and had planted fruit trees, rows of cabbage, and gourds. They had even built a chicken coop near the new sauna!

In China, if you are accepted into the family as a friend, you are cherished and celebrated, especially if you are a teacher. If you are outside that magic circle of acceptance, you are just another competitor for space and resources. But if you are an enemy, you are in peril. One of the first folktales I heard from my students was of the kindhearted farmer who ploughed up a snake during his preparation for spring planting. The poor snake was still hibernating and too sluggish to escape harm so the farmer put the creature in the folds of his jacket until it became warm enough to release. The snake revived, bit the farmer, who promptly died leaving his family destitute. The moral to the story, dear children, is never show mercy to your enemies. I may have been unwittingly gauche on outings due to cultural misunderstandings, but tried not to create any situation where mercy might not be shown.

Not all outings were taken for pleasure. Shortly after the beginning of each semester all the teachers were bundled into the college van by English-speaking Xiuping, a representative of the Foreign Affairs Office, to go to a nearby clinic for our mandatory medical exam to make sure none of us were contagious or harboring a potential medical emergency. Most of us were fit and none of us wanted to submit. We were primarily afraid of having blood drawn after the tragic situation in Henan and other poor provinces in which lucrative blood donor programs had re-used HIV-infected needles, infecting whole villages with the HIV virus. The teachers were uneasy. There were other concerns, not voiced, regarding general sanitation in Chinese hospitals in the early days of the 21st century (a condition that has improved greatly since then).

I'd undertaken a complete physical with my local physician before I left California, and brought his report with me. Sorry. It could not be accepted as official because it did not display his seal or "chop," the unique impression of characters made by a carved stone stamp dipped in a sticky red substance. The issuer's official chop accompanied most Chinese documents, personal or private. Without the personal chop, the document was considered fraudulent. One teacher brought her doctor's report that she had taken the trouble to notarize but even this was considered suspect. No chop, no authenticity. Our protests were in vain; we could either comply or go home.

"Oh well, this is China," someone commented ruefully as all six of the new teachers filed into the van to be delivered to the clinic. It was a phrase we would repeat many times over that year.

The white-tiled clinic was crowded but Xiuping swept us by the other patients. Our first stop was in the urinalysis area where we were handed plastic cups and sent to the squat toilets downstairs. Toilet paper was not provided in most public toilets so we all carried our own. We filled our cups as directed, wrapped them up as well as we could in our own TP, carried them up the stairs full of jostling clinic patients, and set them in a row directly on the reception counter. The test was for diabetes, so strips of litmus paper were added. When the tests had all proved satisfactorily negative for everyone to see, we were instructed to toss cup and contents into a wire waste paper basket in the corner of the waiting room.

With rueful backward glances at the leaking basket, we were directed to another room, placed on beds, and hooked up to a diabolical tangle of wires, suction cups, and clamps for the ECG exam. Once my heart appeared normal, my liver came under the scrutiny of a technician who passed a handheld ultra-sound device over my belly. Blood drawing was next. Oh, ouch! The needles seemed as thick as nails! The youngest one of our teaching cadre fainted, and the nurse never *was* able to find an adequate vein in my arm. She was beginning to lose face, and was so relieved when I joked "*mei*

130

you" (there isn't any) that she let me go with my blood supply intact.

The X-ray room was the real spook house, dark except for a 40-watt light bulb covered with red transparent paper. One by one we entered the room with a wizened attendant. To conduct the exam, the light was extinguished and I stood fully clothed on a platform while the machine closed in on me with a sinister whine. The old man kept a claw-like grip on my arm, yanking it to move my torso this way and that. Incredibly enough, the ancient machine revealed a shadow on my lungs, one I'd seen on previous stateside x-rays, left over from a severe case of bronchitis.

I explained this to Xiuping, but the old X-ray technician wasn't buying my story. He insisted I had tuberculosis and would need to be treated or sent home. A clinic administrator was called in to mediate. They had a heated conversation, during which Xiuping translated my claim that I'd had a TB test recently for public school employment, and I tried to look as robust and rosy-cheeked as possible.

"I'm sure it's nothing," Xiuping said soothingly to the clinic administrator. "How about if we send this American back to the clinic every week to teach English to your staff."

Wait—what? We will? After a stern glance from Xiuping, I nodded and the agreement was accepted. All faces were saved and I was pronounced healthy. The promise was important, but understood to be a charade. The x-ray tech had been correct in reporting the shadow, but the college wanted me approved and the clinic wanted Hwa Nan's continued business. Never mind if I really was infected; I could deal with that when I returned home (I did, but even though the shadow was still there, it was unchanged and of no concern). Once again, the Chinese art of *guanxi*, honoring connections and exchanging favors, functioned as it had for centuries.

Understanding how *guanxi* works is central to an understanding of the Chinese process of friendship and doing business. More than just mutual back scratching or media networking, it is a subtle and complicated web of favors and relationships. Built strategically, sometimes even generationally, *guanxi* can minimize the risks, frustrations and disharmony involved in a society where the rules are fluid and systems can be arbitrary. In China, distrust of anyone outside the family is a constant theme in a child's formative years. Building *guanxi* outside the family has been a way to create trustworthy pathways to finding a wife, buying a buffalo, or closing a business deal. It is not hastily earned or received, but developed over a long period of time, and through personal, shared experiences.

Players in the *guanxi* game are patient; the recipients do not expect immediate return, but future gain is guaranteed. Failure to reciprocate is an unforgiveable sin (one that foreigners often commit), but reciprocation can be loaned and borrowed. It is the kind of connection that the Hwa Nan girls were unconsciously building in the 1930s, when they fled to Nanping as war raged through the coastal cities of China. It was the kind of connection they could draw on in the 1980s, when, as old ladies, they began to articulate their bold plan to resurrect Hwa Nan College. They couldn't have done it without the help of trusted longtime friends, both Chinese and foreign—part of a lifetime of mutual *guanxi*.

To watch *guanxi* grow, let's again look back when Fuzhou was Foochow and the college still occupied the lovely campus

132

overlooking the Min River. The country had been at war for years: civil conflicts between new factions of revolutionaries and the ruling elites, wars between feudal landlords, and now war with the Japanese. Foreigners and the missionary presence were under suspicion. Furthermore, Hwa Nan administrators could no longer ignore the bombs being dropped on ports, the occupation of Chinese cities by the Japanese, and the conflict between the Nationalist government and the Communist movement. An immediate flight from Foochow was deemed necessary, a flight that would temporarily move all students deeper into the mountains, away from trade and shipping routes, for safety. What a terrible thing it was to leave their lovely campus; what a feeling of loss! But through the sorrow and excitement of bidding farewell to familiar places, permanent bonds between students and teachers were forged by homesickness. Many of them comforted each other when family members were at risk during the Japanese invasion and occupation. Later, they commiserated during the famine years following Liberation, and shared the degradations suffered by educated people in the Cultural Revolution. It was on the strength of these bonds that Hwa Nan College would be rebuilt.

Chapter 10: Looking Back – 1937 to 1985

"When it is obvious that goals will be difficult to reach, don't give up the goals, but adjust the steps to get to the goals."
Confucius

Japan lusted after China's vast supply of natural resources and they saw their opportunity to make another grab at these treasures when the aforementioned struggles for power divided China during the 1930s. Busy fighting its own internal battles, the Chinese failed to launch a coordinated resistance to the tiny outside invader, only to find that Japan might be small, but the country was advanced, united and intensely focused on dominance. By 1937, Shanghai had fallen to Japanese forces. Nanking, then the provisional capital, followed, and bombing was being predicted in major port cities like Foochow. Hwa Nan administrators anxiously learned that the key port island of Amoy, their southern provincial neighbor off the coast in the East China Sea, was now under Japanese control. Resolve grew within the leadership of the college to keep their female students (and themselves) safe from the probability of a Japanese occupation, an occupation that was rumored to involve violent treatment of soldiers and civilians alike. Gruesome stories of civilian rape and murder were filtering south from Nanking. Difficult and risky as it might seem, the leaders began to arrange an evacuation to the small mountain town of Nanping, 150 miles up the Min River. There the students and staff hoped to take refuge in the facilities of an established medical missionary settlement, be safe from the bombs, and avoid the brutal attention of Japanese soldiers.

The administrator in charge of the hospital there had been none other than Lydia's brother, Dr. Garnet Trimble, sent by the Methodist Board of Foreign Missions to operate the 80-bed medical facility in that small mountain community. Dr. Trimble, his wife, and an American-born son had moved to Nanping in 1916; two more sons were born on Chinese soil. "Hospital treatment is something entirely new to the Chinese," Dr. Trimble had written to colleagues at home. "They don't know what scientific care of the sick is. The only course of treatment they have is to stuff the patient with herbs and food, rub his stomach, pound his back, and make as much noise as possible. If this combination won't cure him, they let him die."[17]

The Garnet Trimble family had been recalled earlier to the States due to the increasing dangers of being foreigners in a country at war, but had left an established orchard, large productive gardens, and various structures that could be utilized as dorms and classrooms. They also left a legacy of goodwill in the neighboring communities. In fact, Trimble roots grew so deeply into Chinese earth that in more settled times one of Garnet's sons would return to visit and one of his grandsons would become a teacher at new Hwa Nan in the 21st century.

The college staff procured several covered barges to undertake the difficult journey up-river against the current and through small rapids. On the appointed day this fleet of primitive wood and oilcloth crafts, powered by feeble two cycle diesel engines, gathered on the banks of the Min in the shadow of the stone classroom buildings, secured ramps to

---

[17] Portion of a letter from Dr. Garnet Trimble as quoted in "The Trimble Boys", a self-published memoir by Robert Trimble (2009).

the shore, and cleared their decks. In a contagion of excitement, rumor, and fear, the entire student body lent their hands to the move. Young Xu Daofeng and Ma Xiufa, as well as other gently raised girls from well-to-do Fuzhou families who had bonded during the mass education efforts, worked alongside sweating coolies to load bedding, textbooks, and cooking equipment onto the ancient boats. A new teacher, Yu Baosheng, a 1923 graduate, who had returned to her alma mater with a Master's Degree in chemistry from Columbia University, supervised the removal of the entire chemistry lab.

The pungent smell of the river mingled with the sense of urgency that surrounded the exodus was both heady and terrifying perfume to these girls, many of whom had been raised in homes of privilege. They were faced with a choice between accepting the dangers of war and the bombing raids expected soon in Foochow by staying with family or continuing their studies with peers in a safer inland environment. One choice put them at risk but with family, the other choice kept them safer but offered only peers and faculty for comfort—a tough choice for deeply-bonded daughters and sisters.

Many families encouraged their daughters to leave with their colleagues, even though it meant a wrenching separation. Thousands of Chinese were fleeing Foochow for the relative safety of the countryside, but the Ma family elected to remain in their traditional home. Xiufa had never been very far from the familiar walled compound of mud bricks and wood pillars that housed the large collection of siblings, aunts and cousins, grandparents, and altars to the ancestors under its overlapping tile roof. She shed tears of fright and longing as she began to understand what distance from her family meant, but with her despair came a frisson of independence. She was tantalized with the allure of becoming part of strong student sisterhood.

"Will I really have the courage to accompany my student sisters and leave my family behind?" wondered Xiufa, as she passed an armload of textbooks to Daofeng. "And our music! How can we accompany our daily hymns of praise without bringing the piano? We must make room for it!"

The girls raced to the top of the hill, made their case to the matron supervising the move and were thrilled to hear her say, "Let's give it a try!" Coolies swore and staff members prayed as the huge black piano was hefted by the workers from its platform in Trimble Hall onto planks on top of logs. Laboriously, the wiry men inched the piano with ropes and rollers down the hill onto the banks of the muddy Min and up the buckling gangplank. Groaning in unison, the coolies gave a mighty heave, and the black hulk settled itself on the barge amongst test tubes and textbooks.

The night before departure one of the girls decided to venture from the campus into central Fuzhou to say goodbye to her family. A dinner was prepared in the family compound with what luxuries could be had in wartime. Cousins and uncles wished her well, and after dark, she slipped on shabby clothes and made her way back to the campus in the protective company of a Hwa Nan teacher disguised as her servant. The Nationalist Party already restricted freedom of movement among those affiliated with Western institutions, and a well-dressed young Chinese girl accompanied by a Westerner took a good chance of being detained by local volunteer security patrols. Hearts thudding, the two brave companions hurried through darkened streets. Their stealth was rewarded with a safe arrival back at the campus where they spent a fitful night on their bamboo mats among rows of their sleeping friends, all awaiting their river adventure the next day. They missed their families already and wondered when they would see their parents again.

At dawn, after a hasty breakfast of *baozi* (a white bun filled with sticky bean paste or meat) and tea, students and teachers filed solemnly aboard. Aided by the incoming tide, the boats shoved off with their cargo of people, books, bedding, desks, and lab equipment—and one mahogany piano! Although many eyes were cast anxiously toward land and the homes they were leaving, their hearts swelled with feelings of pride in their adventure and hope for a speedy return. The puny engines surged against the muddy current as Xiufa sat down at the manacled piano and began to play. Soon, the strains "How Great Thou Art" could be heard in counterpoint to the throb of the pistons.

They would need faith in something beyond the power of the boats and the skill of their captains to guide them through the rapids, both riverine and military, that lay before them. There were rapids upstream in which junks and barges competed for the services from the tow men on land; these men helped pull the great boats forward over the rocks using thick ropes and bamboo poles, wearing little more than sandals made of rice straw. Their first evening on the river, their flotilla was boarded by soldiers and the boatmen placed under arrest. The next morning, lovely Lucy Wang, well-educated and in command, put on a clean dress, marched off the gangplank and up the hill to military headquarters to resolve the matter. The girls watched anxiously for a few hours until they beheld a triumphant Lucy heading down the hill followed by the liberated boatmen.

Xiufa gulped down the cool watery air and dragged her eyes from the direction of the city that housed her family to the looming green mountains ahead. River waves broke over the shallow bough of the barge and sprayed her with the muddy water. She might have even convinced herself that war could be an exhilarating event, and the idea of "roughing it" in round-roofed Quonset huts in a tiny missionary outpost outside of Nanping would be thrilling. She would be with her best friend, Xu Daofeng. She imagined them reading and singing and doing Teacher Yu's science experiments as usual, but in a safer mountainous setting. In addition, there would be other students in Nanping who had fled the scene of possible conflict. It would be a grand gathering of both boys and girls! Her trusted teachers were there with them as well. Had not President Lucy Wang just achieved miracles persuading the local navigational regulators to allow them to proceed up river? Xiufa felt protected and well-led. "China may be man's country," observed chemistry teacher Francis Fulton, "but there's always some woman who knows how to get things done."[18]

In Nanping, the girls slept 12 to a room under large mosquito nets in dorms that housed patients in the former clinic operation. Classes were held on porches, on stair landings, in the ancestral hall—wherever space could be found. Chamber pots were used at night; during the day, the traditional open trough that was flushed through with water from time to time was used. Drinking water was piped into

---

[18] Wallace, p. 83.

the compound from springs in the mountains and was mostly used for boiled tea. Water for other purposes was drawn from wells dug near the gardens and the cooking terrace. A diesel-powered generating system had been set up when the hospital was in operation; now diesel fuel was too difficult to acquire, so kerosene lanterns were used sparingly. No central heating or air conditioning was thought necessary in this setting where temperatures ranged from the low 50s in winter to the mid-80s in summer.

While Ma Xiufa, Xu Daofeng, and Chen Zhongying, another friend from the mass education effort, were sweeping cobwebs from their new sleeping quarters and setting up classroom equipment inside the Quonset huts, the situation at home in Foochow was becoming more volatile. The Japanese conquered and occupied the city, then later inexplicably left it in the hands of the Nationalists. A fire was set in one of the Hwa Nan classrooms and the building severely damaged. Bombs fell along the channel from Mawei on the coast to Foochow, 13 miles inland, in an attempt to destroy shipping lanes. Chinese soldier boys, sometimes reluctantly recruited, struggled with poor training and equipment. Resisting the well-equipped, mission-driven Japanese foe seemed almost impossible.

And, in one of the Japanese air raids to subdue the city, the entire Ma family was buried under the collapsed mud and brick structure that sheltered them for so many generations. Her beloved family who strove to teach her the ancient concept of "eat bitter"—to endure great hardships in order to achieve something prized—was now teaching her the bitterest lesson of all. Xu Daofeng did her best to comfort the weeping Ma Xiufa, but it was a loss beyond comfort.

Occasionally daring staff members made their way back to Foochow for news, and to check on the deserted campus. Teacher Marion Cole wrote home, "At least 700 bombs have been dropped on Foochow. I've seen wars out here before, but never this air-terror, and never such deadly determination on both sides. I can honestly say, I never knew fear before this."[19] The city of Foochow fell a second time to the Japanese in 1944. Payne Hall on the old campus was burned to the ground. Perhaps, the girls thought, war was not such a thrilling adventure after all.

Staff members and students of Hwa Nan would continue to occupy their Quonset hut campus from 1938 to 1944, under the whine of low-flying aircraft and the worry of slowly dwindling supplies from down-river. There they concentrated on their studies as well as social service and mass education work in the nearby community, emphasizing child rearing, diet, and sanitation. They used Yu Baosheng's chemistry lab to test water and their knowledge of nutrition to encourage good eating habits even in the shortages of war. Xu Daofeng and Ma Xiufa graduated and stayed on to teach until they could continue their studies elsewhere. There was really nothing else to be done. Although America's entry into the war led to a Japanese defeat and surrender to the Allies, war in China continued to rage between Chiang's Nationalists and Mao's Communist armies.

When staff and students returned to Foochow after the Japanese defeat in 1945, it was to a ruined campus and runaway inflation. Both Xu Daofeng and Ma Xiufa pursued

---

[19] Marion Cole to "Friends,"1939, Archives of the United Board for Christian Higher Education in Asia, Special Collections, Yale Divinity School.

careers elsewhere in Foochow; many other faculty and graduates remained in the shelter of their alma mater. Ever the optimist, Lucy Wang used their persistence under dangerous conditions in Nanping as a reputation-maker for the College. With shrewd survival instincts, she forged an economically profitable relationship with the shaky Nationalist government under Chiang Kai-shek, who needed well-trained teachers for his provincial schools. Because the financially fragile government had no hope of giving monetary support to public education until the war was over, it could only promise to give "encouragement and support" to private educations institutions and their outreach services—not with money, but with much-needed protection.

To strengthen her political connections, President Wang offered to serve on national reconstruction committees. She sought every opportunity to remind government leaders that they could use schools like Hwa Nan for leadership training in their attempts to construct a more civil society. Even though it meant making some compromises on class content, she understood the necessity of having Hwa Nan under the umbrella of the government. Thus, the emphasis on dogmatic Christian education shifted to an emphasis on secular community service. The curriculum began to reflect a specialty in courses seen as suitable for women: child development, home economics, teaching, health, and nutrition.

"Service is as essential to life as knowledge," Carol Chen, once a contender for the role as president of the college, wrote to skeptical overseas supporters, nervous about the civil struggle that was destabilizing the country. Throughout the 1940s the majority of the college budget was still funded by the American Board for Christian Colleges in China, in hopes that "normalcy" would return. In the face of countrywide struggles between the Nationalist and Communist forces, Hwa Nan students and faculty feigned normalcy by exhibiting a passive non-involvement in politics, a strategy that kept them safe from factionalism and its backlash.

As the balance of power began to slide from the U.S.-supported Nationalists to the Russian-supported Communists, public political cautiousness and private fears intensified for all organizations tarred with a Christian brush. Finally, partly due to conspicuous corruption within the leadership of the Nationalists and the popularity of the Red Army to the peasant population, that balance tipped in the direction of the Communists. Persistently holding on to the reins of his own popularity, a triumphant Mao Tse-tung declared the establishment of the People's Republic of China to cheering throngs from a balcony overlooking Tiananmen Square in October, 1949. Missionary schools, seen as bastions of imperialism, were no longer welcome in the new Communist educational system that would be nationalized strictly along Soviet models. Nevertheless, the Communists wisely kept what was practical of those unpopular bastions, utilizing the Western-trained Chinese faculty and stately college campuses built by imperialist money in a businesslike fashion.

In 1951, direct communication between Hwa Nan and her patrons was cut off when the U.S. government prohibited sending funds to China. All foreigners were expelled from local colleges and the era of missionary proselytizing, treaty

143

ports, and Western domination of the Chinese economy ended. Hwa Nan was swallowed up along with two other colleges to form Foochow National University. The institution that had truly been a "fostering mother" to Xu Daofeng, Ma Xiufa, Chen Zhongying, as well as Yu Baosheng, and hundreds of far-flung sisters of that alma mater, ceased to exist—but its spirit went underground.

Even after Liberation, requests rolled in from diverse employment sources for former Hwa Nan graduates. No matter what government was in charge, the college was held in high regard. As Lucy Wang had hoped, graduates were known for their spirit of willing service during the mass education project in 1938. Their community outreach to villages around Nanping had built positive recognition of the role women might play as future teachers and community leaders.

Xu Daofeng found work in the new People's Republic in a local high school as a mathematics professor; Ma Xiu Fa became a high school administrator. Chen Zhongying attained a Ph.D. overseas and was offered a college teaching position that embraced her specialty in classical languages. Dr. Yu Baosheng, who obtained a Master's Degree from Columbia, and later a Ph.D. from Johns Hopkins, became a chemistry professor at Foochow University. Other friends and graduates secured jobs in customs, the post office, and shipping companies, jobs formerly held by well-connected male applicants. Some Hwa Nan alums fled China when the Communists took command of the government, completing advanced degrees in other countries. All carried with them the intention of service inculcated by Lydia Trimble and her belief that receiving an education carried with it a

144

responsibility to contribute to society. They also carried the memory of challenging war years in Nanping when commitment and optimism had been so well modeled by their teachers.

In the long run, the arms of the fostering mother nurtured the women's imagination far more deeply than the crushing grip of the new Communist People's Republic of China which alternately invited and brutally punished innovative thought and initiative. In 1956, Mao invited thousands of ex-patriot Chinese back to help rebuild the Motherland. They were encouraged to "Let a Hundred Flowers Bloom" by giving criticisms and suggestions to Mao about his policies and reforms. Unfortunately, a little of that went a long way with The Great Helmsman. A brief year later, those who had come forth with opinions in conflict with Mao's were disgraced, jailed, tortured, and executed. Through the years of Mao's disastrous social campaigns, such as the Great Leap Forward (1958-61), the Chinese people struggled to match his ambitions, but the reach was too broad and Mao's visions too ungrounded. Famines and purges resulting from idiotic steel production schemes and ruinous agricultural "reforms," killed millions.

As his revolutionary social campaigns became more grandiose and grotesque from the 1950s through the 1970s, memories of their peaceful years at Hwa Nan College may have calmed the minds and sustained the hope of those graduates who managed to survive these campaigns. However, beautiful Lucy Wang could not be comforted. She spent some years as librarian at the new Fuzhou University, but quit in despair of Communist party policies. The commitment and optimism she generated and modeled in

145

earlier decades deserted her in her last years and she became bedridden from a lingering illness. Lucy was worn out. Some said it was grief.

The Cultural Revolution (1966-76) was Mao's last attempt to shake up society and eliminate false identities of class or status. The Chinese flag bears a large star representing the Communist Party and four smaller stars. These stars stand for students, farmers, manual laborers, and soldiers.[20] During the Cultural Revolution, these classes were given power over all other professions. Chinese citizens stained with education or privilege were stripped of their positions, humiliated, beaten, and tormented by students or vindictive peasant neighbors in a way that made the former war years seem relatively benign. Educated Chinese who were sent to remote villages to work as hard laborers or herd sheep, comforted themselves by remembering a time when education was revered and teachers cherished. Students became Red Guards with self-appointed military power. Xu Daofeng, because of her impeccable command of English, was branded an international spy and put under house arrest in her classroom by the students in her school. She and two colleagues were beaten, forced to kneel, and utter long diatribes of self-criticism. They were fed only weak gruel and constantly threatened with death. Both of Xu's colleagues broke under the harsh treatment and committed suicide, an all-too-common solution for educated Chinese who felt hopelessly trapped in a net of disgrace and abuse.

---

[20] Information on the meaning of the four stars varies with the source consulted and from the period in which their different roles were valued. Sometimes small businessmen have claimed to be one of the stars; at different periods, teachers have been included.

Chen Zhongying would be packed off to a cabbage-growing collective where she was made to dig and clean latrines. Dr. Yu Baosheng was demoted to janitor in the university where she had been a senior professor and valued researcher in polymer development. Experiences such as this either embitter or embolden, but the Chinese are proud of their ability to "eat bitter." When the chaos of the Cultural Revolution subsided and scholars began to cautiously peek out of their prisons and hiding places, blinking hopefully as lights went back on in educational institutions all over China, Xu Daofeng, Chen Zhongying, and Ma Xiufa blinked, too. Scholars who had been deprived of any academic endeavor for over a decade were hungrier than ever for education and contact with the world outside of China. Was it possible to breathe new life into the dreams of Lydia and Lucy, and actually foster the mother college that had fostered them?

It was Yu Baosheng who answered that question. Dr. Yu had been labeled a "Rightist" in the Cultural Revolution and was not deemed completely rehabilitated until 1979, after which she began biochemical research that led to the establishment of Foochow University's Institute of Polymer Science in 1984. Beyond the laboratory, she was able to create the kind of chemistry between the far-flung alumnae that would catalyze the rebirth of Hwa Nan College. Her formula? "We needed a combination of money and heart that is born of friendship," she confided. "When you have many people, you can solve any problem."[21]

---

[21] Dr. Yu was many times interviewed and honored for daring to reopen a private women's college with limited funds and resources. Her position was that she always had many people helping her. "People are the most important part of the plan," she stated in an interview in *Fujian Daily* newspaper, March 1985.

Chapter 11: Taking a Look at Aging and the Scattered Generations

"The house with an old grandparent harbors a jewel."
Confucius

If Yu Baosheng's endearing words that ended Chapter 10 had been uttered by a member of China's Minister of Civil Affairs today, he might have said: "When you have many people, *you have many problems to solve.*" China, the fourth largest country in the world geographically, currently claims 1.35 **billion** people, increasing hourly. Compare that eye-popping figure with the world's largest country, Russia, at 146 million or the second largest country, Canada, with their tiny 35 million and the concept of "many people" comes into sharper focus. America ranks third in geographic size, but even if the U. S.'s 318 million were added to the population figures of <u>both</u> Russia and Canada, the total population wouldn't come close to China's nose count.

So what do figures like that look like on the ground? What daily challenges are born of high population density? Come with me on a trip to the Sunday Bird and Flower Market where goldfish, turtles, budgies, and puppies hope you will take them home. Kittens are tied to a short length of twine to keep them from wandering off and tropical plants threaten to entangle you if you stand still too long. In addition to the flora and fauna, merchants squatting on bamboo mats that define their territory are selling everything from paper cuttings to antique pottery in the courtyard.

Public transportation is cheap and available in China, so let's take the bus to get in a flea-market mood. But look sharp! This is can be a high-risk activity and calls for strategy. The practice of "queuing up" has yet to become a custom among Mainland Chinese. Even as the bus speeds up to the curb, the waiting passengers begin to jostle and elbow each other for the first chance at entry when the accordion doors wheeze open.

Seats are limited, but squeeze-in standing is permitted as long as doors can be closed without severing an arm or leg. Bus-boarding is fiercely competitive, engaged in with the enthusiasm of a national sport by young and old alike. Unpracticed in pushing and shoving by my line-loving culture, and no equal in this joust, I have learned to stagger on after the tussle, looking as haggard and frail as possible. Then a kindly youth, schooled in both respect for the elderly as well as the competition for limited resources, might dutifully give me his or her seat. The initial satisfaction seems to lie in securing the space. Once won, it can be relinquished in the name of virtuousness.

Seated or standing, hang on tight! The bus lurches fearlessly into traffic, swerves, brakes, accelerates through small spaces between cars and trucks, and spins around traffic circles with centrifugal force. Does the rare opportunity of an occasional empty stretch of road present itself? The driver will then make up for all the delays with a grind of gears and burst of floored accelerator speed that will leave you breathless.

"Too rough!" you declare? Okay, let's get off the bus and take a taxi. They are cheap and plentiful. But with 10 million more vehicles being added to the roads of China *every month*, a great deal of freeway driving is more jam than flow. And no allowances are made for the age of the driver as in the case of an elderly passenger on a bus. No young driver yields to an elderly one; in fact, are there actually any elderly drivers? I never saw one. Driving on China's roads is not an older person's activity.

After our exhilarating ride, we're energized and ready for some lively haggling. Until 2008 when the area was razed for redevelopment, we entered the Bird and Flower Market through pillared gates that led the visitor into an alley lined with a jumble of plants, caged household pets and birds, and aquariums. Farther off the alley stood a more sedate row of shops selling carved teapots and garden statuary. Eventually the alley opened up into a vast area where people set up tables to sell kites, porcelain, antiques (fake and real) stones, undies and kitchenware. No, no—never pay full price! Start by offering half of what the seller asks for. Bargaining is lively and expected; saving face is as important as saving money.

I once found, at the Bird and Flower Market, a stack of men's sapphire blue briefs with a tiny pocket right smack in the middle for carrying condoms. Across the front of the underpants was an emphatic message in graceful Chinese characters admonishing the wearer to carry and use condoms for safety. They made excellent money belts. You never knew what you were going to come away with from the Bird and Flower market, although in 2011 I came home with a hitchhiker I didn't know I had.

On that Sunday, Shelley and her mother had invited me to go to the *new* Bird and Flower Market now located on the outskirts of town near a huge shopping complex, and selling many more breeds of animals and exotic plants. It was a delightful outing and I brought home a spotted yellow orchid. But on Monday, I developed a bumpy swelling and rash on the inside of my elbow and fingers as well as some red spots on my face. The rash grew scaly and expanded to long red streaks running up and down my arm. Little blisters sprouted along the lines and, to a lesser extent, on my fingers and face. By Wednesday, my concerned colleagues were avoiding sitting next to me at mealtimes. The school nurse (who looked about 14 and may have been) declared it a serious blood infection. A nurse friend in the States, to whom I'd appealed to for advice also worried it might be blood poisoning. Time to call Z. Z. Chen to the rescue.

Z. Z. Chen is a well-respected hematologist affiliated with the Fujian Institute of Hematology, with offices in the Union Hospital across town. Dr. Chen is cosmopolitan in his tastes, worldly in experience, and a generous friend of the foreign teachers of Hwa Nan. He usually travelled in a black sedan with a driver and one or two female interns, and it was in this style that he picked me up at the college gates a few hours after receiving my call. Although blood interested him, rashes didn't. He pronounced this a skin disease. He would take me to the best dermatologist in Fujian Province. The car deposited us at the entry of the gigantic hive-like hospital in which he worked.

Union Hospital boasts over 2,000 patient beds occupied (sequentially) by 80,000 inpatients in a single year. The facility is also on record for serving 1.9 million outpatients a year (this was about the population of Austin, Texas in 2013). Dr. Chen cut a swath through the waiting throngs (people in bandages, people hooked up to rolling IVs, people sneezing), and procured a treatment booklet for me from one of the registrars in which my diagnosis and treatment would be recorded. He steered me through the teeming waiting room, up flights of stairs and along corridors, past a busy ward filled with patients and their concerned family members, until we arrived at the dermatology department. The small waiting room was noisy with several people waving their treatment books and vying for a doctor's attention, but Z. Z. Chen brushed them aside (often done in many settings in the name of courtesy to a foreigner), strode into the doctor's inner office and presented my arm to a short, square, grey-haired woman in a white coat. The best dermatologist in Fujian Province examined my arm silently for a few seconds, wrote something on my record book, opened a thick diagnostic manual, written in English, and tapped a stubby finger at an entry entitled "Paederus dermetitus". Then, without a word or a smile, she turned her attention back to the jostling crowd of patients who were thrusting body parts towards her.

The entry in the diagnostic manual described the result of an encounter with a rove or "blister" beetle in words that exactly matched my symptoms: long red welts originating from a swollen area and mirroring each other as an ink blot would, with the addition of small blisters and a scaly surface. The rove beetle does not bite, but is cloaked in a poison ("more toxic than cobra venom" proclaimed one Internet source I pulled up later) that is its armor against predators. We speculated that I had unwittingly picked up the insect from one of the exotic plants at the Bird and Flower Market, brought it home on my person and pressed it in the fold of my elbow sometime during my slumbers. While the tiny beetle struggled for liberation, it may have left a trail of its venom along my arm and on the sheets where my fingers and face picked it up. After hearing the diagnosis of the school nurse, I had been imagining hospitalization and maybe even amputation; instead, I was sold a tube of ointment at the hospital pharmacy that cost $2.50, had my picture taken with my benefactor, Dr. Chen, and sent home on the bus. Apparently, I was going to live.

Death-by-rove-beetle is not a common occurrence locally. In fact, rove beetles aren't even native to China. Today, pollution is the most common killer. Pollution-related respiratory illness is on the rise and 'malignant tumor' is now listed as the leading cause of death according to the Chinese National Bureau of Statistics. Typical of countries that have shifted from agriculture economies to industrial ones, the illnesses of poverty have been replaced by the diseases of affluence: diabetes, cardiovascular disease, and cancer. Most dementia cases go unreported but experts worry that Alzheimer's disease may cause the biggest challenge yet to scattered families and the range of geriatric care options that are still in their infancies.

Foreign investors are promoting apartment complexes for active affluent seniors as well as high-end assisted living facilities but the idea of a nursing home for frail elders is incongruous with the Confucian ideal of grandparents being cared for by their offspring. Nursing itself is viewed as a low-status job and turnover is frequent. Early in their children's lives, adults let it be known (incessantly, it seemed to me) that it is their parental duty to care for the child now and the child's duty to care for the parents later. American children might have heard this constant refrain as a burden, but the kids I taught in 2000 seemed to be emphatically grateful to their parents and frequently stated their intention to provide a home for them.

Playing the "old person" card worked better during the days when Confucius was teaching his political and moral doctrines. Unlike other philosophers, he focused on everyday concerns, preaching personal development of character, respect for elders, and a return to traditional virtues. His teachings, kept alive by his disciples, became the dominant political philosophy in the latter half of the Han dynasty. He encouraged the rulers to model reverence and solicitude toward their wise and experienced older subjects. "When the ruler treats the elders with respect, then the people will be aroused toward filial piety," he advised, as one of the basics for a civil society.

But the current rulers are interested primarily in economic expansion and that is the domain of the young and middle-aged. To again paraphrase Dr. Yu Baosheng, when you have many *old* people you have *even more* problems to solve, a recognition that is dampening ancient traditions and fostering new opportunities. Being old no longer guarantees a position of power as it once did in the traditional family and is, instead, becoming a position of liability for the younger generation and the country.

In 2000, my students were eager to introduce me to my first "Old People's Day," a time when elder citizens were encouraged to enjoy the out-of-doors by flying a kite or climbing a mountain. Since I paced the classroom along a concrete floor four hours every day, I chose the kite-flying option. After class, we walked down a high-walled lane overhung with trees to the nearest major traffic artery. There we boarded a bus that would take us to a park along the Min River where the breeze was fresh and the kite vendors plentiful. Oh, the thrill of green grass and open air after all

 day in the classroom! That a foreigner was involved in this outing did not escape the notice of the vendors, and the price of kites tripled. Gryphon and Grace bargained fiercely, foreshadowing their futures as successful entrepreneurs, and we soon had several kites aloft. "It is better to fly kites than to fish," said the poet Li Po, urging toilers to gaze at the heavens rather to keep eyes downcast on the earth. We agreed with him wholeheartedly.

In ancient days, this holiday was called the "Double Ninth" (ninth day of the ninth month in the lunar calendar), and was linked to the concept of longevity because the word for 'nine' has the same pronunciation as *jiu* which means 'everlasting.' Emperors used the number on royal robes and architectural decoration to insure the eternal strength of their dynasties. Double Ninth day is wrapped in a myth involving a mountain-dwelling devil who caused a deadly plague to befall the hill people and a good son who set out to avenge the death of his parents. Guided by the immortals and armed with his sword, a sprig of dogwood, and chrysanthemum wine, the young man climbed the mountain, slew the devil, and paved the way for a longer life for the villagers. The day originally included eating *chongyang* cakes (a glutinous rice cake made with nuts and other treats) and drinking chrysanthemum wine with ones' elders, preferably in cozy proximity to a mountain.

In 1989, the day was modernized by the Communist government and morphed from "Double Ninth" into "Old People's Day." My young students in the year 2000 clearly enjoyed it as much as I did, in spite of the fact there was no sign of *chongyang* cakes or chrysanthemum wine. By 2011, my last year teaching in China, the status of old people had declined among the upwardly-mobile youth population, and I heard not a murmur of celebrating this festival with kites or cakes. The shift in attitude toward the elderly may be because the growing number of old people represents a major problem to be grappled with, rather than an achievement to be celebrated. Estimates of the growth of the aging population are skewed depending who will benefit from what figure, but in 2011, *Xinhua*, the official news agency of the Communist government, predicted a population of over 200 million people above the age of 60 by 2015. Current reports put the population of elderly at 126 million, or one in every 10 people.

In China, as in other entrepreneurial economies, knotty social problems can often be turned into lucrative business opportunities. Recently there has been an upsurge in the establishment of retirement homes for the elderly, both private and public, specializing in providing housing units and residences geared to the affluent aging. The homes provide meals, activities, and eventually nursing care for those who can afford them. Sometimes adult working children contribute money to provide a higher level of care than the parents could otherwise afford. This is a new variation on the requirement of filial duty so essential to

Confucian ideals. It can be liberating for the old and the young alike.

Like Hwa Nan's Old Ladies, most survivors of 20th century life in China are a sturdy bunch, likely to go on living until age 80 or beyond. Grinding poverty in the service of wealthy landlords or businessmen weeded out the weak in the old days. Those not dead from exhaustion, poor nutrition, disease, and opium addiction were faced with revolution and civil war as the century wore on. Occupation of parts of China by the Japanese led to more suffering and death. For three more decades, after what the West calls "the Communist takeover"—and the Chinese call "Liberation"—more famine and chaos followed as Mao experimented with delusional social policies. Some scholars estimate as many as 40 million people starved or were murdered between Liberation in1949 and Mao's death in 1976 (a much smaller figure is reported by Communist historians).

After Mao's death and the power struggle that followed, Deng Xiaoping assumed control of the government and in the 1980s introduced sweeping economic reforms to encourage private enterprise and foreign trade. Throughout the 1990s, the economy continued to boom and the patriarchs of extended Chinese families watched their offspring leave threshing floors and rice paddies for cleaner, better paying jobs in urban areas where growth was most dramatic. Many others were able to afford to send their children away to urban schools, from which the young people rarely returned. Confucius admonished children not to travel far while their parents were still alive, but modernization and economic growth has encouraged exactly the opposite.

Many of my students were from the countryside. Some families had achieved a certain level of affluence, but some needed to pool their resources in order to pay the expenses of a child who showed academic promise in hopes of a better life for the whole family. College-bound kids were reminded constantly that they were there at the pleasure, and frequently at the hardship, of other family members, and needed to repay the family for this opportunity when they began working. Many were the first members of their families to attend college, and certainly the first to learn a foreign language. And many more were women. Exciting gains, to be sure, but as more young, better-educated women spend their best energies in offices and factories, rather than in the home, who will care for the babies and who for the elderly?

That the One Child Policy would lead to greater economic prosperity for all was the intention of the policy makers in 1986, but they did not anticipate creating a gender imbalance. In China, there are 120 male births for every 100 female births, whereas the world average is 105 males to 100 females. Using these figures, the Chinese government, which usually whitewashes bad news, projects that by 2020 the country will have over 30 million more young men of marrying age than young women. This could result in a subculture of rogue males, a dangerous underclass of men who are unable to find wives and thus function outside the orderly restraints and protections of their own family structure.

Just as worrisome is the new 4-2-1 family pattern, in which a young adult can have as many as four very old grandparents and two aging parents, all depending on that one child for care and support. And where is that one child? No longer nearby, plowing a soggy field before planting time, or raising ducks in a pond. The lure of bright lights and consumer goods, and a job with which to make enough money to buy those goods, is a powerful draw away from the ancestral village and the old people who still call that village home. Even money sent "home" is not an adequate substitute.

Consumer lust is more than a natural consequence of economic growth; it has now been formalized into an economic strategy. Imagine government policymakers musing over their cups of fragrant green tea, asking each other, "How can we shift from our dependency on *exporting* goods to the rest of the world, to growth based on a *domestic* demand for products?"

"Yes," agrees another. "The new middle class in our cities is now eager and able to buy the same products China is providing the rest of the world. But people in rural areas do not consume products because farmers grow most of what they need, store surplus for later use, and trade with neighboring villages for things they can't grow or make."

"So," the musing goes on, "why not remove the farmers from their land—and that's easy, since technically all land in China is owned by the people, i.e. the government—relocate them into urban centers using incentives and subsidies, then attract factories to that area where they can make real money? When more people have a greater monetary income, there will be a huge new market for domestically-made consumer goods!"

And, incredibly, this is what is being done. In Communist countries that govern by fiat, solutions can be developed quickly and announced as policy to be put into immediate action. Catchy slogans help promote the policy to an accepting public. However, some solutions are more complicated and difficult to execute, with unintended consequences not evident until years later. Many China watchers are eyeing this new direction with suspicion while the foreign press seems to take a lively interest in China's failures, transgressions, and aggressions, coupling even success stories with a skeptical spin.

Peasant demonstrations spring up here and there protesting the loss of their land to accelerated urbanization, but nostalgia for the fantasy of the simple country life of yesteryear, the theme of so many country ballads in America, is almost nonexistent among Chinese of middle age and income. They have excellent memories and are still reveling in their escape from the rustic, the dirty, and the insular. Only the elderly want to stay in the countryside because it is familiar territory. If it is the moral duty of the children, especially the sons, to care respectfully for aging parents, then migration of young men to the cities has frayed that thread to traditional responsibilities. The old folks don't want to follow the young to the cities, and the young refuse to return. Although most of my students knew and loved John Denver's tune "Country Road", few urban Chinese share the sentiments expressed by bluegrass legend J. D. Crowe when he sang the ballad *Old Home Place:* "Why did I leave my plow in the field to search for a job in the town?" Country music, with its themes of trucks, faithful dogs, mama, and nostalgia for lost loves will never top the charts in a country gone mad for modernization.

I was baffled as to why the word "countryside" created such a negative reaction in the Chinese, when to me it meant historic villages, meadows and forests for hiking, and hospitable people. When I told my 2000-2001 students I was from a small rural town in the foothills of northern California, they cringed with sympathy and condolence. The next year, I came armed with pictures of my county's tiny twin towns in all their quaint glory, photos of Victorian houses surrounded by trees in a blaze of autumn color, of carriages clip-clopping down Broad Street, of peach fields in bloom, of deer grazing on green hillsides, of water tumbling over granite rocks in the Yuba River canyon.

The disbelief reflected in their eyes and comments made it clear they recognized these pictures as exaggerated visual propaganda, something a Chinese Chamber of Commerce might produce. This was fairyland compared to their ideas of country living. "How can your river water be so clear?" they challenged me. "Why is the sky so blue? Who keeps the streets so clean? Where are all the people?"

I explained that, in fact, my rural county was growing, with people eager to move from the crowded streets of sprawling urban areas into a wooded county with fresh air and less population density. They rolled their eyes. To them, the countryside was dirty, backward and boring.

It is increasingly the locale of much dissatisfaction, as farmers feel the economic boom has passed them by. For centuries, peasants were taxed arbitrary amounts from 10% to 40% of their income to help support the imperial government or the landlord. Taxes are essential to any government, so when the Communist Party took power they continued the practice, albeit using the money for more social services for the people. As income disparity between rural and urban workers increased (in fact, more than doubled in the last 30 years) discontent has also increased accordingly. In 2005, an average city dweller was making about $1000 a year; the person toiling to grow his food in the countryside only made about $300 annually. In an attempt to improve rural conditions, the government launched a campaign in 2005 to make the countryside cleaner and more modern (although it was harder to reduce the boredom factor). To help balance the income difference, all agricultural taxes were abolished. There are now more lucrative manufacturing businesses to tax than to squeeze money out of farmers. By 2006, most Chinese villages could be accessed by decent roads, and had electricity, running water, and phone coverage—unheard of luxuries in the countryside before the 21st century.

To see firsthand what it was that repelled my students about the countryside, two friends and I rented a car and drove east toward the remote seaside villages dotting the ragged coast of Fujian Province. We chose to go without benefit of a Chinese guide, who would have been dumbstruck at our choice of destination anyway. Tourism in China seemed to be undertaken solely for visiting famous and dramatically-restored destinations and having one's picture taken there: the Great Wall, the terra cotta soldiers at Xian, and the Temple of Heaven (which was heavily damaged by Red Guards during the Cultural Revolution and is now reconstructed of imported Oregon pine). Seldom do tourists go off to explore on their own; this is always warned against as "dangerous" by the industry. But how dangerous could exploring be in a country where most people were small and no one but the military police carried guns? My two traveling companions spoke some Mandarin, so we figured that would be enough to break the ice with the villagers and keep us from getting hopelessly lost.

Concrete and brick houses in various stages of partial construction huddled together in colorless oblongs to form the villages. The dirt streets were littered with containers and plastic bags; clearly the city street sweepers with their green carts and bamboo brooms did not serve this area and there was no plan for dealing with the introduction of plastic products into village life. Occasionally pigs and goats poked through the trash, searching for edible treasure. We stopped here and there to walk around, leaving our bright red sedan standing alongside the tiny lanes like a rosy Amanita mushroom. Our party of three, one ebony-black young man with dreadlocks from Cameroon, one curly-topped marketing specialist from Chicago, and me, a small blonde older woman, attracted clusters of curious country folk wherever we went on foot. Staring villagers crowded around us to examine our clothes and comment on our hair. With little in the way of recreation or entertainment in these villages, we became the major attraction. Attempts at conversation went unrewarded; perhaps they only spoke the local dialects.

We planned to picnic at a temple on a hillside we'd seen from a distance, but found it abandoned, vandalized, and used as a latrine. Okay, how about the beach? The sight of three foreigners eating their picnic lunch on the litter-strewn pebbles soon drew a solemn, silent audience. When we stood up and gathered our things, we discovered our clothes were dotted with small oil stains from the pearls of black sludge peppering the sand and stones. The watchers found this hilarious—how ridiculous these foreigners were to sit and eat on a beach! We departed, polka-dotted and pointed at.

The next community on our route supported itself by harvesting seaweed from offshore beds. The workers were returning from their workday in small boats and barges, rubbing cold hands and struggling out of tall rubber boots. When Izzy, the Cameroonian, tried to join in the after-work soccer game, the national prejudice against blacks demonstrated itself by more jostling and tripping than Izzy was prepared for. Lack of exposure to any race except Han Chinese, as well as recent resentment over government involvement with chaotic African regimes being courted for their resources, have combined to exacerbate a strong anti-black sentiment. When the crowd began to enjoy the teasing of Izzy more than the game, we elbowed our way toward our car and fled. Clearly, exploring this particular countryside was not the lark we'd envisioned.

Nevertheless, it is where two-thirds of those 200 million rural elderly are choosing to remain, even if they have offspring in cities. Big city life is disorienting to the rural elderly; they lose their sense of community, their sense of place. "Apartment complexes are noisy and too confining," they complain. "The markets are too big, the streets are crowded, and we have no connections in the city." So in small villages all over China, rural elders are caring for each other in the absence of younger relatives. Sixty-year-olds help eighty-year-olds get through their remaining days. Who will help the sixty-year-olds when *they* are eighty is a question for the future. For thousands of years Confucian directives regarding the sons' responsibility to family elders provided China's social security net, but people are realizing this can no longer be relied upon, with children both fewer and farther away.

But wait! Private and foreign investors recognize that in every need there lies an opportunity. Market research shows that while older Chinese are frugal and often unwilling to spend money on month-to-month residency in a retirement home, many would be willing to buy property in a retirement development providing services for the elderly. Publicity campaigns are being launched to change attitudes about old people's communities. Joint ventures are springing up between overseas assisted living operators and local real estate brokers, albeit mostly in urban centers. Riding on a bus one day, I spotted English words on banners fluttering from the walls of just such a new development. The English language is often used to imply worldliness and sophistication (although the result may be the exact opposite if read by a native English speaker): "California CEO Circles" one banner proclaimed. "Orange County Acres of Forest Resorts" touted another. Still another assured the buyer of "The V-Life: Victory, Virtue, and Variation." There is money to be made.

When the family roots are already in the city or nearby towns, generational issues are less complicated. Parents can be installed in adjacent apartments and many newly affluent couples buy two high-rise 'homes' in the same building, one for themselves and one for older relatives. Local parks and community centers provide the arena for the street life left behind in the old neighborhood or village. Annual festivals can be celebrated without extensive travel.

But when families are divided by geography, urban workers' busy city lives don't permit frequent trips to visit relatives in the countryside. Their elders feel neglected and unrewarded for the money and time spent raising these people as children. To address this issue, a law went into effect in 2013 allowing elderly relatives to sue their offspring for not visiting regularly. The term "regularly" and the amount of the fine for this offense have not yet been determined—nor has the question of financial support for aging farmers left behind without a pension plan.

The sound of a baby's cry is a universal siren song for old ones everywhere, and it is the lure of grandchildren that most frequently motivates an elderly couple to move into the city to assist the new parents in their time honored role as caregivers to the family infants. If the grandparents can't be enticed into the city to care for the newborn, the baby may be delivered to them in their village when maternity leaves expire. There the child may remain, visited at least annually during Spring Festival, until able to attend school. In my Free Conversation classes, students Primrose and Dottie could work themselves into a fountain of nostalgic tears recalling happy days in the rural villages of their grandparents, although they pined for their parents. Alice won a speech contest with a poignant story about the pride her stooped arthritic grandmother took in keeping the family courtyard clean. Mary spoke repeatedly of her grandfather saving money out of his tiny income so she could continue her schooling.

Many of my urban students' families still lived in multi-generational households, and those from the countryside accepted being handed over to Granny as babies. Grandparents raising grandchildren in the States usually results from some kind of disaster in the middle adult generation. Not so in China. The concept of family is so much broader and more permanent than our mutable nuclear families in the West.

As my student Clara explained it "Yes, we only saw our parents once a year at Spring Festival until they were sent to live with Mama and Baba in the city when they reached school age, but that was true of the neighbor children and our cousins, so to us it was normal. We felt surrounded by an almost boundless family."

I felt wistful recalling my devoted but older English parents who emphasized independence and education for me, their only child, because "we won't live to see you grown." My family circle consisted of just us three; beyond that, there were only some seldom seen cousins in Canada. I had been raised like an orphan-in-training.

If the older generation was unable or unwilling to live in the city, and the parents did not want to send their newborn to the ancestral village, daycare or nursery schools became the solution. Affluent urban families might even be able to manage a combination of grandparent care and nursery school, although without Granny to go home to, some children spend as much as twelve hours in a nursery school setting while parents work, shop, and commute.

I often wondered about the Old Ladies' families. Were Chen, Xu and Ma grandmothers? We certainly never saw them with beribboned little ones at the mixers occasionally put on by the Foreign Affairs Office, or handing around pictures of grandchildren at honorific banquets. Did they have family still living in Fuzhou? Were they expecting their children to care for them when they could not care for themselves? These questions would have been seen as too intimate to ask directly, so I listened to see if I could catch any of my Chinese teaching colleagues talking about their grandparents. I waited patiently, ready to slip in a few questions about plans for their grandparents' care or what role they expected to play in their grandparents' end of life. And that's how I came to hear the story of Laura, her family of origin, and the puppet show for Grandmother.

Chapter 12: Looking Closer at One Girl's Life
Laura's Story

The old man on the porch lit the string of firecrackers dangling from his fingers as we drove into the courtyard. Smoke billowed and sparks flew into the air around him. A blue military "Mao" jacket hung loosely on his slender frame and a wide grin rearranged the wrinkles on his face. When the firecrackers exploded just inches from his hand, he dropped them and shouted in Mandarin what we hoped was a welcome.

"Don't worry,' said Laura. "My father is just giving you the traditional Chinese greeting in your honor. Welcome to our family compound."

As we stepped over the high threshold, traditionally designed to trip up wandering ghosts, I pondered the fact that, since firecrackers were also used fend off evil spirits, I'd better try to look as benevolent as possible. Inside an adjacent courtyard a woman in black rubber knee boots was sloshing water over the carcasses of recently slaughtered goats (pictured on p. 170). She, too, smiled broadly, bucket in hand, a row of decapitated goats' heads neatly aligned on the slab behind. She seemed to be enjoying the grisly task, one that would have made me cringe. I often felt like a sissy when confronting aspects of everyday life in rural China.

Members of Laura's family were mostly farmers who toiled in the rice fields around the village as well as supplied goat's milk yogurt and goat meat to hotels for Chinese travelers in the area. Hotels approved for guests designated "Western aliens and overseas Chinese" were not buyers, as Americans or Canadian visitors had yet developed an appetite for goat. Living together in the compound were Laura's birthparents, the grandmother who raised her, her younger brother, his wife, and their two children. An older sister lived nearby with her husband's family.

Wait...an older sister and a younger brother? That doesn't fit the formula of the One Child Policy. We know that if a peasant family has a girl first, they can keep that child and

try again for a boy. If the second child were also a girl, the family had a hard decision to make.

How could they survive if they kept a second girl baby and then had no son to care for them in their old age? There is no Social Security system in China. No Medicare. Only male offspring were bound by tradition to plow the family fields, tend their graves, and perform ceremonial duties for ancestors in the afterlife.

Can you see how these time-honored beliefs lead to the undervaluing of girls? Back in the day when country women had eight or ten children, there were usually enough males in

170

the mix to satisfy tradition. Raising a girl meant feeding a child who would then leave her birth family when she married and work only for her husband's kin. Now, under the One Child Policy, peasant parents had only two chances to get the male who could carry on the family lineage and be depended upon to support and care for his parents in their dotage.

In cities, prospective parents often consulted medical sources regarding the gender of their prenatal child. In rural villages without access to ultrasound testing, that decision had to be made at the birthing bed. Now that infanticide was considered illegal, and the cold "baby water" bucket that was kept nearby in the old days to dispose of unwanted females was no longer in use, there were other ways that could achieve the same purpose.

Laura had been the second girl. Oh, pity the parents whose dual responsibility it was to obey the civil law and also honor the demands of tradition! Laura's parents felt they did not have the luxury of individual choice. They were not hard-hearted people, but they understood that the hardness of life required individual sacrifices to be made for the good of the whole family. They must not keep a second girl baby. They had to make way for the opportunity to try again for a boy. How they wished the child would be given another chance to be reborn under better circumstances! But fate dictated this outcome; the mother turned her face to the wall and let her husband deal with the logistics.

One method used in the countryside to deal with newborns who could not be kept was similar to the ancient Greek and Roman practice of 'exposure.' In those civilizations, a defective or unwanted baby would be placed

171

out on a sacred hillside where his or her fate would be decided by the gods. There being a shortage of sacred hillsides in Laura's village, a common practice was to leave unwanted newborns in or near the open communal latrines. There, the foraging animals would often make short work of the unwanted child, thereby sidestepping the need for a family member or a midwife to be guilty of infanticide. Laura was on her way to her destiny in the arms of her sorrowing father when Grandmother heard the news of the baby's gender.

Grandmother was an aged woman with white hair and bound feet, both the matriarch and also the dependent oldster of her family. She was known in the village as a woman of kind heart and good deeds. Born in the years of warfare and famine, she had dutifully abided by the harsh rules of rural life for many decades before and after Liberation. She accepted China's need for population control and the government's policy. Yet something steely moved in her at this moment and Grandmother came to life. "Not this one!" she thundered, as she hobbled on her tiny feet after her son who carried the small bundle.

Whether he was astonished by her rebelliousness or relieved by the demand his mother made, no one knew. In any case, he handed the infant to Grandmother. A story was concocted that would be widely repeated throughout the village about her taking in an extra girl child from a remote arm of the family. In a country where complex social requirements are often in conflict with individual preferences, such transparent stories, if agreed upon by all, are an essential buffer against a dehumanizing bureaucracy. In this kind of culturally sanctioned duplicity, there was often both a private and a public story, known and accepted by all, for expediency or even survival.

After a few years, the long-awaited son was born who would carry on the family name and make sure his parents' spirits were tended in the afterlife. Because of Grandmother's intervention, Laura grew up much like an only child, perceived as separate from the other family of four by some silent agreement she didn't initially understand. She belonged to her grandmother, slept in the same bed with her, accompanied her in her village rounds and sat beside her at family dinners. As she grew older, the situation slowly became clearer to her, although no one told her directly. Laura watched wistfully as the mother braided Older Sister's hair and fed Little Brother tender morsels from her own bowl. Her grandmother was affectionate and attentive, but Laura often wished for a chance to sit on a maternal lap, even for an opportunity to cringe at the paternal rage feared by her siblings. Mother's decision, however, was irrevocable; once made, she needed to close her heart to her daughter. The story of Laura being an adopted orphan must be upheld.

In spite of a delay in entering school due to an injury that was slow to heal, Laura did well academically in primary school and junior middle school. When she passed the *zhongkao* and qualified to continue on to the number one senior school in a nearby town, she begged her Grandmother to let her continue past the age of compulsory education. It would mean selling some old family wood carvings that had not been smashed by the Red Guards during the Cultural Revolution to buy Laura's books and uniforms, and to pay for transportation and possibly accommodations at school.

Grandmother reluctantly agreed, but she later began to

grumble. "A certain amount of education is fine but is senior school necessary?" she muttered. "Why not just get a job in the local shoe factory and find a nice boy to marry there? That is enough for a good life."

But Laura's pleas had prevailed and she continued her education, an achievement not shared by either of her biological siblings. Grandmother acquiesced but remained skeptical about the worth of all this time spent in school. "You don't need an education to be a success," she maintained.

As Laura began to blossom as a student, even against the background music of Grandma's complaints, her father began to cast a cautious but hopeful eye toward her progress. Slowly the caution melted his resistance and the ordinarily aloof Zhang Wei became increasingly animated about her achievements. Aha! Laura saw that this might be something she could do to earn his respect and capture more of his attention.

Laura was amazed to learn her father had also been a good student, completing senior school and qualifying for medical school that was then only an additional four-year course of study after that. Alas, his family was very poor and needed him to work in order to help support them all. Zhang Wei applied for scholarships. Yes, he qualified financially, he was told, but his father had worked as a repairman in houses of landowners before Liberation. Any dealing with landlords or people of wealth and power was enough to damn a person as a "Rightist" or a "Capitalist Roader." In those days, it was essential to be from pure soldier-peasant-worker roots. His father was considered suspiciously technically accomplished and had rubbed shoulders with a few too many landlords. For this sin his father was suspected of being an "enemy of the people," and by association, so was Zhang Wei. He was denied the scholarship; it would go to someone who had no connections with the old ruling classes.

Determined to continue his education, Zhang Wei entered a medical training program and tried to make a living selling rice cakes while he took classes. Business was brisk, but between making the rice cakes, selling them, and continuing to be part of the rice planting and harvesting cycle, he had little time to study and eventually had to drop out of the program. Sorrowfully, Zhang Wei accepted his fate and his filial duties, made more and better rice cakes, and eventually they provided him a successful self-perpetuating business.

When a distant family member with expertise in raising goats moved to the area, the enterprising Zhang Wei saw another opportunity and contracted to supply local hotels with meat and yogurt. Now he was a businessman farmer, confident that he could support his family, but still casting backward glances at the faded dream of medical training. China is not a place where one goes back to school in mid-life, but it *is* a place where offspring carry the burden of their parents' dreams. When his daughter, acknowledged as such or not, began to show signs of academic advancement, that dormant dream began to grow again. Perhaps his daughter (for now, surely, the pretense could be allowed to fade) might be the one to inherit his future as a medical professional.

Zhang Wei had smoked most of his life, quit several times, but always began again on the eve of any qualifying test that marked the path of Laura's progress. He could see his daughter was bright and well-motivated, but as he watched her leap the hurdles on the way towards their hopes

175

of college, he relived his own anxieties and disappointments. He was a bundle of nerves through the summer of her senior year, when the National Exam was given to determine who would go on to what college.

Laura was nervous, too. In fact, she always became ill the day before tests were given, and since this was the biggest test of all, she became very ill. Studying, watching father begin to smoke again, being anxious and nauseated—all those factors conspired against her attempts to qualify for a four-year college. She never attained the necessary score. She took the *gaokao* two years in a row and, even though she had been one of the top students in the local high school, she could not achieve a high enough score to attend a university. Laura's intelligence and drive were never in question, but a single test is given nationally and it is difficult for country kids to compete with their city cousins. Rural schools tend to be poorly-funded with underpaid teachers and shabby equipment, leaving those who attend them less able to qualify for higher education.

Thus Laura enrolled in Hwa Nan College, one of many surprised girls who had not done well on the National Exam after many years of shining in their local elementary school classes. After graduation from Hwa Nan, she found a job in a private high school that recruited foreign teachers. Over the years she'd made many friends from English-speaking countries and today, she had invited some of them to her village to see a puppet show given for the pleasure of the gods in gratitude for recently sparing Grandmother's life. The old lady had taken a treacherous fall in the now indoor latrine, a tiny concrete room with a hole in the middle over which the user squatted. Grandmother's old knees could no longer reliably support a squat. She lost her balance, fell against the concrete wall, split her scalp and lost consciousness.

Family members had prayed for her recovery, promising the gods a puppet show if all went well. It is well known, Laura explained, that the gods love puppet shows, so with Granny on the mend, a troupe was located and a stage set up in the middle of the village square. A leaning tower of gold embossed paper money was stacked in front of the stage, to be ignited at a strategic moment in the presentation. It is equally well known that burning paper money ensures wealth and status for ancestors in the afterlife.

But before lunch and puppets would we like a tour of the house? We would! The kitchen was a spacious outdoor space under a canopy and sported a couple of huge pottery water jars, a concrete sink, a two-burner propane stovetop and a wood-burning oven. Female family members busied themselves preparing the midday meal, the biggest meal of the day.

Partly under the staircase in the main room a round, wooden table was set with rice bowls and chopsticks for at least 10 people. A smaller room contained two massive pieces of wooden furniture: a chair fit for a giant, and a gargantuan settee that insured the sitters would be dwarfed by its size and chilled by the hard shellacked wood. It seemed an odd furniture style for a country of small people, but this combination appeared in most of the homes I visited. Up the wooden stairs, the family slept in various configurations on grass matting spread across wooden beds, enclosed in white mosquito netting, each illuminated by one low-wattage bare bulb. The house was built of concrete and porous bricks, reflecting little in the way of Western comfort or décor but it gave the family luxuries not previously enjoyed, and for those they were proud and grateful.

And wasn't the best decor of all a full table laden with delicious food? We descended the stairs to the sight of steaming dishes of green vegetables, stuffed dumplings, pungent soups and rice. Fujian province cooks are famous for their broths made from scratch and every part of the beast on which the broth is based can be found in the soup bowl— beaks, feet, fish heads or pig's ears. Chinese hospitality demands that the guest be served the most treasured morsels at the dinner table, be it the eyeball of the fish or a slice of gelatinous black sea cucumber. This sometimes posed diplomatic challenges when dining with Chinese friends or colleagues, but Laura had cautioned her family about the persnickety food preferences of her American teachers and everything looked soothingly familiar.

"Our parents taught us to cherish every part of the pig," I was once reminded by a Chinese colleague dispensing soup into my bowl, after I expressed alarm over the recognizable porcine parts the soup tureen held. Sometimes at banquets my ladle would contain half a chicken's head or a duck's foot. Even the words 'local specialties' gave me a queasy feeling, because they could mean river snails or frogs cooked in fragrant wine or *chou doufu*, a very foul-smelling tofu that had been fermented in brine. Buddha Jumps Over the Wall Soup contains shark's fin, sea cucumber, and other creatures from the sea simmered with ginseng in Shaoxing rice liquor. I had recently visited a snazzy new restaurant that offered a menu translated into English with an electronic dictionary. I was delighted to read that I could begin with Buddhist Ritual Procedures Onion Soup, continue to an Explodes the Pork

Chop Sandwich and end the meal with Dissolute Sweetheart Forgets the Kindness Fruit. Wine? How about a nice Carbuncle Red? *Man man chi! Bon appétit!*

After the meal, Zhang Wei tried to organize his offspring and guests for a photograph, a feat that could be compared to a Keystone Cops routine with Laura arranging wisps of Grandmother's hair to its best advantage, adults trying to assign each other position in the grouping by status, kids snatched up to be displayed by proud parents. Once pictures had been taken using everyone's camera and to everyone's satisfaction, it was time to head to the village square for the puppet show.

The stroll took us past mud brick homes with tile roofs, personal garden plots growing bok choy, mustard, and cabbage, courtyards stacked with split wood and dried dung for cooking fuel. Constellations of black eyes stared out from windows at the foreigners. Although western visitors had become a familiar sight in the bigger cities in 2000, there were still many villages in which residents had never seen a Caucasian except on television. "*Lao wei!* (Old foreign person!) was whispered from house to house, and we felt like a cross between movie stars and two-headed aliens. Remember, "old" is a term of respect, but "foreign" is a word close in meaning to "alien." Toddlers who had never beheld any human face that was not framed with black hair and studded with dark eyes wailed and buried their heads in their grandmothers' laps at the sight of our light eyes and hair.

But look! The puppet show was in full swing! Jointed doll-like figures danced upon the small portable stage, controlled by wires in the hands of the puppeteers standing on a box behind the background curtain. The villagers, seated on the hand-built stone walls that bounded the square, laughed and talked while the puppets, in satin gowns and long flowing sleeves played out their comic or tragic roles. Accompanying the drama were three musicians. One sawed on an *erhu* with a bow, another reflected the tempo of the stage action by hitting gongs, cymbals, and drums with varying levels of intensity, and the third blew a horn producing a reedy rambling series of notes.

A light rain fell, but still the paper money piled in the square burst into high flames when it was ignited. After a while, the antics of the puppets with their falsetto voices  began to lose their grip on the audience. We wandered back to the family compound where Grandmother was napping. Laura seemed an integral part of her extended family, all vestiges of her former separate status erased by time. She had been through emotional trials that would have put most westerners on the therapist's couch for decades, and yet this big-hearted woman seemed to magnanimously accept it as one of the many painful adaptations to the family that allowed it to remain solid.

By the time my decade in China had passed, Laura had married a man she admired, and the couple had a child of their own, a girl who they cherished and nurtured together, employing a conscious combination of Chinese traditions and modern ideas of childrearing. As I watched Laura raise her daughter, I wondered how she sorted through the events of her own childhood, separating the gold from the dross, not letting her role as daughter cast a shadow on her new role as mother.

I was curious about how Chinese parents often passed the ownership of kids around for the good of the whole family, without apparent psychological damage. I pondered the absence of "special needs" students in the college setting and the almost complete absence of identified attention deficits or learning disabilities in my students. As a former school psychologist in California, I had assessed many students for ADHD or learning disabilities so that they could request special accommodations and modifications for their disabilities in the regular classroom. Not so in China. A human rights watch group has reported that handicapped children are rarely provided with opportunities to overcome barriers in public school and many more disabled young people are excluded from a mainstream education completely.

I was fascinated with Chinese childrearing practices that in some ways seemed so rough and rigid, but had produced the warm, generous girls I knew in class. As my young Chinese friends matured, married, and began their own families, I was able to get a closer look a child's beginning, from the womb through the early years of socialization.

Chapter 13: Looking Around – Views of Motherhood and Daycare

"He who is in harmony with the Tao is like a newborn child."
Lao Tzu

My Chinese friend Jane was pregnant. Her ordinarily round face was taking on moon-like proportions and her formerly tiny abdomen pushed proudly against the confines of her over-blouse. Family and friends fussed over her, giving advice, reminding her of the old childbearing traditions, while her husband hovered paternally in the background, relieved not to be the center of this attention.

I had met Jane in 2000 when a group of foreign teachers sought a Chinese tutor and, in spite of our abysmal talents with her native language, she and I became friends. At the time, she was a student teacher at a huge university nearby, working on a Master's degree in philosophy and also working as a teaching assistant. The school provided a small salary and housing in a staff dorm, but Jane needed more money for clothes and for replacing the tank of propane she used to cook in the hallway. Each dorm resident bought and filled his or her own propane tank that was then attached to a two-burner gas plate. A concrete sink and counter along the wall completed the communal kitchen arrangements for the young. Apparently other dorm residents were stressed for money too, as Jane's tank was frequently stolen in spite of a complicated knot of chains and locks with which she tried in vain to secure it.

Her tiny room in the featureless concrete residence hall held a kitchen table where we worked, a single bed surrounded by a curtain, and some wooden trunks for her belongings. The biggest difference between Jane's room and those of my students was that it was hers alone, a luxury newly-experienced in the life of this young person. As we climbed the stairs to her floor, we ducked under massed tangles of electrical wiring, not included in these post-revolutionary buildings in the mid-1900s, but added later after electrical utilities became in common use.

In such a setting and with such a schedule, boyfriends were hard to cultivate, even for an attractive, intelligent woman like Jane. We shopped for snappy clothes in the new department stores springing up in central Fuzhou, and sat in trendy teashops featuring carved antique reproduction furniture, but her Prince Charming remained elusive. After several years of unsuccessful hunting, Jane fell back on the time-honored tradition of letting one's family assist with matchmaking and a suitable marriage was arranged with a handsome young man from her hometown who was on his way up.

The groom made good in the world of business, and the new couple was soon able to buy an apartment in one of the new condos being erected all over town. Typically, the apartment was just a concrete shell at the time of purchase; it was up to the new owners to provide everything from wall and floor coverings, to sinks and toilets. Jane enjoyed the task of choosing wood laminates for the walls, tile for the floors, fabric for drapes and plumbing fixtures for bath and kitchen. It made her feel very adult, and furthermore, an adult with discretionary income, a new luxury in her life. In addition, she retained her university teaching job on a part-time basis to make sure she remained viable in her profession.

After the nest was feathered and the construction uproar and sharp tools were gone from their home (thought to have a very negative influence on an unborn child), Jane and her husband were free to start a family—a family consisting of one, precious child. They had already discussed whether they would strive for a girl or a boy and decided it was not important to them. This was a new world in which women could be educated and successful. Even if older family members might burn incense in temples to request that the ancestors influence the gods towards a boy child, Jane and her husband agreed they could raise a child of either sex with equal enthusiasm.

"We just want the baby to be healthy," Jane declared, echoing the timeless hopes of parents everywhere.

Now that I had to take a cross-town bus to see Jane, we did not spend as much time together. For a few weeks before the baby's due date, she could take part of the 90 days' paid maternity leave then provided by law, and she used it to stay close to home. Strangers freely dispensed advice when they encountered a pregnant woman, so being out in public was trying. Also, dangerous things could happen.

"What if I went out and someone touched me on the shoulder?" she worried. "This could be very bad luck according what I've been told!" So many superstitions surround a pregnancy and, in spite of her higher education, Jane wasn't taking any chances. Don't touch anything with glue on it, stay away from scissors, don't eat shellfish or pineapple. Oh, the list was long and the perils many.

Finally, the great day arrived. I knew a little bit about the traditional Chinese birth process. Women were encouraged to squat, if possible, while giving birth. Silence was advised since a mother crying out might attract evil spirits. A necklace might be placed around the baby's neck before the umbilical cord is cut to assure the baby's life remains in the necklace, not the cord. Jane, however, would have her baby in the modern Hospital for Mothers and Babies in downtown Fuzhou. Whatever combination of magic and good medical attention the family employed, a beautiful, healthy baby girl was born to her and her husband, and a few days after the birth I was granted permission to visit.

Jane occupied a simple metal-framed bed in a ward of seven other beds, most of them filled with postpartum women or their family members. In the bed across from Jane lounged a middle-aged male, feet up and comfy. Jane's mother and mother-in-law took turns attending her there, and would accompany her home when she was discharged. Baby girl slept elsewhere in her little wrap and cap, impossibly tiny and delicate. Jane was contemplating both a Chinese and a western name for her baby, invoking a bright and successful future. Names are carefully selected to reflect these hopes, as many believe names can influence everything that happens in life. A name of combined meanings might be selected to enhance the child's spiritual makeup or to satisfy a grandparent. However, these would not be formally bestowed until the Red Egg, or baby-naming party, was held when the child turned one month old. Red is the color of good luck, eggs a symbol of fertility, and the party formally welcomes the child into the family. It also underscores the historical uncertainty the first month of life.

According to Fujian Province tradition, that first month of a child's life is one of quiet and confinement for both baby and mother, absolute and complete. South Chinese tradition dictates that during that time the mother and baby will not be separated, will not stir from the same bed, will receive no visitors outside the family and will be fed a diet of rich soups and herbs. The older generation keeps a beady-eyed watch to see that these traditions are followed.

"Don't wash your hair," they warn. "Don't brush your teeth. No bathing. Stay in bed and keep the baby warm with your body." If the rules are broken, dire consequences are predicted.

"What could I do?" Jane asked me later. "I was afraid to go against their advice."

She did confess to sneaking quickly into the bathroom to splash water on her face or brush her teeth when the elders were cooking, hoping that this action did not spell disaster for either her or her baby girl's health. This reclusive month is followed by the happy celebration of bestowing of the name and serving red eggs to guests, a lucky luxury in old China. Sometimes a "milk name" is temporarily used, possibly a disparaging nickname to foil the evil spirits in their desires to capture human children.

Babies must be kept quiet and restrained so as not to create a liking for frenetic activity. They are frequently swaddled in layers of clothing. Musical mobiles and brightly colored toys might come later, but in the early months of life the emphasis is on a calm environment and limited stimulation. Bouncing the baby, or even holding one upright during the first few months, was taboo.

Once I tried to quiet the crying baby daughter of a Chinese teaching colleague, whom I'd offered to hold while her mother retrieved forgotten homework papers from the campus across the street. The infant was presented to me on her back, but began to holler immediately, so I hoisted her onto my shoulder and patted her on the back while we walked in the foreign teachers' courtyard. The gatekeeper's wife was on me in a flash, scolding me, repositioning the howling bundle horizontally on my upturned arms. Eventually, babies are carried strapped upright to the back or front of an adult, or just in someone's arms or lap, but never far from a human body. In 2000, no plastic baby carriers or front-facing strollers separated an infant from the physical presence of the person holding him or her. Their range from parent or grandparent was not much longer than an arm's length.

Even playpens were small six-sided bamboo enclosures about the size of an office wastebasket, set up in the doorway of a shop or tiny residence so a toddler could watch passersby within the safety of the pen. With the soaring number of American kids diagnosed with attention deficit, hyperactivity, or attachment disorder, we might do well to consider how some of our Western childrearing practices affect our kids. In the name of independence (our own and the child's) our babies have their own rooms, are pushed facing forward in complicated strollers looking toward the limitless world, are amused with a cornucopia of plastic, noise-making toys. I think of my first child, hauled to a Paul Klee exhibition I wanted to see that was closing at the San Francisco Museum of Modern Art on day seven of his young life. He was constantly passed from hand-to-hand of admiring friends, and put down to rest in a crib festooned with mobiles and a cartoon-printed bed sheet. It's a wonder that his young nervous system survived the barrage of my good intentions (which it did).

187

I visited Jane and her daughter Hui, again when she was about two years' old. Jane's husband was not at home as he needed to travel a great deal for his job in the export industry. This is a common situation in a country where men are expected to follow the money. Jane didn't like it but it was a reluctantly accepted situation among upwardly-mobile young couples. A grandmother lived with her in the apartment to provide companionship and help out. When I arrived, this very aged woman was reclining on the wooden coffee table. Jane explained that Grandmother preferred resting on a hard wooden surface as she found the modern bed and mattress set they bought her too soft and uncomfortable.

Young Hui was being toilet-trained and, even though the bathroom had a Western style toilet and a fanciful child's potty seat, I watched as Jane squatted on the tile floor with her bare-bottomed baby, making the shhh-shhh noise Chinese mothers use to encourage their children to urinate. At that time, children were permitted to pee whenever the urge arose, so getting them attached to only using a sit-down toilet could be problematic. Pants, overalls and snowsuits for children were made with split crotches so the child could be toileted on demand without removing the layers of clothing in which they were often bundled. In addition to the convenience factor, many Chinese believed that, in spite of the allure of the new Western toilets, squatting over a hole was simply a more sanitary and healthier way of relieving oneself.

Fortunately, the child seemed to be right-hand dominant. If she had preferred using her left hand, it would be her parents' duty to discourage this use by any means possible. The character for left-handed also means "improper" or "out of accord" and left-handedness is associated with bad luck. Even though 8-15% of the world's population is left-handed, Chinese children are required to use their right hands, and are corrected very persuasively if they do not. Fitting in and conformity is the guiding principal, not individuality. "The tall tree gets felled and a singing bird can be shot down," warns an old folk saying. Don't be different, and don't attract attention to yourself.

Jane was raising her daughter in the traditional Chinese expectations of cooperation, conformity, and excellence, but with some modifications. The old ways called for an authoritarian parent: stern, scolding, frequently dispensing physical punishment. Most of my students had been struck or beaten by their parents at some time during their lives, but they interpreted it as a sign of parental commitment to high standards of behavior. Chinese parents do not obsess over their child's self-esteem or their degree of attachment or their level of stress. They assume their rights as parents include making demands, expecting obedience and doling out punishments. And yet there seemed to be little lasting resentment about harsh treatment. In fact, my students consistently voiced a deep attachment to their parents combined with an enduring sense of obligation: "Our mothers suffered to bring us into the world," they intoned, "now we must submit to their authority."

An old folktale called "The Bad Mother" supports the notion of discipline as love. It tells of a poor boy who began to steal cabbages from a neighbor's cellar to bring home to his hungry mother. Happy to have the succulent leaves atop her rice, the mother didn't question where her penniless boy was getting them.

Finally, the boy was caught and sentenced to death by the village elders. He expressed a dying wish to suckle at his mother's breast, but when she offered it, he bit it off. "You failed to nurture me with parental harshness and discipline," he accused his mother. "If you had punished me when I brought home the first cabbage, I would not be dying today."

Shame and blame can be the deadly duo of Chinese behavior management practices. Criticism is given publicly to increase its impact and make sure it is part of the collective memory. Less successful siblings are compared with more successful ones at the family dinner table. When something went wrong in my friend Hong's factory, management put all its energy into who was to blame and how they should be punished, rather than how the problem could be corrected or prevented. This concept is so deeply internalized that the 2012 Olympic athlete Wu Jiangbiao, sobbing uncontrollably, apologized to journalists for "shaming the Motherland" by winning only a silver medal, not a gold, in men's weightlifting.

Jane preferred a less authoritative position, one that taught by example, encouragement, and what is referred to as "teaching by holding her hand." Much attention has been focused on the phenomena of the "Little Emperors:" singletons, often male, born to indulgent parents flush with increased spending power, swamped with attention from two sets of grandparents, and occupying a virtual throne as the only child. In such a social setting, any child could become self-centered and demanding. But most Chinese children are raised with the expectation that they will behave respectfully to their elders, share resources with their peers, obey their teachers, and conform to the expectations of their social environment. I have watched some very self-indulgent boys grow into considerate young men as society exerts its influence. Interconnectedness and the primacy of the group are concepts still valued in China, over the Western ideals of individualism and personal freedom. Surrounded and saturated over time with Chinese cultural values, even self-centered individuals may morph into at least benevolent dictators when they mature.

Jane was lucky to have funds and family members to help her with her infant daughter. She, along with her affluent neighbors, could afford a combination of grandparent care and nursery school; such affluence enabled Jane to keep her university job. In many families, if the older generation was unable or unwilling to live in the city, and a parent did not want to send their child to the countryside, daycare or nursery schools provided the only solution. Without a granny to shoulder the childcare responsibility, some children spend as many as 12 hours in a nursery school while parents work, shop, and commute. In fact, fulltime residential childcare facilities are available even at preschool age, where a young child can avoid the spoiling influence of doting grandparents and get a head start learning the skills that success in society demands.

"What would twelve waking hours away from home be like for a little one?" I wondered. To answer that question, I scheduled a visit to a preschool where some of Hwa Nan's early childhood education students were completing internships. I'd heard that even small children are expected to sit attentively for long periods of time and are taught to behave as an orderly member of a group, with unquestioned obedience to their leaders. Was this true? How would it be accomplished? This I had to see for myself.

The day of my visit dawned warm and humid. I had arranged for another teacher to show a movie "for listening practice" to my class while I taxied to the address of the daycare center. I was met at the entrance by a committee of daycare dignitaries, presented with a bouquet, and spent the required few minutes drinking weak green tea in a gesture of hospitality. In 2001, a certain amount of fanfare and formalities were always observed when a foreigner visited any place of business or institution. It made me feel a bit sheepish and like an imposter; I preferred being treated like an interested colleague rather than someone who must be impressed. By 2010, institutions did not commonly go to such ends. The Chinese have abundantly proven themselves to be generous and worthy hosts, the pinnacle of this proof being the 2008 Beijing Olympics, and could now be more relaxed.

My guide (hostess or handler, I wasn't sure) escorted me to the classroom area for four-year-olds, explaining that about 250 children from ages two through five attended this neighborhood daycare. Some children were dropped off at 7:00 a.m. in the morning by parents on their way to work, while others came later with grandparents. I watched as oldsters delivered their precious grandchild for the beginning of the structured part of the day, handing them over to a nurse who checked two small hands for cleanliness, ten fingernails for length, foreheads for heat and each tiny tongue for color and texture (a traditional diagnostic technique). If there were irregularities, they were dealt with then and there, or the child was sent home. Once inspected and approved, each child joined in the dance-like exercises being led by a teacher in the play yard using various kinds of shakers and clackers that the children swung around and beat together in an attempt at cadence with the music. The goal was unison and they were getting there.

"What were the songs about?" I asked. "Enchanted castles or barnyard animals? Magic dragons?" No, all the songs were about loving the Motherland, respecting teachers, soldiers and policemen, being loyal to the leaders, and cooperative with their classmates. No Eeensy Weensy Spiders or Peter Cottontails for them. Those were creatures you squashed or ate. You didn't have a personal relationship with Henny Penny or the Three Little Pigs; they were dinner. The kids seemed joyful and coordinated as they danced, proud of their role in important Chinese civil matters.

Once all were present, the teachers clapped their hands and the children bunched towards the door, eventually moving single-file into classrooms of 30 to 35 pupils in each room. In the room I visited, one teacher and one assistant were giving a Mandarin lesson to five-year-olds using frequent choral repetition. Later, the children used magic markers to practice writing simple characters drawn for them on the blackboard by the teacher. Catchy little ditties accompanied by tambourine and piano were constantly used to keep their attention. All of the songs taught lessons in citizenship, grooming, and the importance of group harmony.

Occasionally the teacher sang, "I praise Xiaomei for working so hard at writing," and the students would echo, "*We* praise Xiaomei for working hard, too!" Of course, the tables could turn and the teacher could sing, "I criticize Yifan for being noisy and bothering his neighbors," and the other students dutifully chimed in with, "*We* criticize Yifan for being noisy, too!" Powerful conditioning for little minds!

After a bowl of noodles and veggies topped with a pigeon egg, it was time to rest. Thirty-five little bottoms were placed on red plastic potties, then the children were bundled off to

their naps in sea-green cots with identical blankets. They slept two to a cot, side-by-side but head-to-foot and were cov-ered with identical cotton quilts. There were no stuffed toys or binkies, no tears and no fussing. The nap room was silent as I tiptoed out and joined the staff in their bowl of lunch noodles, quiet conversation, and a short snooze on couches or chairs. I was surprised to find that both my students and my Chinese teaching colleagues always napped after the noonday meal. Shopkeepers slumped on their counters, yardage merchants sprawled across rolls of fabric, banks were closed from noon to 2:00

p.m. At first I was somewhat scornful about that tradition, taking the position that naps were for babies, but soon learned to appreciate its wisdom and its pleasure.

After naptime, the children engaged in an activity that looked like play but was actually practice. They were given paper hats folded out of newspapers and challenged to move from one side of the room to the other through a throng of other oncoming preschoolers also wearing hats, without allowing their hats to fall off. They dodged, they ducked, they veered, enjoying the activity, but also seriously trying to honor the purpose of the activity. Such good preparation for negotiating the sidewalks and bus stops in a city of over six million people!

Just when I thought they couldn't have much more fun, the hats became pretend steering wheels in chubby hands. The object was to "drive" any which way through the mob without hitting or toppling anyone. It seemed pretty much in the style of Chinese drivers on the streets of the city. Now I knew where they began their training.

Then it was time to paint a picture to take home to Mama and Baba. Pots of primary watercolors were placed on low tables that seated eight or nine children. The teacher demonstrated how a flower should be painted and with what colors. According to Chinese belief, this was no time for abstract finger painting nor individual expression, but the prescribed copying of an agreed upon representation. It was explained to me that the child may be permitted to develop creativity *after* he or she has mastered the approved form of artistic expression, not before. Almost identical paintings of a single flower were presented to each delighted parent or grandparent who picked up the child after clean-up and a story-reading session. Time to go home and enjoy a few hours of family togetherness, even if it were around the TV set. Then it was off to bed—often a shared family bed—to rest up for another new day.

Chapter 14: Looking Back – 1980s to 2008

"Perseverance is the foundation of all action.
Success is the coming together of all that is beautiful."
Lao Tzu

Like the slumbering family in its collective bed, the notion of a private college for women took a three-decade nap. From Hwa Nan's closure in 1950, until the new days of China's "open door policy" in the 1980s, no such private accredited college existed, largely because a China closed off to the rest of the world had no need of the skills that depended on international communication and business relationships. In those pre-opening days, propaganda posters of muscular cheering young people, fists raised in triumph, still festooned the brick walls of public buildings. Streets were filled with bicycles and darkly clad pedestrians. Colored or patterned fabric was thought to be evidence of individual vanity, a quality scorned in a collective society. Small boys in red bandanas played ping pong on rough hewn tables with a row of stones serving for a net. Carts piled high with produce were pulled by men, not beasts, while girls in braids joined their cadres in calisthenics under the ubiquitous portraits of a benevolent smiling Mao.

But as the choking dust of the Cultural Revolution began to settle in the 1970s, the rough and profitless labor of being a student-peasant-soldier-worker was losing its charm. The experiment in social leveling, so optimistically begun, had ended in chaos and destruction. Once the Gang of Four (the quartet, including Mao's wife, who were thought to have committed the harshest crimes during the Cultural Revolution) were in prison and Mao Zedong was safely preserved forever in his glass coffin in Tiananmen Square, tiny Deng Xiaoping was acknowledged as "Paramount Leader." This wily survivor, a mere 4 feet 11 inches tall, began to allude to the glories of Western-style wealth. Foreign dignitaries of a capitalist persuasion suddenly found themselves welcomed to the once-mysterious Middle Kingdom, toasted by grinning Communist Party members at banquets, and wooed as partners in business opportunities.

China had the manpower that was willing to work for practically nothing if only they knew what to do. The capitalists knew very well what to do with cheap non-union labor, and quickly recognized the advantages of moving their production overseas. They also recognized the difficulties. Chinese housing was still austere and allocated by one's work unit. Most apartments measured in the neighborhood of 300 square feet and the residents frequently had to share communal toilet facilities. Electricity, mostly added externally after construction, was still only available for low-watt bulbs (that frequently exploded when they burned out), television, and the occasional refrigerator. Would their on-site project managers be willing to relocate to those living conditions?

In 1984, Fujian Province became one of several locales targeted for rapid economic growth when Deng Xiaoping's new policies of expansion were enacted. The banks, the media, and every inch of land would continue to be owned by the government, but businesses could be privately owned and competitive. The building trades flourished, and soon new factories making shoes, ready-made garments, machinery, and vehicles sprouted on the periphery of Fujian Province urban centers. A simultaneous demand soared for office workers who were able to speak practical English, not the formal language of academia, to overseas customers. The government was promoting a campaign called The Three Selfs: self-reliance, self-administration, and self-propagation. If women could be trained in the international language of business English and in the technicalities of office management practices as well, wouldn't that be the very embodiment of the Three Selfs, and a benefit to the Motherland? And how about some new perspectives in child development? A broader education in nutrition would be needed in a country that would soon be able to expand its appetite further than the rice bowl and the cabbage patch. Won't business people demand modern clothing design to address the thirst for color and individuality in dress? Oh! Wouldn't it be exciting to provide this professional training through the resurrection of Hwa Nan College for Women, to sing its old songs and believe in its mission of service and inspiration?

These were the sentiments and suggestions that Dr. Yu Baosheng, deep into her 8th decade, murmured seductively into the ears of Hwa Nan alumnae as she traveled to Beijing, to Hong Kong, and to America in the early 1980s. A white-haired woman with a sweet smile, a kind heart, and an iron will, Dr. Yu had graduated in 1923 from old Hwa Nan College. She went on to earn advanced degrees at Columbia University and Johns Hopkins, then returned to China as her mother had bid her to do. She attained the role of professor and director of Fuzhou University's Institute of Biochemical Research. Ruthlessly demoted during the Cultural Revolution to the role of janitor in the same department she once chaired because of her Western education, she was finally declared fully rehabilitated in 1979, and began reinventing her life from where she left off.

Resilient as a ping pong ball, she began by initiating a laboratory for biochemical research into polymers. These are the chemically-produced chains of molecules we recognize as resins, polyester fibers, and many kinds of plastics. Unlike the mutability of the polymer molecules she studied, Dr. Yu stayed loyal to the Communist Party in spite of the abuse she received when the Red Guards were purging the country of the "Four Olds" (defined on p. 86). In the service of strengthening Party ties after her rehabilitation, she attended the People's Congress in Beijing in 1984 as a provincial representative. There she met with many other older Hwa Nan graduates to whom she presented her scheme. They listened, they became bewitched by her dream, and the dream took shape.

How Yu Baosheng and her colleagues went about badgering potential donors for funds, procuring land, and constructing a campus on a very small budget makes for unexciting reading and will only be recounted briefly here. The women employed a combination of intelligence, charm, and determination, often laced with serendipity. The father of a former graduate whisked some land on Nan Tai Island out from under the noses of developers who wanted to buy it and donated it to his daughter's alma mater. Wealthy overseas alums were tapped for foreign money. Former graduate Dr. Liu Yunghuo was persuaded to leave her position as a clinical psychologist in Los Angeles to oversee the proposed Childhood Education and Counseling Department. Dr. Liu had fled Fujian Province with her daughter during the war and made her way on foot to Yunnan

Province, then America, a feat that required enormous courage and luck. Now she would return to a new China with a new sense of purpose.

Chen Zhongying and Xu Daofeng, friends from the old missionary school and the 1939 flight to Nanping (Chapter 10) were two of many professional women who volunteered to work with little or no pay. Chen Qionglin, He Xiaozhi, Zheng Yuanxuan, Zhu Heying—names we Westerners have trouble pronouncing and remembering—joined hands with others to support the effort. When government agencies recognized the fact that Dr. Yu was not only very serious but well-connected politically, both provincial and municipal treasuries supported the building fund. As a private school, Hwa Nan could charge tuition (about the equivalent of $32 in 1986, now almost $1000, depending on the department), although about 25% of the enrollees were dependent on scholarships.

Various international organizations contributed, as well as sympathizers from the 13 Chinese universities operated by American church groups in the pre-Liberation days. Foreign teachers were recruited from the U.K., America, and Australia through the United Board for Christian Higher Education in Asia and the Amity Foundation. Amity, originally a Bible-printing company, had enlarged its operation in China to provide medical education, clean energy development, and microfinance to rural communities. The Foundation also screened, trained, and paid people willing to go to China to teach English (only a B.A. in any subject area was needed). Many of these teachers fell in love with the country and its young people, returned to teach year after year, and lent continuing financial support as well. The men and women hired were expected to keep their religious views out of the classroom for fear of endangering the neutral status of the fledgling school. Actually, the students, many of the staff, and most of the Fujian government officials cared little about religious affiliation, as long as the foreign teachers and the money kept flowing in.

And flow in they did. In 1987, Dr. Jeanne Phillips, a clinical psychologist and former mentor of Dr. Liu, was invited to deliver a series of lectures in the new department of Childhood Education and Counseling. An unexpected teaching vacancy sprung up, and Jeanne stayed on to teach English. Enthralled with the lives of the Chinese staff and students she befriended, Jeanne returned annually in spite of a worsening cardiovascular condition until into her late 70s, and was still at Hwa Nan when I arrived in 2000. She was broadly-educated, incisive, and generous with her laughter, her support, and her loyalty. A male friend, asked to point her out at a large party quipped, "She's one of the oldest persons in this room and also one of the youngest." Jeanne's early years at the college were compensated by room and board. The room was a section of the unheated concrete classroom which was curtained off. It contained a cot, a chamber pot, and a few nails on which to hang her clothing. Later, when the college was able to provide the foreign teachers with a dorm across the street in a former merchant's house, Jeanne occupied a large room with a sleeping alcove. In her sitting room, she entertained, taught, scolded and counseled faculty, her students, and floundering new teachers like me.

One who came through the Amity Foundation was Sue Todd, an octogenarian from North Carolina, who taught English with a Southern accent and a ready sense of humor.

A young couple from Oregon brought their lively golden-haired daughter who charmed the neighborhood residents with her antics. She returned, tall and sophisticated, to teach English in her young adult years. Dr. Betts Rivet, an educational psychologist, arrived in 1992 and stayed eighteen years. Betts said her final goodbyes three times, each time intending to live an active stateside life, only to return as many times to lend her good cheer, fearless energies, and administrative expertise to the college. She taught organized, highly-motivating classes in both English and Early Childhood Education. Students loved her lively style. She also recruited foreign teachers, baked bread for their tables (when it was not an easy-to-find commodity), spear-headed building projects, and oversaw the fourth-year transfer program to Centenary College in New Jersey. Betts's dear friend, Kay Grimmesey, a former missionary to Burma, became a faithful returnee as well, bringing years of steady experience as a junior high teacher. Laihar, a Singaporean of Chinese extraction, returned many times, and is well-loved in the classroom for her lively, but strict, traditional teaching style and her compassionate heart.

The college offered four major departments to its incoming students in the beginning: Health and Nutrition, Clothing and Design, Childhood Education, and Applied English. Sometimes the incoming students chose their majors (or their families did); sometimes they were placed by the administration to fill an under-enrolled department. When a handful of students were "recruited" for a new Home Economics major, they grumbled and complained about being trained as maids. But none refused the assignment. Chinese students are used to doing what they are told to do.

Resisting authority could lead to a dangerous loss of face for the person enforcing the rules and resulting retaliation. Because it was only a three-year professional college, girls with scores on the *gaokao* that did not qualify them for university could be admitted. Many came from Fuzhou but over a fourth came from out-of-town and needed dormitory accommodation. These dorms, hastily expanded to nearby rented buildings as the demand increased in the 1990s, were often dismal, dirty, and dark; many a homesick student cried herself to sleep in her damp dormitory bunk. But close friendships were born in these conditions also. When I assigned my third year class a senior thesis topic entitled "Millstones, Milestones, and Touchstones," which required them to describe important events and people encountered during their three years at Hwa Nan, I was treated to endless examples of the richness of dorm life.[22]

The majority of the faculty and administration in 1986 were retired alumnae of old Hwa Nan. As the college grew in enrollment and then in graduates, the Old Ladies were assisted by "young faculty," new alumni from the resurrected Hwa Nan willing to work for low pay out of a sense of obligation to the school (and to build an all-important resume). Sometimes the school sponsored their travel to earn a four-year degree in exchange for their promise to return and teach. The young faculty and foreign teachers

---

[22] I assigned this topic in 2003 because I had read former senior theses on contemporary issues from the past few years. Most of them made no sense, having been completely copied from fragmented Internet sources without regard to grammar or syntax. I figured they could not copy events from their own lives, and was rewarded with a difficult, rambling reading task, but one full of rich and insightful content. I wish I had saved their writings.

were encouraged to develop bonds with their students and to model humane and ethical values that would positively impact their development. This was not expected of professors in big public institutions where lecturers droned on from behind their desk at the front of the class, and then disappeared when the bell rang. As the college grew and the need for teachers increased, a more detached part-time faculty was recruited, ironically from Fujian Teachers' University, the school that had swallowed up old Hwa Nan in the 1950s.

The 1986 campus bore little resemblance to the beautifully-landscaped cluster of arched and pillared buildings at the original college campus. The whitewashed concrete and cinderblock buildings of the second version of Hwa Nan were sandwiched in between a public swimming pool and the once-elegant Foochow Merchant's Club, now falling to rubble and occupied by several extended families of squatters. The "Forty Families," as they were known, sold beer and sodas from plastic ice chests stacked in the once-graceful porticos, played cards on its steps, and put up bamboo tripods on which to dry their laundry on sunny days. Inside the gates of the campus, two large classroom buildings, a general assembly hall, a formal reception room and large cafeteria were arranged four to six stories high around a central courtyard. A tiny women's lavatory consisting of a trough, through which water was flushed, and a spigot for hand washing. The one student dorm necessary at the time was located on the top floor of Classroom Building #1. The Norfolk Island pines and small floral displays that had been planted around a tiny central gazebo and along the edges of the quadrangle were a welcome ruffle on the otherwise plain surfaces.

A tall narrow stack of rooms built of porous terra cotta brick housed the administration offices of the Old Ladies, each unheated room furnished simply with an old wooden desk and a wooden chair. When I arrived in 2000, ferns grew in the decomposing brick, roof tiles were askew, and a mimeograph machine had been added to one of the rooms. No one could accuse the Old Ladies of luxury, although there was a large board meeting room in one of the more substantial buildings. A library of musty out-of-date books occupied the damp basement of Building #2. Seldom open, and presided over by a dragon lady who viewed the students as potential thieves, the collection was made up of donated and left-behind books, ancient magazines, and a few English classics, often in digest form.

In spite of the lackluster appearance of the campus, Hwa Nan continued to attract foreign teachers in larger numbers than the huge state universities. This was partly because Xu Daofeng and her admirable staff managed the Foreign Affairs Office like mother hens, helping renew visas, arranging travel plans, and providing field trips and outings to local places of interest. The 10 to 14 foreign teachers the school housed each year were treated like family, taken into homes, and bailed out of trouble when they trespassed or got lost.

As a result, students who came with widely differing school backgrounds and fragile self-esteem were taught by a wide variety of native English speakers whose mission was to build their confidence and promote more independent thinking. Small classes (35 compared to the 50 or 60 in many senior schools), and even smaller conversation groups, gave

206

teachers a chance to know their students well. Jeanne Phillips stated in a report to the United Board, "The number of foreign teachers has been a vital distinction in building Hwa Nan's early and continued success." Foreigners teaching in key universities around town clamored for an invitation to our lively tables at mealtime. They viewed our resource room with its shared computers and copy machine with exclamations of envy. Other university administrators and school-for-profit principals were notorious for changing the contracts, the class size, or the expected number of classroom hours after an overseas teacher arrived. The Hwa Nan administration honored their arrangements and provided a community in which their teachers thrived.

A rambling old stucco building across the street from the campus provided private rooms for the women foreign teachers along with a few satellite apartments for men and married teachers. Antiquated bathrooms, the library/TV room, reception room and a resource room were all shared. This latter area was stocked with instructional books, song sheets, and maps that could be borrowed or copied on the Foreign Affairs Office's sporadically-functioning copy machine[23]. I often spent time in the resource room as a newcomer, anxiously flipping through the well-thumbed English as a Second or Foreign Language books, hoping a more experienced teacher would appear to give me tips on how to make my lessons more punchy. I was seldom disappointed. Although there were few textbooks in the early

---

[23] China's copyright laws are very weak and rarely enforced. Anybody's work is everybody's. The prevailing attitude is that it is more efficient to copy something already developed and made by another than to be original. And why innovate, when your ideas are unprotected and can be stolen?

days, teachers gradually brought books from home. The more experienced teachers improvised their own materials and gleaned ideas of the many Internet ESL/EFL sites. Bedrooms and sitting rooms were on the top two floors, large reception room and offices on the ground floor, and kitchen, laundry and dining area were in the basement. This arrangement kept our thigh muscles strong and fit, in spite of the fact that we had both a cook and laundress who doted on us.

There were 50 stairs from my second floor room to the dining room/laundry area. Every time I left my coffee cup in the microwave, or forgot to add my jeans to the laundry basket, it was a 100-stair round trip. The mornings I was on water duty in the old dorm, where we boiled water for drinking and washing dishes in a huge aluminum urn, I'd be up and down those stairs several times, turning it on, checking on it, turning it off. My classrooms were in two different buildings on campus, one up 44 stairs round trip, the other an 88-step round trip from the campus courtyard. The English Department was on the top floor of one building; if you needed to pick up a tape recorder or video this added to the elevation gain and loss. One morning I counted how many stairs I'd climbed and came up with a total of 766 by the time I got back to my room after lunch for a nap.

Prospective teachers, now motivated more by curiosity and novelty rather than Christian zeal, find their way to Hwa Nan through word-of-mouth and the Internet. They usually represent two different stages of life: post-graduate, but before settling into marriage and parenthood, and post-retirement, but with enough curiosity and verve to take on a whole new challenge. And what an effervescent mix of personalities and backgrounds they can be! Osaze, from

Nigeria, chose China as an alternate to America when he failed to qualify for a U. S. entry visa. He was aghast when he realized how completely different the two countries were: people ate with chopsticks not knives and forks, they used characters to write with instead of the alphabet, *and* they had an aversion to dark skin. Osaze was befriended by Jackie, a tall, shy ex-servicewoman from the Midwest who shared his skin color but not his culture.

Jorgen and Lila, Scandinavians now living in Australia, provided lively piano music and delicious Danish pastries on weekends. Mary Margaret, ever the gracious hostess, tried to raise the level of social intercourse at dinner by providing lovely table settings. Fredrick came from a small stateside college that kept itself afloat by offering transfer opportunities to Asian students; entry standards were low there for overseas students and the financial contribution from their families was high. Occasionally, a few of the faculty from that school would find themselves heading to Hwa Nan on a short-term consultation junket to enjoy Fuzhou cuisine, local massage parlors, and to be able to return home with colorful stories and pirated DVD's. None of the foreign teachers taught the same way: a standardized classroom experience did not exist at Hwa Nan in those days as far as I could tell.

Adventurous friends of mine, eager to share the experience, followed me. One was Ann, a highly-skilled college English teacher and administrator who joined me in creating a Fuzhou gynecologists' "saloon." Doctors from the Women and Children's Hospital had called Hwa Nan to ask if some foreign teachers would help them run an evening "saloon" (they meant "salon"), in which the medical faculty could practice English. How we enjoyed our evenings with this bright and sometimes bawdy group! When the hospital remodeled and began a promotional campaign, Ann and I were featured in their glossy color catalogue, pictured earnestly consulting one of their specialists, even though we were clearly far beyond our child-bearing years. Jenelle, also a seasoned teacher, was indignant at Chinese attitudes towards cheating. "We're just helping each other," they protested when she scolded them. Never very interested in being surrounded by women, Jenelle left after one semester but returned to China to teach in Qinghai Province with a teacher she met at Hwa Nan. Norma, a marriage and family therapist with a generous heart, became everyone's soft shoulder. When the SARS epidemic began to close down public institutions, she stayed on to complete a theatrical production being worked on by her students.

Carol, a former Waldorf teacher with a strong connection to the natural world, yearned the whole year in Fuzhou for the sight of a starry sky or some piney woods to walk in. When cajoled into teaching an English class for preschoolers, she was aghast to learn that the parents demanded two hours of focused, directive instruction for their five- and six-year-olds. Carol knew that Rudolf Steiner, the philosophic founder of Waldorf education, would have been aghast, too, as he believed education at that age should be about socialization, imagination, and active play. She later learned that well-to-do families in some of China's major cities are beginning to agree with him and flocking to schools employing Waldorf and Montessori methods for both their children's early education and to acquire new parenting perspectives themselves. Tiger moms in transition!

The Trimble thread between past and present has proven the most enduring. Remember Garnet Trimble, Miss Lydia Trimble's nephew, who had established the medical mission in Nanping described in Chapter 10? This was the haven to which the Hwa Nan student body fled in 1938 to escape the Japanese air raids. Dr. Trimble and his wife were raising their three boys in China before Garnet was recalled to the States during the war. Upon his return to the States, Dr. Trimble became the college physician at what is now the University of Puget Sound in Tacoma, Washington, and the couple bore a fourth child, Margaret. Continuing their lives as students and then adults in the Pacific Northwest, the Trimble children made good in their professions and set up the Charles Garnet Trimble Fund at the University of Puget Sound, from which three Trimble offspring graduated (Robert, J. Edward, and Margaret). The Fund annually grants a UPS graduate in Asian Studies full transportation costs and a living wage to teach Oral English at Hwa Nan.

Better yet, Gordon Trimble, great-grandnephew of Lydia, after a successful career in economics and politics, has returned to Fuzhou for the last several years to teach at Hwa Nan, assisted by his wife, Sonia. His father, Robert, one of Garnet's sons born in China, visited Gordon during his term at the college, witnessing the growth and substance of Great Aunt Lydia's dream. Best of all, the University of Puget Sound offers its graduates a year-long Pacific Rim/Asia Study-Travel Program, during which the students visit Korea, Japan, Indonesia, China, and other Asian countries. During that year, they have twice spent a month at Hwa Nan College, receiving instruction, writing papers, and resting up from their rigorous travel schedule.

I was teaching third-year students when the first group of Pacific Rim kids arrived the day before Thanksgiving in 2008. Excitement had been running high: third-year students with good English skills had been selected to be 'buddies' for these American college students of more or less the same age. The cultural differences between 21-year-old Chinese girls and American kids at that time were vast. My Chinese girl students were electrified with both delight and terror. The fact that some of the visiting students were boys heightened the anxiety in their female cohorts. Preparation of a gala Thanksgiving dinner for the 25 visiting students, their Chinese buddies, and selected Hwa Nan faculty, under the supervision of the indefatigable Betts, was going well. Mixers were planned and field trips organized. At the hour of the travelers' arrival from Ulan Batar, Mongolia, the Chinese girls were gathered at the college gate dressed in their stylish best. The bus doors opened and the American kids tumbled out, all tangled hair and rumpled clothes, sporting the ratty backpacks and unlaced shoes of scruffy young vagabonds everywhere. I groaned. Would the Americans' tattered appearance be disappointing, even offensive, to their welcoming buddies? I needn't have worried.

"Ooooo, they're so lovely," whispered my student, Ivy, who stood next to me. "So tall and so fair!"

One of my Chinese students felt so badly for her American buddy, she tried to buy him a shiny new pair of shoes to replace his broken-down boots. He gently refused her offer. The concept of being offspring of the upper-middle classes, who could well afford a fifth year of college traveling in Asia, but preferred (and were able to choose) the grunge style of dress was unfathomable to my young student from the countryside.

When I first arrived at Hwa Nan the pay was low (about $200 a month US, plus room and board) but there were opportunities to earn a little more on the side if one was willing to take on more work. Frequently the work was more like play and provided delightful cultural insights.

"Brown rice?" laughed the Chinese businessmen I was tutoring one year. "No such thing!"

So I asked a visiting friend to bring a small bag of brown rice with her from California. After examining it in disbelief, the businessmen whisked us off to a fine restaurant to try this exotic food. But it took much longer to cook than white rice, the other dishes were cold by the time it was ready, and they were put off by its chewy texture.

"This was not a product that will have economic success in China," they predicted.

In the decade I was there, I tutored students, coached immigrating adults headed for Canada, edited awkwardly-translated papers to be presented at international conferences, taught Saturday classes for elementary school kids, did the voice-over for a China Travel Service video, and had a brush with relocation counseling. Other friends acted as models in fashion shows or as "experts" in TV ads. In later years, our salaries increased but so did our workload, making outside jobs less appealing.

The story of Hwa Nan's growth and progress from 1986 on through the 90s and into the 21st century is full of advancement and setbacks, heroes and villains, mistakes and corrections. Yu Baosheng, Liu Yunghuo, and some of the other original Old Ladies have declined and passed away.

Chen Zhongying became president, Ma Xiufa was vice-president, and Xu Daofeng took charge of both the English Department and the Foreign Affairs Office. A listening center equipped with headphones was installed so students could listen to English recordings, and a computer lab was cautiously developed. Enrollment increased and departments were added. The governing board somehow purchased another complex of buildings to accommodate the expanding number of departments but there were irregularities in the contract and money stood to be lost. Inevitably, it became clear that the demands of administrating a modern college with multiple majors and overseas transfer programs were becoming too complex for the remaining Old Ladies. The strengths they brought from the past century were very different from those needed now in this new Pan-Pacific, techno-dominated world. But hand the reins over to the young faculty? Not on your life.

"We are in transition," they acknowledged. But the wheels moving the transition forward turned very slowly. A professional administrator was hired but soon became overwhelmed and "ran away" as the Chinese say, sparking rumors that college funds accompanied his departure. The future of the college looked grim. An appeal for assistance was made to Professor Lin Ben Chun, a distinguished educator, translator, and a former student of Dr. Chen's. She knew he was retiring soon from a major university in Fuzhou. Could he become acting president during the transition period? The loyalty between teacher and student lasts a lifetime. He could not refuse.

Lin Ben Chun understood that if the college were to expand and be competitive in the 21st century, major changes had to be made to bring it up-to-date. He asked Betts, Kay, and myself to be his consultants, to attend board meetings, give him input, and help out in any way we could. I helped a young faculty member develop a campus-wide questionnaire designed to collect suggestions for the school's future. Professor Lin recognized the need to develop more clearly defined departments and curricula, publish a college catalogue of classes, and to establish some kind of consistency within the Hwa Nan educational experience. Betts, Kay, and I attempted to hold "Scope and Sequence" planning sessions with baffled department heads who were used to spontaneous and unilateral decision-making in their own domains. Lin massaged friendships and connections and corrected financial and contractual errors. With his excellent English and quick wit, he became a liaison to stateside schools and funding sources. Here was an example of another professional academic, on the threshold of relaxing into a well-deserved retirement, who donated many hours and positive energy to the preservation of the college.[24]

Almost any direction in which the college wished to improve or expand required a bigger campus, a campus that would collect all the departments and dorms into one central location. Dorm space had been rented all over the hillside neighborhood, classroom space was divided between two locations, and departments were being added willy-nilly.

---

[24] I was told that Lin Ben Chun had been sent to a remote village in Mongolia during the Cultural Revolution to herd sheep. Because of his educational background, he organized a school and taught the village children. When the CR was over, the grateful villagers helped him financially so he could return to school himself. In 2012 he was awarded an honorary doctorate from Morningside College in Iowa, the college that graduated Miss Lydia Trimble in 1904. He is now Dr. Lin. His contribution to Hwa Nan is incalculable.

Sometimes competing heads of departments demanded their own domains; sometimes favors needed repaying, and sometimes positions were created for reasons other than merit. This common practice, referred to as "bureaucratization" by Chinese educational experts, frequently undermined quality in colleges large and small. Four more majors were added to the original quartet: Tourism and Travel, Shoe Design, Foreign Trade, and Home Economics. The latter was unpopular because the students suspected they were being trained as housemaids, but it was strongly promoted by a friend of the college who was a member of the International Federation of Home Economics. Business English split off from Applied English and became a separate department, each competing for their quota of foreign teachers.

The college library had been deemed too small for a school of its size, and a Ministry of Education official ordered us to increase the number of books on its shelves by half—immediately. With no warning, members of the young faculty and willing foreign teachers were bundled into the college van and transported to a new book warehouse one afternoon. We were told to load up as many books as we could carry into the waiting van—no time to make lists or confer on what was needed; the object was quantity. It was like a game of Supermarket Sweep, only in a bookstore, and it was not a game. But where to house the books in the Nan Ti campus so the students had access but the dampness didn't?

The Chinese government would soon help us answer that question. Even before the new millennium, government officials were evaluating its system of higher education and preparing a plan to restructure and refinance its key universities. Higher education in China had taken a beating during the Cultural Revolution and was still scrambling to catch up in reputation and in teaching methodology. China's leaders yearned to be able to boast a number of world-class universities. In order to do that, money must be spent, schools enlarged, and curriculum geared to the economic and social needs of the quickly-developing country with its new technological needs. In addition, options must be provided for the burgeoning population of young men and women determined not to stay mired in the sticky mud of rice paddies. There was some speculation that the Chinese Communist Party wanted to separate students from workers and get them out of the inner cities in case they shared new revolutionary ideas. These concerns eventually led to the concept of "university villages" on the periphery of major cities to which institutions of higher education could be relocated.

By 2005, rumors spread predicting a new university complex, encompassing major and minor schools, would be created near the village of Minho, forty-five minutes east of Fuzhou. It would conform to the nationwide movement to restructure and expand higher education and would include the major colleges and universities in Fuzhou. This is a case in which the government, as the agent of land ownership for the people, does what it deems necessary for the common good. They simply identified the land needed for the project and took it, granting the farmers who had worked it for generations a small compensation. Minho farmers were informed that their fertile river bottomland would be covered with concrete and that a new center for higher education would grow there instead of the green vegetables they had been tending. Glowering peasants waving posters protesting the loss of their land stood in their fields even as the earth-moving machines crawled over their cabbages. The farmers argued they were inadequately reimbursed for the use of the land, but there was really no contest. The Chinese government is the absolute authority and rules by fiat, never by consensus or electoral majority.

By another miracle beyond my comprehension, Hwa Nan College was granted a parcel of that land, guaranteeing the privilege of building a campus in the new University Village. Although there was general excitement about the project, I found it painful to visit the site with its surly inhabitants still tending their crops and fishing in their small pond. Nevertheless, architectural plans were drawn up, funds were again cajoled out of wealthy donors and supportive organizations, and in 2007 building began in earnest. The nearly impossible goal? Have the new campus ready for occupancy before the school's 100th anniversary celebration coming up in June 2008. Anyone who has ever been involved in a building project knows that deadlines are a fantasy and it is probably wise to double both the time and money budgeted.

When June 2008 rolled around, the new campus was just beginning to take shape. It was decided to hold the centennial celebration there anyway in spite of the fact that only a few buildings were finished, none were furnished, and piles of construction debris still littered the un-landscaped grounds. A light rain fell the morning of the anniversary. Attendees at the gala picked their way along planks set on top of muddy paths, admired the few completed buildings, and marveled at the architect's conception of the finished campus. Red banners hung from unglazed windows, columns of balloons swayed in the breeze (below). A rainbow of umbrellas protected their owners from the lukewarm drizzle.

The heroines of Hwa Nan, the remaining Old Ladies, sat on the front row of folding chairs facing an outdoor stage. Behind them sat the young faculty (now proudly playing a recognized leadership role), mixed in with foreign teachers, behind them visitors, graduates, friends of the college, and the curious. Leaders old and new gave speeches, students and graduates performed folk dances, and deafening music was amplified from rented loud speakers. What an achievement! What a gala and stirring occasion for all!

When the ceremonies were over, we walked about the new campus, picking our way carefully on planks over uncovered ditches. The new administration building had

 been named Trimble Hall after the founder and her generous family; the foreign teachers' dorm, overlooking a small pond, had been upgraded to the status of "International House." I secretly wished there could be a monument in the entryway to the tiny cook who labored so faithfully for us at the old campus, shopping, cooking two multiple-dish meals a day every day except Sunday, brewing up herbal teas when we were ill. But in 21st century China, cooks are not memorialized. Instead, the new elevator was the main attraction.

By the fall semester of 2008, some of the classrooms at the new campus were ready for occupancy, new dorms could open to house more lavishly-laden students, and the former campus on Nan Ti Island became increasingly forlorn and deserted. A few straggling enrollees of the Food and Nutrition department, needing to use its ovens and chemistry labs, continued to hold tutorials there; the former foreign teachers' dorm housed those students and provided space for a children's Saturday school.

Our old cook and her husband had retired to a modern two-bedroom apartment closer to the original campus, partly financed by public funds designated for housing retirees. This diminutive woman, who had hugged me in a most un-Chinese show of affection when I gave her sweaters and Size 4 shoes I was unable to bring home at the end of a semester, had proudly furnished and decorated her retirement home in grand style with yuan skillfully saved from her tiny salary (in 2002, about $50 US a month).

Relentlessly, the old neighborhood surrounding the 1986 campus was being demolished and rebuilt with high-rise condominiums and slick little boutiques. No more the morning march music, no more excitement of the arrival of first-year girls, no more Old Ladies in their austere brick tower. A new era for the ghosts, elderly heroines, and young students of Hwa Nan was soon to begin elsewhere.

Chapter 15: Looking Around – Unforgettable Students, the Festive Calendar

"Teach these triple truths to all: a generous heart,
kind speech, and a life of service and compassion.
These are the things which renew humanity."
The Buddha

Struggling to communicate comfortably in two languages as structurally and tonally different as English and Chinese requires a large measure of courage, focus, and persistence. My students were taking on a second language like the young heroines they were. We sorted through phrasal verbs, practiced punctuation (a relatively new concept in their written language and sparsely used), and grappled with grammar. When I began teaching in 2000 I was eager to know their personal stories. I was continually amazed at their resilience and sense of obligation.

Some of the girls hated English or had no talent for languages, but were there because their parents demanded it in hopes of financial advancement of the whole family. Several had fathers who had been working in restaurants in the U.S. for many years, sending money home to support them and their mothers. Maybe if Maggie could get a good job in a foreign trade company she would be able bring her father home. Fran wept as she described her feelings of guilt at being here in the relative luxury of a college campus while her father and mother worked so hard in the muddy fields at home. In describing the future, *all* my students declared they wanted to make money in order to provide a home for their parents. Was this the Confucius ideal that had been drummed into them, or were they really the devoted children they professed to be? And what would their priorities really be when they began to earn their own livings? My curiosity drove me to cook up speaking assignments that would give me access to their lives before or outside Hwa Nan. And as I plumbed their personal stories, some girls stood out as more heroic than others.

One of them was graceless, boyish Ginger. In her fearless but innocent way, she had become involved in a romance with one of the foreign teachers, but unfortunately for her, a married one. He was older, more experienced, and had used all the usual forms of seduction: dinners out, flattery, promises of a life together in the future. Even halfway around the world on another continent, the absent wife somehow got a whiff of the affair and soon appeared at the gates of Hwa Nan, breathing fire and informing the world of her matrimonial position. Ginger was devastated. Outpourings of sympathy and attention from her classmates amplified her misery. The male teacher was scolded, released from his duties, and returned to the custody of his wife, but Ginger wept on. There were rumors of pregnancy. Her family denounced her as ruined and turned her out of the house. How would she live?

A Chinese-American couple took her in, kept her safe and tried to bolster her collapsing self-esteem. The American, Clifford, had taught English in Fuzhou some years ago, married a local woman and they were expecting a child. Under the influence of their kind reassurances and good food, Ginger's innate survival skills kicked in. Soon she was taking lessons in a kind of kung fu martial art called Da Dao or "Big Saber." This form of brutal fighting was used in the pre-Liberation days by civilian militias; now plastic retractable

222

swords have replaced steel ones when practicing for exercise and balance. It was through this practice that Ginger translated her sorrow into angry yells and thrusts (probably with the banished lover in mind), and regained her composure. We will see how she later put this resilience to good use in the competitive world of global commerce.

Gryphon was the C- student with the A+ giggle that could infect the whole class with laughter. She was clearly the beloved and cosseted child of her family and demonstrated well-developed skills in the art of good intentions, making excuses, and expecting to be forgiven for late assignments or undone homework. She bubbled over with giddiness and goodwill, and what she lacked in academic motivation she more than made up for with her ebullient personality. This would serve her well as she, too, entered the realm of international business after graduation.

When two of my oldest U. S. friends took a week out of their independent tour of China to stay in the foreign teachers' dorm with me during a National Day holiday, I invited those students who hadn't gone home for the week to spend an afternoon with us practicing their conversational English. Gryphon was among them, and later insisted that we all take a bus ride to Jian Bing Park on the Min River where we could enjoy an evening sing-a-long, complete with bonfire. Whether my friends enjoyed being packed into a rampaging bus and sitting on the dirty river sand in the humid evening air or not, it was an experience unlike any other they'd had on their trip. When it was over, Gryphon threw her arms around the shoulder of these good sports with proclamations of undying love.

Gryphon began seeking employment in the city of Xiamen about three hours drive south of Fuzhou a few months before the end of her third and final year at Hwa Nan. A dazzling island city once known as Amoy, Xiamen is a showcase of modernity and economic success. One hundred and eighty miles away, across a choppy stretch of East China Sea, the residents of Taiwan still debate with the issue of whether to remain independent or become part of the People's Republic of China. Xiamen is the mainland model city that shouts, "Look at our material success and join us!" to Taiwanese who resist returning to the Motherland. Many graduates would have chosen to live in Xiamen, but only people with work permits for that area were allowed to do so.

Under the system of *hukou*, still in effect in 2003 when Gryphon was about to graduate, an individual was registered in his or her place of birth and needed elaborately-arranged special permission to work elsewhere. Called the "caste system of China" the *hukou* was thought to be essential to control the stability of population distribution. Now that so much of China's work force is on the move in search of economic advancement, the *hukou* has become impossible to enforce, although it can be invoked as a reason to dismiss a redundant worker (as one of our gatemen was to discover following a theft in the courtyard). In any case, recent government plans to urbanize huge chunks of China's rural population and move them into shoddily-constructed towns have made the concept almost obsolete.

Not a problem for young Gryphon, with her privately acquired residency *hukou* in Xiamen. "With money or influence, anything can be arranged," I was assured.

"Almost anything," I thought, as I pictured Gryphon squirming and giggling her way through job interviews and hugging the astonished businessmen on the way out. She brought me a continual stream of English advertising brochures from companies with which she had interviewed. They were treasures of electronic dictionary-created hyperbole.

And then she settled. She would sell stone. Stone? You mean the figurines made out of the lovely rust-red Shoushan stone carved and sold in antique shops? Little trinkets formed out of soapstone and sold as jade in tourist markets? Fake amber amulets? No. Building stone: granite, marble, slate. The brochure from the company she had chosen waxed eloquent about the quality of their product: "Upon presented before you the beautiful stone is like a daughter to be married, any language to describe her turns excrescent and cadaverous before it." I think they meant the words would seem flawed and lifeless, but one could never be sure.

I visited Gryphon several times when she was getting her toe-hold in Xiamen and the stone business. She changed jobs as frequently as she changed apartments. She worked tirelessly, but managed to include me in a few business lunches. Her apartments were always in the concrete-shell stage; she never stayed long enough to decorate. Although she complained about long hours entertaining European builders, and seemed to be constantly on her cell phone to prospective buyers, her bubbling optimism never faltered. Was this frenzy of initial activity enough to earn her a permanent place in the stone business? Only time would tell.

Lori was big-boned and serious, with a broad face and upswept bangs. Her father owned and operated a factory in a nearby town that made sandals for export. She had accompanied him many times to the huge trade fair in Guangzhou, and was learning English so she could help expand his business. The shoes were sold to Middle Eastern countries as well as Asian ones, but English was the international language at the fair, on the phone and on the Internet.

One day she asked me to accompany her to her father's showroom and help her develop some verbal selling points she could use to present the shoes at the trade fair. On the appointed day, Lori collected me in the ubiquitous black Chinese-Volkswagen Santana driven by a scowling chauffeur.

We were delivered to a brick building outside of town in which the shoes were displayed. I looked aghast around the showroom: hundreds of decorated flip-flops of every color, thong sandals with rhinestones and plastic flowers, sandals with open toes and closed, sandals that laced up and sandals that buckled. Lori stood earnestly by, notebook at the ready, awaiting my inspired expressions of praise for each pair of shoes.

Several hours later, on the way home when we stopped at a restaurant for my reward dinner, we both got a lesson in the difference between asking "*do* you like" and "*would* you like" when inquiring about a guests' menu preferences.

"What do you like to eat?" she inquired. So I cheerfully began to list my favorite dishes hoping she would choose two or three. Soon the table was filling up with heaping platters piled with *jiaozi* (dumplings), *chow baicai* (Chinese cabbage with garlic), *kung pao ji ding* (spicy chicken with peanuts and veggies), *qie zi* (eggplant). Uh-oh—foreign language error! I was only able to stop the flow of food coming our way when

I explained the difference between the word *do* in her question, which invited a wide range of possibilities, and *would,* which required more of a choice. We carried home a great deal of food in plastic boxes because of that grammatical subtlety.

Victoria tugged at my heartstrings. She was willowy, earnest, and long-winded. Other girls would sigh and exchange subtle glances when Victoria told a story because she embellished every sentence with flowery phrases. She swooned over any film clip shown in class that hinted at romance. In fact, they all did in 2000. I used a teaching video series that involved anecdotes in the life of a mature couple and their grown children: young adult son and his wife still living at home while they worked to establish careers, an older daughter who was a successful businesswoman living independently and dating, and the third a teen boy. Whenever a husband on the video would greet his mate with a hug, or a date would plant a goodnight kiss on the single daughter, or the teen son would flirt with a girlfriend, my whole class would dissolve into nervous giggles. In their family lives, those actions were never witnessed. Chinese families are very close, but seldom openly affectionate. This was racy stuff.

Victoria frequently came to talk to me as soon as class was over, to clarify a point or ask me a question. Eager for me to know and love the best of Chinese culture, she brought me recordings of classical zither music with hand written cover notes. Beautifully rendered in her draftsman's print, the notes described the mood the composer has been trying to convey. She seemed more attuned than the other girls to all things artistic and wanted to be valued for who she really was. Her parents, mathematicians and engineers, were dismissive of her sentimentality and yearned for her to mirror their own capabilities and interests. Sensitive to their disappointment, she turned elsewhere for validation.

Victoria could not have known when she gave me the poem by Tang dynasty poet Wang Wei, copied in her delicate calligraphy and translated into English, that I had been going through a moody time before I came to China. Those buoyant days of rafting and skiing I had loved so passionately were behind me. I still enjoyed floating easy rivers, but rowing whitewater and hauling equipment needed for longer river trips had become daunting. Local backcountry skiing territory was being purchased by big outdoor sports companies that cross hatched the land with groomed tracks and charged to use it. My kids were grown and gone, and the profession of school psychology was becoming more of a data-driven position laden with hours of testing, due process concerns, and hair-splitting diagnoses. Younger sweeties had followed opportunities and directions open to them and men my age seemed too old in many ways. I was wondering where I would ever find intense joy in my life again. And without intense joy, I thought, what was the point?

The poem, An Autumn Evening in the Hills, was a typical Tang dynasty nostalgia piece, full of beautiful images and longing. But it whacked me out of my pity party with metaphorical jolt at the end:

> Through empty hills new washed by rain
> As dusk descends, the autumn comes.
> Bright moonlight falls through pines,
> Clear springs flow over stones,

The bamboos rustle as girls return from washing,
Lotus flowers stir as a fishing boat casts off.
Faded the fragrance of spring
Yet, friend, there is enough to keep you here.

If I had been in a different frame of mind, those quiet airy words might have breezed right by but the last two lines seemed to blow the door of my mind wide open to possibilities. I'd enjoyed decades of roller coast living with of its joyful thrills and sharp descents, but maybe it was time to learn to enjoy subtler pleasures. Maybe I didn't always have to be on some grand adventure. The fragrance of *my* spring had faded, there was no denying, but my autumn could be a whole new awareness of rustlings and stirrings, learning to appreciate shadows as well as moonlight and the patience of silent stones as well as flashy moving water. I marveled at Victoria's perception and her choice of this poem, out of thousands of Tang poems, to give to me.

Before I left in 2001, I asked Anita, a student accomplished with the brush and ink stone of calligraphy, if she would render the last two lines for me on paper suitable for making into a scroll. She was, in fact, the winner of the Miss Hwa Nan contest in which Shelley performed her signature drum solo. Anita prepared a stunning script in big characters, had it backed by celadon green silk and hung on black rods. It hangs in my home to this day as a reminder to me that there is always something to keep me alive and engaged.

One of my most outstanding students aspired to greatness and asked to take the name Fan Garo, after a heroic female Japanese cartoon character who was her ideal. She lived up to her moniker in leadership, generosity, and high attainment. Shadow, on the other hand, cut class frequently, snoozed when she did come, and was good-naturedly inattentive. A few years later, she arrived at a student reunion in a suit and high heels, already an executive in her father's company. Apparently she hadn't needed to be attentive.

Ginny should have carried a little umbrella because life always seemed to rain upon her. Her father had died when she was younger, forcing both wife and daughter to fall back on disgruntled family members. Ginny's mother returned their resentment with bitterness, and taught her daughter well in the process. This pretty young girl always expected the worst. She was a standoffish and gloomy and seemed to spend little social time with peers. Many weekends she would offer to help me shop or sightsee which seemed to cheer her up for a while, but sooner or later the cloud would cast its shadow, gloom would descend, and she would wrap the cloak of her sorrows around her like a comforting shroud.

If Victoria, the poet, tugged at my heartstrings, Alicia was a heart-breaker. A diffident girl from a peasant family who was at Hwa Nan on a small scholarship, Alicia was hardworking and dutiful in her homework attempts, attaining average or above grades on most tests. She always came to class prepared. When I heard she might not be able to return for another semester because of financial difficulties, I used the extra money I was making consulting for Lin Ben Chun to pay next semester's tuition in advance so she would not have the added stress of financial worries as we approached semester finals.

On exam day all the old wooden chairs were moved into straight rows again creating as much space as possible between each student. As frequently as the foreign teachers ranted about cheating being dishonorable, unnecessary, and not allowed, it was common in the Chinese classroom. I was told it could only be dealt with by vigilance and, as insulting as it seemed, two proctors were assigned to a classroom when an important test was being given. I made success as easy as possible by presenting a study guide before each major exam covering exactly what was on the test. We went over it in class. I pointed out that by reviewing the contents of the study guide they should be able to pass with flying colors. I explained that how they did on tests primarily helped me know how to teach them more effectively. I threatened to tear up the paper of anyone I caught cheating. So on examination day I was shocked to find Alicia peeking at notes she had hidden in her jacket.

I demanded the exam paper and the notes be given to me and excused her from class. A tearful Alicia appeared at my dorm door that afternoon. She said she had to meet a certain grade level to keep her scholarship and she hadn't the confidence in herself to take the test unassisted. She begged me to let her re-take the test. Sorry, I told her. I had given her every opportunity she needed to do well on the test and warned the class of the consequences of cheating. She had made her choice.

Later that evening her class counselor, one of my favorite Chinese teachers, also came to plead her case. Sorry, I repeated. I had thoroughly considered the argument that it was a "cultural difference," accepted as inevitable, but I wanted to draw a firm line. No cheaters in my class.

But in the end it was made clear to me by the head of the English department that if a student fails the final exam, she must be given a chance to make it up with another teacher-made version of the test. Really? A student was caught blatantly cheating and I had to write a whole new test to give her a second chance? Yes, was the answer. Grudgingly I complied, prepared a different test covering the same material, and kept a beady eye on her as she completed the questions. Alicia passed with a solid, B but she did not return the next semester anyway. Who knows what happened to my tuition money and whether Alicia continued to use cheating as a strategy for advancement or became an honest penitent.

The teaching year cycled through the South China seasons. I learned Fuzhou actually lies on the same latitude as northern Florida. Blistering summer heat faded to a humid sticky autumn with occasional blustery days when the wind blew away the perpetual overcast and gave us a fleeting glimpse of blue sky. Winter brought rain to the grimy city streets, as well as temperatures in the low 50s, which seemed colder due to the continuing dampness in the air that simply changed it from sweaty to chilly. The students sat all day in their hats and coats; I found a down factory and had a jacket made. We all wore long underwear, as none of the classrooms were heated. These girls, used to unheated homes and dorms became uncomfortable in the heated rooms of the foreign teachers' residence where we held Free Conversation (it was unspoken but understood that foreigners were sissies and needed air conditioning as well as heat in our living spaces). I couldn't wait to get back to my warm room but my students found it unpleasant to go from cold to warm to cold again when they left. Some fell asleep in the cozy atmosphere. By the time spring crept into our classroom, we actually welcomed the heat and humidity, for a few weeks at least, until the heaviness of that combination began to oppress us again. I, of English extraction and a childhood in the Pacific Northwest, was felled by the rising degrees and dampness much sooner than my students who grew up in the mists and molds of a semi-tropical climate.

Throughout these seasons, we shared holidays and festivals as well as the weather. In the West the word 'holiday' implies time off work; in China, they are called festivals because people rarely stopped working (except for Spring Festival, known as Chinese New Year in the West). New to me was Mid-Autumn Festival, celebrated in early September due to differences in Gregorian calendar calculations and lunar calendars. It traditionally involved the family getting together, admiring the harvest moon while nibbling tiny embossed pastries known as moon cakes and remembering faraway family members. The girls told me elaborate stories about a rabbit pounding herbs into medicine on the moon and a woman named Chang'e who drank her husband's elixir of immortality to foil his enemies and then fled to the moon to become its goddess. I found the stories hard to follow (but then imagine telling a Chinese person about Rapunzel or Jack in the Beanstalk). Store-bought moon cakes in gaudy red and gold boxes poured into the Foreign Affairs Office for the foreign teachers. We ate as many of the gummy rounds stuffed with mysterious pastes as we could, but preferred having a beer on the rooftop of our dorm and singing moon songs. On those evenings the strains of "Blue Moon," "I See the Moon," and "Moon River" drifted out over the twilight streets.

The hard-won People's Republic of China was established on October 1st and this National Day was already on the books as an official, but short, holiday when the government recognized that giving people time off from work led to a buying frenzy. Urban dwellers now had more free time and little else to do with it but shop. Sandlot baseball, pick-up volleyball games or swimming in the river were not available options. Society had passed so quickly and vigorously from a feudal to a thriving industrial one that leisure activities had not caught up with the actual existence of new leisure time. Recreational shopping was in. People off work for a few days with money to spend were good for the economy and encouraged, so the first day of October became a four-day holiday—sort of. At school, the time out of class had to be made up on the weekends preceding and following the "holiday" because nobody thought to write it into the semester schedule, with its prescribed number of teaching days.

Imagine a holiday when a billion people are set free for short travels and shopping sprees! One National Holiday, I took a ferry to Gulangyu Island near Xiamen. A commanding electronic voice over the intercom at the landing dock teeming with eager passengers admonished us repeatedly in both Chinese and English: "Arrive the boat with extreme care. DO NOT PRESS OR STRUGGLE!" Alas, the plea fell on thousands of deaf ears as Chinese with RMB to spend surged onto the two-story, pagoda-like boats, pressing and struggling in order not to be left behind. Making tomorrow's disaster headlines seemed more probable than reaching the island as we listed away from the dock, but the struggling ceased once we were underway (there was no way to avoid the pressing) only to be resumed at the debarking dock.

Our next calendar holiday to consider was the American Thanksgiving. After years of annoying my family with dinner table requests for testimonies of thankfulness, I finally had the perfect audience. After presenting an abbreviated version of the first Thanksgiving, I told them to imagine they were at my dining room table. Most of what we eat at Thanksgiving had never been seen at a Chinese table, so it was a perfect excuse for vocabulary building and a discussion of cultural differences. The pictures I had of a huge roast bird, sitting alarmingly whole on a platter, surrounded by bowls of mashed potatoes, and heaps of tiny green cabbages elicited a mixed array of emotions. A whole bird to be dissected at the table in front of the diners? Yams contaminated with butter and sugar? Chinese usually serve fruit or soup for their last course so the sight of pumpkin pies peaked with whipping cream was greeted with delight or a little shudder, depending on the viewer. When it came time for them to write what they were thankful for, I got a cornucopia of concepts:

I am thankful my family and friends give me courage and wisdom.

All lovely animals. All inventions, especially Edison for giving us bright.

Thanks for the farmers supplying food. For the flustrations of life that makes us strong.

For handsome boys and graceful girls.

Thanks for athletes get the honor for our country.

For predestination for bringing us together, for the Internet to make new friends.

For great forefathers, age-old cultural traditions, the Communist

Party and socialism for it give us the stable environment.

235

And a stable government is what most people will declare they want. Our method of changing leadership every four or eight years, tolerating two warring political parties that seem dedicated to opposition rather than compromise, and having a third arm of the government as powerful as the Supreme Court seems madness to them. Lately I'm beginning to wonder about it myself. American voters, who seem resistant to learning about complex issues, are coming to the polling booth in decreasing numbers.[25] Our politicians seem more interested in courting financial support and getting re-elected than in educating and leading. Our two dominant political parties demonstrate more talent for knee-jerk opposition than for compromise. China's one-party socialist state has been able to accomplish stunning gains for its people in a very short period of time. Worth being thankful for, but at a high price in freedom of speech and human rights.

The Chinese Communist Party was also wisely beginning to embrace the secular aspect of Christmas. What a perfect incentive for people to buy more stuff! Plastic Santa and Christmas songs popped up everywhere. Since China now made most of the Christmas decorations used in American homes, why not enjoy them here? Plastic Christmas trees and twinkle lights were everywhere. I read "The Night Before Christmas" to the girls and when they questioned the existence of Santa, I told them about the letter to Virginia O'Hanlon published in the New York Sun in 1897. We learned to sing "Santa Claus is Coming to Town" and "Rudolph the Red Nosed Reindeer." Someone had brought red Santa hats from the U. S. (made in China), and we went caroling to other

---

[25] Only 36% of the voting-eligible public in the U.S. cast their votes on the November 2014 mid-term election day.

classes, carefully singing only the pop songs of the season so as not to attract criticism in this officially atheist country. It seemed wrong not to at least mention the birth of Jesus, but somehow stories of mangers, stars, heralding angels, and wise men didn't blend in easily with Santa, his elves, and a reindeer with a glowing nose. It's an awkward partnership, one we Westerners readily accept but, like a joke that has to be explained, loses much on close examination. I did sneak in "Silent Night" to our repertoire because it seemed more like a lullaby than a hymn.

Nostalgic for this missing aspect of Christmas, a friend and I went to Flower Lane Church for Christmas Eve in 2011. The main sanctuary was packed and we were routed to a side hall where the televised choir was simultaneously piped in. They sang in Mandarin, we sang in English and the blending our two cultures was very moving to us. This was what Christmas was all about! When the congregation settled in for the notoriously lengthy sermon, also in Mandarin, we slipped out into the streets of downtown Fuzhou to experience the other side of Chinese Christmas Eve.

Flower Lane Church, the same ancient stone church from which Meiling drew comfort and Shelley attends, now huddles in the middle of the teeming metropolitan center of Fuzhou, with a population of five to seven million, depending on who's counting. Neon signs flash ads for Haagen Dazs ice cream and Rolex watches. A subway system is under construction with all its attendant disruption. Vendors hawk unrecognizable snacks on bamboo skewers outside of shops selling knockoff Gucci bags. On Christmas Eve retail stores are now encouraged to stay open for a full 24 hours, so citizens unpracticed in the new idea of exchanging gifts, could get up to speed. The streets were packed with eager shoppers, rooting through sale tables on the street and clutching plastic shopping bags. Somehow witnessing this part of our shared cultures was familiar but not as uplifting.

February seems early for a celebration with the name of Spring Festival, but it is observed on the first day of the first month of the *lunar* calendar year. It is China's major holiday and even the dragon of a constantly growing economy is put to sleep for a few days. Workers who have left villages to seek jobs in urban factories and offices flood bus stations and railway cars by the millions in an attempt to greet the new

year in their ancestral homes. Successful Chinese business people board airplanes with gifts chosen to advertise their new affluence. Businesses and banks are closed for a week and schools go on break. College students exchange dorm life in favor of their mama's cooking and a houseful of aunts, uncles and cousins, all of whom have been cleaning and chopping for days to prepare favorite foods of far-flung family members.

Like most festivals, the fundamental object of the three-day celebration is to enjoy mountains of delicious kitchen magic with both frequent and seldom seen family members. Houses were cleaned inside and out, calligraphic couplets have been hung on door frames and the character "Fu" is pasted in the middle of the door to symbolize auspiciousness, abundance, and wealth (picture p. 238). Women gather around the kitchen counters to help roll thin dough circles for *jiaozi*[26], fold the circles around a spoonful of succulent stuffing, then steam or boil them until they are little mouthfuls of satiny flavor. While families slurp Spring Festival soups, dumplings, and cakes made of glutinous rice flour, dragons with many legs dance in the streets and fireworks crackle, in spite of government attempts to ban amateur pyrotechnics.

Because it is a long break for teachers, most of us chose to leave China for a change of pace, but I enjoyed one unforgettable Spring Festival in a Guilin hostel amidst both Chinese and travelers from afar. The fireworks were constant, thunderous, and brilliant in spite of the prohibition. On that trip we also visited the gorgeous terraced rice paddies named "the dragon's backbone," layers and layers of tiny leveled growing plots stacked up on the steeply rolling hillsides in Longshen.

---

[26] Jiaozi are similar to the tasty new-moon shaped dumplings that Americans call "pot stickers". "Pot stickers" are steamed first, then fried, but a jiaozi is a paper-thin dough stuffed with a variety of finely-chopped veggies, spices, and meat, and steamed until the stuffing is cooked and the dough is translucent.

239

In April 2003, we dyed Easter eggs on tables in the foreign teachers' dorm. In preparation for this project, I spread *The China Daily* over the tables. That week, the official government publication had featured gory pictures of the fighting in Iraq, pictures the U. S. papers were probably discouraged from printing. I turned the papers over to less offensive journalism. Stories of crucifixion, resurrection and egg-toting bunnies seemed about as hard to reconcile with reality as the pictures of an American war in the Middle East, so I stuck with colored eggs.

Equally hard to imagine was the task of my student, Martha, during the time of Qingming (early April). It was her duty as eldest child to refresh the family burial vault, sweep around the tall pots that contained bones of ancestors, and weed around the turtle-shaped tomb. Families also arrange offerings of food and tea at the gravesites, as well as burn paper money for their departed relatives. Larger sheets of paper for burning are now being printed with pictures of hairdryers, TV sets, fashionable clothing to reflect the new affluence required to keep up appearances both on earth and in the afterlife. Smoke from lucky incense clouds the air. More subdued than the music and flower-filled Mexican celebration of *Dias de los Muertos*, Asian traditions of honoring the dead emphasize making sure their ancestors are comfortably provided for after death. But in urban areas where the population is running out of space for tombs, the costs of a burial plot have soared. Cremations or burials at sea are being encouraged, and in some cases, mandated, by the government. Even though tombs still dot the hills in the countryside, there will be fewer tombs to clean during Qingmings of the future.

The old grandpa whose birthday party I attended near Yangshuo during May Day break was not yet in the grave, and the family was doing everything they could to keep him alive and well nourished. Our concierge at the Fawlty Towers Guest House (named after the British comedy serial of that name starring John Cleese) had befriended me and my two flirty traveling companions, taken us to his home where he confided he planned to start a school (would we like to donate to this project?), and included us in the festivities. The food looked delicious and we wielded our chopsticks impressively.

"Delicious! What is this meat?" my friend inquired.

"Dog," came the nonchalant reply.

She blanched. "What kind of dog?" my horrified friend quavered, thinking of her beloved pooch left at home in California.

"A meat dog," was the answer. It seems that dog meat is considered heat-generating in the Chinese way of reckoning the elements of "cold" and "hot" according to the ancient system of yin and yang. Many rural families raised meat dogs to make sure their elders' blood was sufficiently warmed during the winter months.

My students remembered the excitement of getting red envelopes filled with money from relatives on birthdays or during Spring Festival. The red envelope is almost as important as the money inside as it symbolizes energy, good luck and is believed to fend off evil spirits. Money should only be given in red envelopes to make sure it be beneficial to the receiver.

"How did you spend the money you are given?" I asked, imagining clothes, CDs, maybe a sweet treat, or special event.

"Oh, we weren't allowed to spend it," they replied. "It was put away for our future education."

Can you imagine this response coming from the mouths of American adolescents? It was spoken without resentment and was a revealing example of the value placed on education by young and old alike. Chinese parents are fiercely committed to their children's advancement and further education. Amy Chua's book, *The Battle Hymn of the Tiger Mom*, lays out in vivid detail how closely she supervised her girls' American schooling and music lessons and caused an uproar in more permissive parenting circles. Self-esteem is defined by achievement. "Good job!!" is not the mantra of Chinese parents and teachers. "Work harder!" is. Consequently, Chinese young adults are streaming into our colleges and universities, armed with excellent study habits and single-minded commitments to top grades and graduate honors.

Chapter 16: Looking Closer at the Graduates' Lives: More about Ginger, Gryphon, Shelley, and Others

Considering the heavy value placed on education, you might expect graduation day to be a time of gathering around the young person with congratulatory hugs and great rejoicing. But caps, gowns, and the solemn tones of "Pomp and Circumstance" are not part of the graduation experience from a Chinese college, nor are there clusters of admiring families snapping photos. All the effort goes into getting admitted to a college; once there, the pressure is *off* regarding school but *on* regarding jobs. Part of the third year challenge at Hwa Nan was landing a supervised internship in a local business, and after that, students never looked back. When third year girls left at the end of their first semester, it was the last I saw of them unless a reunion was arranged when I returned the next time.

Fortunately, reunions *were* arranged and over the years, at lunches and dinners, in Fuzhou and nearby Xiamen and Quanzhou, I kept connected to my students' lives as they changed shape against the background of their country's evolving culture. We would get together for lunch or dinner in a noisy restaurant, its tile floors awash with oils and broths, while they shared news of their lives with their peers and with me. I was always amazed at their steadily increasing maturity and accomplishments.

Ginger plunged into the working world with vigor after she regained her momentum following the romantic disaster described in the previous chapter. She was outgoing and ambitious, so real estate sales appealed to her. After training with a prominent real estate company, she began showing apartment spaces in new developments sold by the square meter, as well as older properties. Even though my Chinese friends would refer to where they lived as their "house," single-family dwellings with yards and two-car garages do not exist in most typical urban settings in China. Too many people, too little space.

"People looked and looked but didn't buy," Ginger complained. "I was expected to be on duty at all times. First-time real estate shoppers were often people in their thirties, eager to stop living with their parents. But with more competition for jobs and the cost of everything going up, it was unrealistic to think they could save enough money to buy a house." Ginger fell out of love with real estate after investing several months of effort with little return.

Her next experiment was in teaching. Private tutorial schools for middle and high school-age kids were springing up everywhere and the demand for teachers was great. The hours were limited by the fact that the "consumers" were in regular school all day, requiring these specialty

schoolteachers to work evenings and weekends when extra-curricular classes could be offered. Many students, already bored senseless from sitting all day in a classroom where information was presented, memorized, and regurgitated, were not highly motivated. Ginger had the sparkle and the force to command the attention of a class but without any teacher training, she was just one step ahead of her students every day—how I empathized with that uneasy feeling!

That didn't stop me from offering an elective Saturday tutorial on basic teaching techniques during one of my early years at the college, as many of my students expressed an interest in how to set up and manage a classroom. Since I barely knew what *I* was doing, one of the veteran U.S. teachers agreed to help me. We talked about the necessity of bonding with the students, clustering the desks in work groups and making sure each child was bathed in encouraging comments. Self-esteem, we intoned sagely, was so important. We stressed pacing lessons for slower learners, using age-appropriate interests to frame up lessons, and tried to explain the difference between punishment and consequences.

Blank stares of skepticism met our lessons. Apparently, none of these techniques would be of the slightest use in a Chinese classroom. In most of their schools, each student in classes of 50 or 60 was assigned a number by which he or she was known. At any age students sat, day after day, in a row of stationary chairs attached to the floor and marched to the teacher's drum of reading from a text and oral drill. Slow learners were shamed publicly, scolded liberally and sometimes physically punished. Such kids eventually dropped out or were left behind, bored and bewildered, as lessons moved beyond their abilities. Achievement levels were recorded in scores alone; nobody doled out gold stars or smiley faces.

I once watched a five-year-old set her dolls up in little chairs facing a writing board. "Oh, how adorable,'" I thought. "She's playing school." Then she got out a stick, whacked each one of her dollies hard across the back of the head, tossed one out into the courtyard, and began her lesson.

Ginger was too effervescent for this role. She enjoyed her students and was inclined to be playful. The teenage students enjoyed her, too, and joined in the play but whether they were learning anything was called into question. Never one to patiently memorize her own lessons, Ginger was reluctant to require the disagreeable task for her students. She hated the evening and weekend hours which took away her social time with friends. It was mutually agreed she would move on. The confines of an office did not appeal to her. What was left?

Ginger decided to go into business for herself. She would sell auto parts on-line.

"Auto parts?" I exclaimed. "What do you know about auto parts?"

Apparently she needed to know very little about auto parts. She only needed to know who wanted them and where to get them. She advertised on the Internet, was prepared to take phone calls—in English—at any hour from people in countries like Iran and Nigeria, and find the part they needed at a reliable factory in the People's Republic of China or Taiwan. Ginger produced, promoted and priced nothing: she was the middle woman who made the transaction possible and easy for the faraway customer for a fee. And she was very good at it! Her business grew, thrived, and yielded a substantial income.

What she was not good at was being a pliant, traditional feminine partner. Ginger was single and in her late twenties when I saw her last at the wedding bash of tiny, fretful Sue. Chinese females in their 30s worry about becoming "leftover women" but Ginger's not into worrying. She is waiting for the rare Chinese male who can meet her on a gender-equal playing field.

Modern weddings like Sue's bear little resemblance to the traditional country one I described in Chapter 9. Although some religious urbanites exchange vows in churches, the predominant setting is a hotel in which the bride appears in a fantasy of red or white wedding gowns, a lavish banquet is held, and the couple is toasted frequently enough so that everyone ends up drunk. The marriage is legalized prior to the banquet through a process administered by the Civil Affairs Bureau. It is at the wedding party where the union is publically recognized and celebrated by family and friends. As in most situations requiring presents in China, money is the gift of choice. At many weddings, I needed to present the red envelope in which gift money always changes hands to a woman at the door who opened it, counted out the loot and recorded it beside your name as you entered. No matching grapefruit spoons or fondue pots for them, nothing to register or return, and a good dollop of public record to encourage the generosity of the giver.

Before the wedding itself, many couples elect to pose for a series of romantic studio photos, costumed and coiffed according to the studio backgrounds selected: sylvan, Grecian, ranch, pre-revolutionary China. I have watched brides involved in outdoor photo-shoots in a park pull on rented wedding dresses over their jeans and sneakers to look deeply into their sweetheart's eyes for the love-under-the-bamboo shot. If the wedding is particularly stylish, there may be a black convertible waiting outside the wedding venue decorated with pink rosettes and ribbons and perhaps huge blow-up versions of Mickey and Minnie Mouse, the ideal couple, in the back seat.

Gryphon's wedding must have been an elegant affair. In her home, she proudly displays two photo albums of herself and her new husband, Ken, dressed like dude ranch cowboys, as Scarlett and Rhett on an antebellum porch, as Chinese aristocracy of old, serious and elegant. Later, when I visited her in the shining port city of Xiamen, she was ecstatic about their new apartment, about their big brown lab named Cocoa, and their car. Words and laughter tumbled out of her as we drove toward a chic row of bistros for an after-dinner drink. "If she wears you out," Ken said affectionately, "just tell her to be quiet. She is so excited to have you here."

Gryphon's ebullient personality and "can do" attitude had earned her patrons representing huge building corporations in Belgium and Italy who wanted to deal with only her in procuring stone for their construction projects. An active employee for one of the main building stone suppliers in Xiamen, Gryphon was someone they could trust to get the best stone, at the lowest price, and on a guaranteed delivery schedule. Besides, when representatives of the corporations came to China, she entertained them lavishly at a hilltop restaurant serving regional food. They were a long way from home, culturally and geographically, and she kept them laughing and happy.

Ken was in the stone business, too, and the couple was moving toward establishing their own corporation, taking their favorite customers with them for starters. Ken had written a brochure in English that was much more readable than the advertising pamphlets Gryphon had shown me as a student. We stopped by a marble warehouse on the way to lunch where Gryphon harangued the supervisor about a delivery deadline. The couple reluctantly visited Europe once a year to meet with clients. "We always come back feeling sick." they lamented. "All those gooey pastries and buttery sauces....disgusting!" They were planning to buy another apartment in the same complex where they lived so their parents could spend time in Xiamen. "We want them to feel comfortable here when the baby comes," they shyly confided. Modern as they are, they wanted their child raised by no one but family.

Some were nesting, some were not, most were independent, many were rolling in yuan. Remember Shelley, the bean in the rice bowl who fell in love with her drumming instructor? Shelley would dazzle me with pictures from her travels in London or Venice or the Czech Republic. Her lively, cheerful intelligence and advanced degree in business was allowing her a quick climb up the ladder of success.

"Who's taking all these pictures?" I asked.

"Freeman," was her answer.

Freeman, the boyfriend Shelley kept secret from her family, with her in the Czech Republic? How did they manage that? Shelley needed to travel for her work representing a leading electronics company and didn't want to go alone. In order for Freeman to accompany her, he needed a travel visa, so they completed the Civil Affairs paperwork and were legally married. In this way, her travel-for-work visa could be extended to her spouse. "Shhh. Not a word of this to Mother," she cautioned. Especially if the word was husband.

She and her mother were still mutually involved in a game of "If you don't ask, I won't tell." The mother remained a busy physician and continued to care for her comatose husband in his hospital bed, while the daughter pursued her life as an independent businesswoman who was gone a lot, even though she retained a bedroom in her mother's apartment. Both parties understood that marriage was a topic best left alone. Shelley's married status simply did not exist in her mother's reality.

I puffed up the littered concrete stairs to Freeman's apartment one night when the couple had invited me for dinner. It was in an old part of town, and filled with plants, posters and artifacts from a bohemian lifestyle: 60s music posters on the wall, a red-heeled sock monkey on the futon couch, a lava lamp, stacks of old books. I had never seen another home in China like it! Freeman kept his hair very short with a tuft on top in defiance of the standard Chinese businessman's haircut.

Shelley and Freeman clearly enjoyed both having me over and taking me out. I think I was one of their few respected elders who knew the secret of their marriage and approved heartily. I was a comfort to them; I gave their relationship authenticity. They took me to restaurants I didn't know existed, we dined on food I never would have ordered, and I invited them to the foreign teachers' New Year's Eve party.

One dreary day we drove through a persistent drizzle to a nearby village to visit Freeman's mother, a retired teacher and a Mao apologist who still believed in the infallibility of the Great Helmsman. Freeman drove Shelley's new car accompanied by the same spousal advice and complaints an American wife might offer from the passenger seat. We parked on a muddy street, zig-zagged around puddles on foot and climbed the echoing stairwell to his mother's third floor apartment in a concrete block apartment building. This she shared with her other grown son, who appeared to be a more *noir* version of Freeman (black leather jacket, beer in hand, eyes glued to the TV). Like mothers anywhere, she produced bowls of Freeman's favorite foods and heaped our arms with oranges, dumplings and dried mushrooms when we left.

Another time we walked through a labyrinth of decaying concrete buildings to the studio of an artist friend of Freeman's whose specialty seemed to be sculpted genitalia and chamber pots. In his pictorial brochure he revealed, in a delightful example of written Chinglish, why he was drawn to the chamber pot as the source of his inspiration: "(it is) a antiquated object that's have already lost self factual function for a long time. It's further keeping the matrix character of China traditional culture down, bears the humanistic sensibility. And also the chamber pot demonstrates it's decorative effectiveness in the historical sense, put the personal sentiment and Zeitgeist up." In the courtyard of his studio was a rocking horse in the shape of an erect penis, beside it rode one in the shape of a vulva. Apparently all this attention to potties and erotica paid off very well. I'm told the artist now has his own successful gallery in a fashionable part of Fuzhou.

Shelley and Freeman lived very different lives but seemed to harmonize perfectly when they were together.

Freeman was the bright, independent thinker who was dubious and expressed concerns about some of the consequences of China's economic success. He was determined not to sacrifice personal fulfillment for financial gain in his own life. He had a small shop and was in the processes of developing a modest studio in which to teach music and make recordings. Shelley had become a successful quality control and sales assessor in the flashier world of tech equipment, but admired him for his beliefs. With him, she could let her hair down and play. Her mother trod gently around conflicts in Shelley's approach to traditional issues, such as choosing a mate and obeying one's elders' wishes, using the universal parental strategy of ignoring what she didn't want to know. Neither Shelley nor Freeman wanted to parent a child, so for almost 10 years the charade was useful to all involved.

But toward the end of my endless rewriting and revising of this book, I was thrilled to receive an announcement of their wedding, followed by a personal invitation. What a temptation, but so far away! So expensive to get there! A long time coming, but such a short event! The couple would be deeply preoccupied with arrangements and ceremony. I would have precious few opportunities for a really connective visit. In the end, I decided to be there in spirit, but not in body. I begged for pictures and stories from Shelley and from friends who would be in attendance.

This committed and unconventional twosome decided on a traditional Christian church wedding, to be held in the same old stone church on Flower Lane that provided a spiritual home for Meiling during her pregnancy. Shelley looked ravishing in a floor-length pink strapless gown with a white rosette in her short dark hair that allowed a tulle veil to tumble down her back. Dressed in a black suit and a blue-striped shirt, Freeman appeared solemn. But the twinkle in his eye and the red bow tie he affixed to his collar reminded me of the impish Freeman I knew; I almost expected him to wink at me from the picture. The church was filled to capacity. A choir of red robed young choristers stood against the left wall filling the nave with the magic of choral music. Behind the minister, who, friends told me, droned on and on in lengthy cautions and blessings, floated red and pink balloons, echoing the colors in Shelley's bouquet.

After the minister pronounced them husband and wife, Shelley and Freeman turned and walked to their mothers sitting in the front pews on opposite sides of the aisle and embraced them both. Traditional Chinese weddings include a *kowtow* (kneeling, sometimes placing the forehead on the floor), or at the very least a deep bow to the groom's parents and ancestors, but this couple took turns putting their arms around each mother in a tender hug. Their embrace expressed love as well as respect, was a symbolic act of inclusion of both mothers into this union, and was a statement that their marriage was a commitment to their families as well as to each other. I'm told the congregation was awash in tears—but not for long, as the party reconvened at a nearby hotel where flowing tears gave way to flowing champagne and smiling faces.

In contrast, gloomy little Ginny continued to simmer in her own unhappy juices. She returned to her hometown after graduation and moved back in with her sullen mother in her dark, uncomfortably furnished apartment. The furniture was large and wooden. Little light penetrated the windows covered with dusty evergreen drapes. Being there helped me understand why it was in gloom where Ginny was most comfortable. It felt like home to her, but not to me. She worked as an office assistant for a ceramics company that made vases shaped like swans, Easter egg planters, and figurines in the shape of abstract female figures in swirling gowns. Last week she processed an order from The Netherlands for $26,000 worth of ceramic chickens to be used in floral displays. She complained that her supervisor criticized her mercilessly and required that she work long hours.

I met up with again her in a busy manufacturing town, where she, and I and Alexis, a student from a different class, visited an elaborate museum dedicated to establishing the kinship between the People's Republic of China and Taiwan. The museum presented many examples of the cultural and genetic links between Fujian Province and Taiwan, establishing a strong case for Taiwan giving up their independence and being absorbed by the Communist system on the mainland. It was filled with grandiose propaganda, including photos of Chiang and Mao in happy cooperation.

In another room, trumpets sounded from a video showing armed conflict. The inscription read "In 1945 the Chinese people defeated the Japanese invaders with support from the international anti-fascist front and Taiwan returned to embrace the Motherland." It did? This insistence on shared roots is part of a national educational effort addressing territorial expansion.

It was the same argument used to justify "the peaceful liberation of Tibet." That hapless country was helpless in the face of the invasion of Han Chinese, with their weapons in

1949-50, and currently with an infrastructure of roads and housing for a massive influx of workers who were sent to settle there. Taiwan, in spite of its proximity geographically and ethnically, has so far resisted invitations to rejoin the Motherland and is in a much better position to defend that resistance.

Alexis, a serious girl committed to doing right, studied the exhibits carefully. "We are like family," she declared, reflecting popular opinion of Mainland Chinese, but not of the majority of Taiwanese. "They really are a part of our country!" She and Ginny seemed to hit it off as they clucked about the misguided notion of an independent Taiwan.

When I left the next day Ginny presented me with a big box containing treasures from her factory: a ceramic swan vase, a swirling white-glazed woman. She was proud to be able to be generous with her former teacher, and as awkward as it was to carry such a present on the bus, I was grateful to see her in that light. Back at the dorm in Minho, I put water and flowers in the swan; the water leaked out all over the wooden desk, marring the finish.

This honest young woman was nervous about seeing her boss siphoning off materials, finished products, and even capital from the big U. S. company that the woman was supplying with goods. This is a common occurrence in China and is a source of frustration and anger in the stateside manufacturers. "Quality fade," a term coined by Paul Midler in his fascinating book "Poorly Made in China," occurs when the ingredients used to make a product are thinned or altered for the local factory supervisor's profit. It is certain to occur unless the company sends its own quality control people to oversee the process. My poor former student felt pinched (and maybe even a little envious) between what she knew was not right, even though it was profitable for her boss, and her need to retain the job.

Some years later Ginny married and had a lovely little girl of her own. She wrote me of her worries that she was too strict with her daughter and asked for my advice. This was not surprising news because children of unhappy mothers often take the brunt, physically and psychologically, of their mothers' depression. It may become generational, with the children exhibiting more behavior problems and academic difficulties leading to more blame and punishment. Was Ginny, raised by an embittered mother herself, capable of giving her daughter the affection and positive regard she needed to break the pattern? She was certainly not alone, if I could believe my students' stories of harsh treatment in the hands of their well-meaning parents. Ongoing e-mails and pictures sent from Ginny are a testimony to her resilience. She speaks lovingly of her daughter and has found contentment in both her family and her job.

Starry-eyed Victoria, the sentimental girl who had given me the Tang dynasty poem, had already shown signs of decline when I encountered her as a third-year student in 2003. A seasoned writing teacher had needed to go home mid-year and I was able to take her place and have the pleasure of teaching written English to the class of students I had begun with in 2000 teaching Listening and Speaking. Most of the students had matured, some had dropped out, but Victoria had shrunk.

"Victoria! What happened to you?" I inquired after I witnessed her sitting listlessly, day after day, in the back of the class.

256

"Oh, teacher," she wailed, "I have lost my passionate!"

In June 2001 when I left at the end of my first teaching year, Victoria had given me two studio shots of her taken at the end of senior school. She was dressed in yellow with yellow ribbons in her swept-up hair, and was posing in the coquettish postures typical for feminine photos. With her hands gracefully arranged along the side of her face and her up-turned eyes, I did not recognize her but she seemed pleased with the effect. During the summer months her engineer parents encouraged her to take math classes; they were still hoping Victoria would fall in love with slide rules and stress gauges.

In her second year at Hwa Nan, she began to hear voices telling her fantastic stories and suggesting unusual behavior. With difficulty, her parents located a doctor who specialized in mental disorders, not a common specialty in China where conformity is valued and uniqueness is ignored. He placed her on medication. It was impossible to be sure what she was taking from what she told me, but it seemed contraindicated according to the symptoms she described. She was no longer a waterfall of romantic notions in class. In fact, she was frequently absent, turned in mediocre work when present and was more isolated than ever from the rest of the girls. She seemed to be fading before my eyes.

A few years later, we met during a lunchtime reunion of the class one of the students had arranged. The chatter was lively and the laughter washed over the table like waves. Most of girls were excited about their work, new boyfriends, and possibilities for advancement.

Victoria told me mildly that she was an office assistant in a big company. "Life is okay," she assured me in a low monotone. "I'm used to my medication. Work is easy. I still live at home with my parents." She had indeed lost her passionate.

Under different circumstances Sally's passion for teaching the young had combined with her parent's desire for her to pursue a career in business. She began as a teacher at a progressive nursery school that combined the best of Chinese traditions with those of Montessori and even Rudolf Steiner of Waldorf education fame. Her talents were recognized, and by the time of my last visit, she was director of a three-story preschool with a waiting list for admissions. She seemed calm and confident as she proudly showed us the children's individualistic art projects and calligraphy. I smiled at the painted footprints on the floors and stairs to help instill patterns of walking on the right side and queuing up.

Fan Garo's sense of duty was expressed not with sword-waving conquest (as a first-year girl she chose to assume the name of a Japanese female warrior), but with the offer to buy me a new pair of sneakers at English Corner in 2008, when she noticed mine were in a disgraceful condition. She and her best friend, Bessie, both my enthusiastic students in 2002, had heard about my return to Hwa Nan and came to surprise me at the weekly Friday evening conversation-sharing event held outside the gates of the old school. Anyone in the community who wants to practice English can come and engage in conversation. Since Hwa Nan had a larger number of foreign teachers than any other college, we attracted a regular crowd.

Traditionally, students honored their teachers with loyalty, respect and sometimes with care or support. The

Mandarin word for 'teacher' is *laoshi,* literally meaning 'old teacher', signifying both Chinese values of age and education. Bessie and Fan Garo were kind-hearted traditional young people, demonstrating their traditional Confucian esteem by offering to get me properly shod.

I protested that I just wasn't much of a shopper but they insisted on taking me to the biggest sneaker store in the Dong Jie Kuo area, the center of downtown Fuzhou. After our shopping expedition we shared cups of tea at a nearby park. The two women told me they were feeling discouraged. Each had a job in a foreign trade company, but prices for all consumer goods except food was on the rise, particularly real estate. "We went to school and got a good job like we were expected to do," they complained, "but everything is so expensive now, we still can't afford to buy a house. We are too late!" They were still in their 20s and I assured them they had many years ahead to buy houses, but their voices echoed the lament of many Chinese who grabbed at wealth just as it was becoming inflated and out of reach.[27]

Lori, now a useful partner in her father's shoe business, sent the company driver to take me to a celebration of Buddha's birthday in her hometown. We ate a huge meal prepared in woks and stacked bamboo steamer baskets over fires in back of the house, then walked to the village to watch women heap the neighborhood temple altars with bottles of

---

[27] As I finish this book in 2015, things looked even grimmer as Chinese stock market investors, whipped into an investing frenzy by state media, watched with dismay as the value of stock indexes took a series of breathtaking dives. In August the government unexpectedly devalued the yuan in an effort to boost the country's slowing economic growth in export goods. Trouble ahead, warn the China watchers.

oil, fruit, whole chick-
ens and Coke for
Buddha. Tall red
boxes of fireworks
provided by pros-
perous village bus-
inesses were stacked
high in the courtyard.
As evening fell, the
townsfolk paraded
through the streets
bearing artifacts and
statues from the local
temple. Then the
men in Lori's extend-
ed family gathered

where the fireworks were set up on a launching platform and
lit the wicks. Ohhhh...Ahhhh...the sky above us was
illuminated by explosions of sparks that rained down on the
delighted celebrants.

The biggest changes came for two young friends who
were not students at Hwa Nan College. One latched on to me
on a train going from Fuzhou to Shanghai. Travel distinctions
such as First and Second Class had been abolished by the
communist system but replaced by Soft Sleeper (a stateroom
with two made-up sleeping bunks) and Hard Sleeper (two
three-tiered bunk beds in an alcove facing each other, their
thin pads covered in green plastic. Hard Sleepers
compartments were three-sided with a ladder at each end
and completely open to the passageway). There was also Soft
Seat and Hard Seat, but this was an overnight journey, so I

decided on Hard Sleeper in order to mingle with ordinary travelers. Mingling can be intense and unavoidable on a train crowded with curious Chinese and I was glad to finally confine myself to one person when Erica introduced herself and asked if she could practice her English (which was advanced and thus a pleasure for us both).

Erica was at student at Shi Da, the big university down the hill from Hwa Nan, and was going home to Shanghai for the summer. She was a mature, intelligent girl, comfortable with self-disclosure and direct conversation. My bunk was one of the top ones, so we sat on someone else's ground-level bed (as did everyone else) and talked away the trip. In the baggage car was an antique buffalo skin trunk filled with Bird and Flower Market purchases I was bringing home, along with my conventional luggage, and without her help I never would have found it again as it was unloaded at a different terminal. The only thing constant in most of my travels was my confusion over Chinese transportation systems of organization, different in every city and impossible to understand without a local.

Having collected my baggage, she put me in a taxi to the airport and promised to keep in touch. She was as good as her word and every semester I returned, Erica and I shared meals, conversations, and adventures. She invited me to judge a *jiaozi*-making contest at the huge university she attended. I invited her to the foreign teachers' Christmas party where we played silly games and sang carols. She included me in her class outings and called me in tears when she had lost her bid to become class monitor, a move towards acquiring Communist Party membership in the future, and an essential step to advancement. Never mind...the next year

Erica was offered a scholarship to study in the Philippines, and took it as sort of a unique route to other possibilities. She stayed in the Philippines, completed her degree with distinction and later landed a job in a key university near Shanghai, specializing in international affairs.

One auspicious week, a junket from the British Parliament passed through and wanted a tour of the university campus. Erica was assigned to the task and her destiny revealed itself. She made an indelible impression on one of the visitors, a bachelor Member of Parliament, who asked to see more of her after the tour. He then sought permission to communicate with her when he returned to London. The communication grew frequent and the couple began to suspect that, in spite of the extreme differences between their backgrounds and their cultures, they were soul mates. He arranged another visit to Shanghai; Erica visited him in London. By the time he asked for her hand in marriage, family and friends who knew the couple were jubilant. Their engagement pictures were taken and gala celebrations were held in Shanghai and then again in England. When she e-mailed me to exclaim that she was marrying an MP, I thought she was talking about a military policeman.

We agreed to meet in People's Square in Shanghai the next September and look! here she comes across the wide expanse of flagstones in knee-high boots and a charming red felt hat, the picture of cosmopolitan confidence. Her intention had been to spend six months in China and six in England, but she found she was gone from China now more than she was present. We strolled about a nearby commercial area and she was the picture of a sophisticated shopper. Erica occasionally sends me pictures of her and her MP in state gatherings with

European dignitaries, poised, happy and completely grateful to never again have to aspire to Communist Party membership.

Xia also made my acquaintance in a public place, this time by admiring my scarf on a wintry street in Suzhou, a town near Shanghai renowned for its classical gardens. I had joined traveling friends who were staying at a modern Ramada Inn and had convinced me to do so, too, even though this was not my usual accommodation style. Since Chinese have no problem asking questions about the cost of things, even the amount of one's salary, Xia asked how much it cost per night. She was aghast at my answer. I was a little aghast myself, as I didn't usually spend that much on a bed and I much preferred a hotel not primarily populated by Western tourists.

"My mother is a well-connected accountant in Suzhou. She could arrange for you to stay in a businessmen's hotel around the corner for one-third the cost," she confided.

The catch? Xia was a teacher and didn't like the job. She wanted to be a travel agent. Would we let her be our tour guide in Suzhou and environs? Suzhou was a well-preserved city of contemplative gardens with names like The Humble Administrator's Garden and The Master of the Nets Garden. Ancient waterways laced the town and were overhung with traditional buildings. Sounded like fun to me, so the next day, I moved to a much more basic but inexpensive hotel. Then we sallied forth to see the sights Xia had to show us.

The truth of the matter was that she wasn't a very good guide yet; her inside knowledge of major gardens and sites was still rudimentary. But we rode local buses, took a rickshaw, walked over arched bridges and ate in little noodle shops. I was delighted, but my friends were clearly disappointed. They had hoped for a more professional and informative tour.

Still, by the time we'd spent two days together, Xia and I were friends enough to share other excursions. We met in Guilin for 2008 Spring Festival, spent New Year's Eve in the hostel there and travelled to Yangshuo with a young Frenchwoman who was attending a university in Beijing, her tuition paid for by the French government. Her freewheeling lifestyle and attitude were a revelation to Xia. In the company of these two, other Chinese young people gave us insider's travel tips: we should stay at the grooviest hostel, we were to call 'Farmer Tang' if we wanted to float down the Li River on a bamboo raft. It seemed that Farmer Tang led two lives. He grew rice and veggies in his fertile paddies surrounded by fern-frosted karst peaks but when contacted by "a friend of a friend," he dropped his hoe, pulled on his North Face jacket, pocketed his cell phone, and gave his customers an unlicensed but intimate tour of the villages along the Li River, dodging the packed and amplified pagoda boats that toted tourists by the hundreds up and down the waterway.

The following year Xia agreed to meet me in Jingdezhen after Nicole Mone's novel *A Cup of Light* had inspired me to visit the seat of imperial porcelain production. Europeans in the 1800s regarded Chinese porcelain as artistry of great beauty and luxury, particularly those pieces decorated with blue pigment under the glaze. Our hotel had a dazzling mural made of porcelain tile squares depicting the methods of this production and their history. Museum workshops demonstrated the process of turning and painting and firing in kilns built into the hillside. We scoured a huge emporium in town for treasures but found only poorly copied mass-produced versions. Jingdezhen was no longer making dishes for royalty, and was now like every other producer of cheap pottery coffee cups and vases available on the world market.

One year Xia took me to her family home in wintry Suzhou where we all wore heavy down jackets every minute of the day, inside and out. Her parents, now retired, were both previously employed by the state, one as a doctor and the other as an accountant. They followed me around with a tiny electric heater for fear I couldn't cope with normal conditions in a place where it was traditional not to heat houses, even though a light snow fell during the evening. They were right. I was miserably chilly, even though they gave me their spare bedroom (piled with decades of possessions), even with the feeble heater running all night, while Xia slept with her parents. I was tempted to join them.

Eventually Xia emigrated to Australia. She acquired a teaching—not a travel agent—job in a Catholic school there, added a boyfriend to her repertoire, became involved politically, worked towards citizenship, and hoped to bring her parents over soon. Her last communication with me described her excitement about voting in the next election. She was appalled at the impact of the rightwing and nationalist "One Nation" party. "You have no idea of the idiots out there, casting their votes without any knowledge about the policy of the party or where the party is leading them!" she wrote, sounding fully converted to the democratic process.

I was changing, too. The Desiderata urges us to "take kindly to the counsel of years, gracefully surrendering the things of youth" and I was trying. Once back in the States, I bought a small kayak suitable for use on easy rivers and lakes and let my boat partner from our days of whitewater guiding take possession of our shared Avon raft. My grown children were smoothing out the wrinkles in their relationships and working lives. Rather than backpacking in foreign countries, my travels were becoming more domestically-focused. The one exception was a trip to Venice where a friend was spending the winter on his sailboat waiting for permission to sail to Russia. My mission was to procure *smalti*, intensely colored high-fired glass squares, to use in a newly acquired artistic interest: making Venetian glass mosaics. I was finding "reasons to remain here" as Victoria's poem had foreshadowed.[28]

"Are you going back to teach again in China?" asked friends who knew my history of see-sawing between Asia and America as the first decade of the 20th century drew to an end. I would shrug and answer vaguely. The truth was, I was afraid the Fuzhou I met and loved in 2000 was being steadily demolished year after year in the name of economic progress, and I didn't want to witness it. Confucius said, "Old age, believe me, is a good and pleasant thing. It's true you are gently shouldered off the stage, but then you are given such a comfortable front stall as spectator."

Did I really want a front row seat to watch the destruction and transformation of the things I loved about Hwa Nan College and the old neighborhood? I wasn't sure. But when my good friend Carol retired and confirmed her

---

[28] To re-read the full poem by the great Tang master Wang Wei, refer to Chapter 15, The last lines read "Faded the fragrance of spring, Yet, friend, there is enough to keep you here." Those words struck me like a bell.

long-held desire to accompany me to Fuzhou, I swept away fears and complaints with the excitement of a planned return. It was time for me to teach at the brand new campus to which the college had fully moved in 2009, and experience University Village for myself.

View of the new Hwa Nan College campus in University Village

The International Faculty House stands on the pond promontory in the middle of the picture. The administration building, named Trimble Halls, is on the right; the other buildings are dorms and a student union. Classroom buildings cover the opposite side of the campus, outside the picture.

Chapter 17: Looking Around Again—At the New Campus, New Students, and a Modern City

"Everything has beauty, but not everyone sees it."
Confucius

Early light sifts its way through the draperies as I drift between sleep and wakefulness. It is 2011 and I'm back in China for my fifth (and what would be my final) teaching semester, in spite of saying my sincere farewells in 2009. I'm a little disoriented. Dawn in the new University Village campus is a different experience from the mornings I relished on Nan Ti Island in 2000. My windows are equipped with pull-cord drapes. The strident patriotic music and amplified exercise commands that used to assault my ears have been replaced by a tentative electronic tinkling of bells from a central broadcasting location nearby. This is followed by an insipid music box ditty that is repeated over and over until I'm driven from my bed and slam into the bathroom—*my very own tiled bathroom*. There's a lot less sharing in the new foreign teacher's dorm than there was in the old.

I run a comb through my hair and pull on loose, light clothes for my morning walk. Scorning the unpredictable elevator, I walk down the three flights of stairs to the ground floor, although I'll be happy to use it on the way back up after class, carrying a load of teaching materials. No gateman is needed to watch over our door in this dorm as there is now a security system in which we use electronically programmed cards to buzz in and out. As I descend the front entryway stairs, I notice the top step has already pulled away several inches from the main building and wonder which is "settling," the stairs or the dorm itself? I glance up at the four-story building, with its grand inscription of "International Faculty House" on the lintel. It looks like a luxury motel and is a far cry from the ancient wood and stucco dorm with ferns and moss on its roof that was my home in previous years.

By now, the young cadets at the police academy in the neighboring campus are beginning their calisthenics. Their self-generated count of *"yi! er! san! si!"* sets the pace for my walk. Even though there have been changes in my absence, the humidity is just as oppressive. The steamy September heat engulfs me as I pick up speed, but instead of the sooty grit of charcoal cook stoves and the exhaust of passing buses sticking to my damp skin, the air is heavy with construction particulates. I walk to the manned campus gate, flash my badge at the disinterested guards (they know the days are numbered until they, too, are replaced by an electronic device) and emerge onto a wide barren boulevard that runs past the new Hwa Nan campus. The buses that ferry students in and out of far away Fuzhou are still silently snoozing in their parking lot, and the highway is deserted except for an occasional cement mixer or truck hauling construction materials. Across the four-lane street is a cluster of grey buildings that make up a technological college. To the right is a wide intersection, beyond which crouch similar clusters, grey and brooding, all part of the relocation of major Fuzhou universities and colleges to the University Village. A few trees have been planted, a few banks of coleus cluster grudgingly around some of the gates, but the overall effect is of the triumph of concrete.

After my morning walk, I return to my room to shower, coaxing hot water from the "on demand" water heater. I take great care getting out of the shower pan though, because in

269

spite of a rim around it and a curtain that requires strategic placement to contain the falling water, the drain has not been recessed, and water seeps under the porous grout edging the shower pan and onto the tile floor. Tile is the ubiquitous floor covering in modern China, *glazed* ceramic tiles, slippery and dangerous. The floor is awash with soapy water and I tread gingerly. Ablutions completed, limbs intact, I descend to the dining room for breakfast set out by rotating fellow teachers, unvaried since 2000, and accompanied by the same peevish discussions about who ordered an egg and didn't eat it, or who forgot to order an egg and swiped someone else's. A precise little teacher with a strong sense of right and wrong has been in charge of morning eggs for over a decade and takes her responsibilities very seriously. Besides the carefully monitored eggs, there is fruit, porridge, and toast.

I have been assigned to teach one class of third-year girls and two classes of 'new girls,' many away from home for the first time. The foreign teachers are being paid more according to national standards now, but the weekly teaching load has been increased as well. Each class is in a different building, and all classrooms come with padlocks and keys. Inside the bare white washed rooms the unbroken windows open nicely, the blackboard is less pitted, but the chalk is just as dusty and brittle. The audio-visual equipment remains clunky and outdated. I still need to lug an old boom box up and down stairs, although now CDs usually accompany the text rather than a tape. Apparently the money had run out when it came time to buy desks, because there they are, the old wooden chairs with their flat writing arms reaching out to me from my previous years in class, still faithfully serving.

To me, it seemed a miracle that a small private school like Hwa Nan was able to afford to establish a campus in the new University Village, since they'd been unable to buy new chairs and textbooks in the entire decade I'd taught there. *Guanxi* must have come into play, resulting in donations from overseas alums and longtime supporters of Hwa Nan. President Chen was now a decorated and respected educator who was no doubt owed some favors. Lin Ben Chun quietly arranged for impressive accomplishments related to the project with humility and good humor. Betts Rivett was a tireless fundraiser with her own clutch of connections. The grateful father of one of Betts's private students bought two large Norfolk Island pines, similar to the ones on the old campus. In 2008, Betts supervised their planting in preparation for the 100th Anniversary, insisting that their placement be well back from the building to accommodate growth. The gardener disagreed; he wanted them up against the building where he felt they would show better for the anniversary celebrations. The matter was thoroughly and communally argued with all present at the planting, but Betts had prevailed—at least while she was present. The landscaper finally agreed they were her trees; she could have them where she wanted them. Now the trees grew tight against the building in 2011, the gardener having planted them exactly where he wanted them in 2008, as soon as Betts left the property.

During the geographic transition to the University Village, the administration had been handed over to the young faculty. The transition between the reign of the Old Ladies, who graduated from Old Hwa Nan in the early 1900s and the reign of the women who had graduated from the resurrected Hwa Nan in the early 1990s was now complete. Zhang Xunjie, the vibrant, well-educated former head of Food and Nutrition, was fully functioning as the new acting president. She had completed her master's degree at Florida State University and demonstrated strong leadership abilities in her department as well as creativity in establishing community partnerships. Sweet, self-effacing Fay, whose wedding I had attended many years prior, was my direct boss, while Shirley, energetic, loquacious and impulsive, took responsibility for the English Department as a whole.

This "young faculty" now at the helm was clearly a new generation of leaders. They set schedules, established a semester calendar, and held frequent department meetings during which they entertained concerns, grievances, and suggestions. They developed a system of evaluation for teachers and administrators alike. This kind of permeability between workers and management was unthinkable in 2000 under the old administrative style, in which decisions were made by leaders with little input from their underlings and the underlings did what they were told to do without question. President Chen, the venerable Xu Daofeng, and Vice President Ma were occasionally transported from town to the new campus to preside over a contest or sit for a commemorative photo, but they had no staffed offices in the large white administration building christened Trimble Hall. Even our old college van driver, Guo Ping, he of the rodeo driving style, was gone. New speed limits, traffic lights, and more cars had taken the fun out of it for him. Guo Ping had trained his young replacement well, however, and the new driver also seemed to enjoy hearing gasps from the back of the van as he strove to keep the tradition of outrageously aggressive driving alive.

Some things hadn't changed. The Foreign Affairs Office was still as helpful and resourceful in attending to our needs as ever. In that office, Nell and Jessica carried on the tradition of listening to our complaints, helping us sort out local travel plans, doling out our salaries and collecting our fees with compassion and patience. The new system of dorm residents paying for phone calls and irregular meals required a certain amount of both. The text for my third year class was the same ancient business guide I had used when I taught at the old campus in 2003, illustrated with women on typewriters and men in wide-lapelled business suits. But my students holding those textbooks were different in many ways. Did I doubt the authority of the outdated print material? They seemed full of confidence as they consulted electronic dictionaries and smart phones. Did I wonder about my qualifications for teaching a business course? They hung less on my every word anyway. Was I professionally attired? They were decked out in clinking jewelry, strappy shoes, and hot little jackets. Was I shrinking to a less commanding presence in the classroom? They seemed to be getting taller and more robust on their diets of fast foods and bubble teas. In the few years that I'd been gone, the overall atmosphere of the student body had become thoroughly modern.

Not all of my students were that slick, it was true; there were still a few pink tracksuits, baggy knock-off jeans and ponytails. But the mode was definitely mod and the more affluent girls strutted their stuff, advertising their status with blonde streaks in their hair, jangling bracelets, and three-inch heels. This would be their last semester in college because the previous month-long internship had been extended to occupy the entire semester. More and more colleges were letting students out earlier in order to hit the job fairs and recruitment centers before the competition. Seven million young people were expected to graduate from colleges and universities by 2014, up from just one million in 2000. Yet deep concerns have swirled around the reported approximate16% unemployment among recent graduates.

The girls' names had shifted to more contemporary favorites, too: Hillary, Alison, Deirdre. There were no Fannys to discourage, no Golden Pennies, or Tulips, or Gryphons— names that brought a smile to my lips—although I did have an individualist called Fever in my first-year class. She had been ill frequently in her previous years and somehow decided on this condition as an identity. When urged to choose a different name, she chose Violet, a name that I associated with the very opposite of her outgoing, assertive personality. Most of them came to college with English names now, as English was being presented at an earlier grade level and was beginning to be a regular subject in countryside schools.

Some new voices even called into question the old Chinese system of education that rested on memorization and regurgitation. Still, most of the girls seemed like baby birds in a classroom nest with their mouths wide open, waiting for the teacher to stuff information down their memorizing gullets. My attempts at exercises that required analyzing or critical thinking had to be presented as play or make-believe. They seemed as resistant to educational risk-taking as ever at first, though not as silent about it as the semester continued.

There were no tears during the early weeks, and a great deal less anxiety about speaking out, although that role often fell to the bold, as it does in any class. The bold were not always the best students either and, on one memorable occasion, a third-year student in Business English class took boldness to an extreme. She was a disdainful, unmotivated learner who constantly distracted her neighbors, so during class I asked her to come and sit in a vacant chair closer to where I usually stood.

"No. I won't," she declared, in perfect English.

I was so stunned it was I who fell silent. Several students came up to me during recess to apologize for her behavior. They explained that Dorothy was from a wealthy family and didn't think she needed to be in school, particularly a vocational school like Hwa Nan. They were embarrassed for my loss of face. After class, I laid down some stricter guidelines with her, face-to-lost-face, but it was another rough indicator of classroom climate change. Was this a positive sign of Chinese women finally speaking up for themselves, or a negative reminder of erosion in a culture of respect for and obedience to teachers and elders?

We held larger "Free Conversation" groups in special rooms in the foreign teacher's dorm instead of our own residential rooms, removing the easy intimacy of having students look at teachers' pictures from home on the walls and see the style in which we decorated our individual space. And we lived in style, relatively speaking. Each teacher now had a suite of rooms with his/her own sitting room, sofa and widescreen TV. Ah, privacy—such an American luxury. No need to watch the news with others who might make annoying comments during the broadcast. But after a while I found watching news and videos in the privacy of one's room to be lonesome. In the old dorm we all clustered around the only TV and shared opinions as well as mouthfuls of popcorn. I missed the necessary sharing in our old funky accommodations because that often led to friendships I wouldn't have initiated or predicted. We enjoyed heat and air conditioning in each of our rooms, and a new cook who sometimes joined us at the dinner table. Our resource room had three computers, a copy machine, and a library still filled with essentially the same ESL materials I'd used in 2000. There were stack and stacks of pirated film DVDs, copied without consequence and sold in stores for a buck or two.

As promised, Carol had come with me to teach this fall semester of 2011. We agreed that what we wanted to do most at the end of the teaching day was to get off campus and into the "real world." But where to go? There was an unconvincing rendition of Student Street a few blocks away, still crammed with warrens of shops selling cheap accessories and knockoff clothing, but all housed under a patchwork roof of tarps and corrugated plastic. There was a designated food court instead of a hodgepodge of food vendors strung out along the street selling everything from octopus-on-a-stick to sliced pineapples.

The fun of searching for hilarious product descriptions and advertising copy was gone, too. Manufacturer's command of product language and English in general was more sophisticated now. In 2000, while browsing on the old Student Street, I was tempted by an advertising sign on a plastic CD rack that offered irresistible promises: "Save your poem over time and create your life. This will make you happy and make you sensefull. Space will be so exciting!"

During a visit, in 2001, to a new Walmart, I bought up a whole rack of anklets when I found each pair sporting a label that proclaimed them "Women's Cocks." Alphabet confusion used to ladle up good belly laughs; now hilarious mistakes were harder to find. I knew I should rejoice that lessons were being so well learned, but I missed the fun of going to Student Street just to read the tee shirt slogans in mangled English.

Well then, let's take a bus into town. It's a 45-minute ride one way, so we need to go on the weekend when we have enough time for a major excursion; no more just descending the "Long Stairs" to the Liberation Bridge across the Min

 River. But lucky us—the bus originates just a block past the campus, so getting a seat for the first leg of the journey is a breeze. Finding a space on the midtown buses to which we must transfer to complete the trip is more of a challenge. The buses are packed with

adult shoppers who have already done battle for their seats or standing room, and have no intention of giving an inch. The return trip is still another story because if even a tiny fraction of the thousands of students who live in University Village decide to come home the same time we do, the buses will be bursting with youthful passengers. There are certain places I identify where it's less crowded to board for the return trip, certain transfers that are more advantageous. A trip to town now requires additional strategies and vigilance.

The buses are bigger and more battered than most cars on the road, and the drivers are well aware of that advantage. Are only youthful daredevils hired to sit behind the steering wheels of public buses? They seem to love the challenge of squeezing into tight lanes, the thrill of pedal-to-the-metal acceleration and lurching stops where people are spilling off the curb waiting to board. We board our bus at its first stop, careen out of University Village onto the main road into Fuzhou, speed by huge new shopping malls outlined in oscillating neon and featuring sexy, two-story photos of international models. We can buy French biscuits at Carrefour, Hagen Dazs ice cream in downtown Fuzhou, and get a cup of coffee at any of the many specialty coffee shops opened within the last five years. There are Rolex showrooms and Prada boutiques and Sketcher shoe shops. When I arrived in Fuzhou in 2000, the big excitement was the opening of Metro, a German supermarket carrying clothes and small appliances as well as food. By 2011, there were three Walmarts, many new Chinese super stores, and a Sam's Club, as well as hundreds of slick and expensive specialty shops clustered in elegant marble-floored malls.

But is there street life? Not much. Not unless you count mobs of shoppers with plastic bags rushing in and out of doorways flanked by young salespeople clapping and cheerleading the customers inside. People are too busy in downtown Fuzhou to stop and listen to *erhu* players or watch men shape intricate insects out of bamboo or have their fortunes told by sparrows. A few favorite places remained: the old style restaurant on the second floor of one of the early main street buildings, where cooks slave feverishly over hot woks. We stop here for a snack, choose a table and note its number displayed in the middle. Then we join throngs of prospective diners lurching past glistening dishes of food displayed on a long counter separating kitchen from customers, shouting their orders and table numbers, pointing at what looks good. In the midst of the chaos, clerks manage to pencil orders and table numbers on a scrap of paper, and when the food is ready, a waitperson miraculously delivers the dish to our claimed spot. The plates are small, almost like dim sum, so by the time we were done ordering, several plates of steaming dumplings, shiny bok choy, and rice-filled pineapple halves decorate our black lacquered dining table. I rejoice every year I return that this eatery is still where I left it.

Bellies full, we walk round the corner from the main shopping street to the area known as Three Lanes and Seven Alleys. An older part of town that managed to stay out of the way of wrecking ball and bulldozer until someone had the bright idea of preserving it, the area has now become a tarted-up version of its former self. I used to love to walk its streets and back alleys, poking through shops full of temple accessories for the home altar, lantern stores, and tight, winding lanes in which families conducted their daily business. Occasionally, someone would beckon me in to admire a blooming plant or a painting in progress. For a while it seemed like it would all be lost to advancing urban development, but miraculously the neighborhood was designated as a "Cultural Relics Protection Unit" and its new life as a tourist destination began.

Of course, first it had to be torn down. Only then could the *new*-old Three Lanes and Seven Alleys be rebuilt as a viable consumer destination. Now visitors to Fuzhou flock to the pedestrian street lined with wooden and stucco reproductions of old Fuzhou. Temple shops, previously stocked with lanterns, braziers, candles and incense, now tout scarves and jewelry, accessories for the modern shopper. Sunglasses, purses and wallets, ice cream, and flimsy plastic toys are more in demand than lanterns. A few homes and temples have been reconstructed to reflect the lifestyle of the ancient merchants, but the atmosphere is carnival. The Starbucks on the main lane, complete with its signature green shade umbrellas, is always packed.

Today perhaps we should leave Three Lanes and Seven Alleys and seek solace in the old neighborhood. After a few more bus connections and a bridge crossing, Carol and I dismount on the busy street below the old campus. A huge yellow Volvo crane peers down at us menacingly as I try to get my bearings. The shops that sold household goods, the video game store, and the old buildings behind them are gone, replaced by a gaping hole and the vertical piers that will support the cluster of apartment towers about to be built. Huddled in the middle of the piers, on an island of undisturbed soil, is an old stone German bank, with arched paned windows and a tile roof. On the corner of the street, the slick glass office of the condominium developer displays a diorama of the finished project. The old bank building is to be the featured centerpiece, lending an aura of internationality to the grounds. The developer is selling condos in advance of their completion on the promise of a river view for all. For everyone, that is, except those long-time neighborhood families living in the sagging brick and wood row houses on the streets behind these towers. Little by little those folks will be moved and scattered among a number of other housing developments in Fuzhou without views of the river or the cooling breezes of the Min.

The old campus feels even more forlorn without the energy of all the girls to perk it up. Some Food and Nutrition classes are still held there until their lab at the new campus is fully outfitted. The students who take these classes live in the old foreign teachers' dorm, but the wooden stairs have a hollow sound. On Saturday morning, special English classes are held in the reception room for children five-years-old and up whose parents are willing to pay for tutoring. A kindly former teacher had volunteered this service to some faculty children a few years before, the demand had grown, and now it had become a moneymaker for the college. Many of the foreign teachers were encouraged to participate. Parents eager to give their children a head start on English were willing to drive them across town for Saturday class and stay to have a kind of "mom's conversation." Racial prejudice raised its head again when a Vietnamese-American teacher agreed to take on the younger kids at the Saturday school.

"No," said the parents. "We want someone who not only speaks English but *looks* English."

Let's walk down what we used to call "Fruit Street" where vendors once sold pineapples and mangoes and watermelons, and hung their bananas to ripen in the tunnels leading to World War II bomb shelters. If I turn my head to the right now, the scene looks the same: old women sit in open doorways on bamboo stools, red lamps glow on family altars, vendors sell unfashionable clothes and incidentals for the home. If I look to the left, I see a wall of concrete and glass dotted with small balconies on which laundry is hanging. The flickering light of TV programs has replaced the glow of altar lamps. This is the first wave of completed condos in a neighborhood that still spans a century of architectural and life styles.

All is not lost. The blind massage parlor is open for business and we ascend the stairs for a rejuvenating back rub. The shop selling huge paper floral displays for funerals is there also, as well as tiny shops selling fabric, 10 different varieties of rice, and bamboo household items. An occasional street vendor tempts us with flowers or herbs. Dark winding alleys continue to beckon. At the end of one we venture down, the neighborhood is celebrating enthusiastically in a tiny Buddhist temple. Carol and I are welcomed in and handed small blue bowls of sweet broth in which floats some kind of cream-colored buds. Nothing to do but drink both broth and bud, and hope its blessedness would protect us from whatever might lurk in the water. We each put 10 yuan in the collection box and continue on our way, happy that at least some of the old neighborhood remains.

What will happen to the daily life in the lanes that wove the community together through shared revelry, rivalry, pleasure and pain, when the lanes are lined with canyons of condos? Xu Daofeng, the former Foreign Affairs Office director, was recovering from a hip replacement that fall so I visited her in her modest apartment near a big new complex of identical towers filled with residential apartments. On the way, I passed a variety of little shops struggling for existence. A few older folks gathered in the sparsely landscaped public grounds, to use yellow and red metal exercise equipment installed in concrete. There was no sign of intergenerational family life spilling out into the street, no roadside barbers, no one mending shoes or cooking their dinner on an outdoor brazier. All the closeness and color of the old neighborhoods was fading from the big apartment units, replaced by designer parks and specifically designated commercial spaces. Village and street life, bedrocks of Chinese culture, will not be available to children raised in condo complexes. No matter how rich the country becomes, it will be the poorer for this disappearance, at least to me.

Back at the campus, I settled in to draw up lesson plans for the coming week using the texts I had been given, plus plenty of outside resources and activities. This teaching year I found my enthusiasm for cookie baking and Easter egg dying considerably reduced. My new students had seen it all, at least virtually, on the Internet and in films, and were much more sophisticated in their tastes. Over the past ten years, they'd all eaten bowls of cereal, sampled pizza, knew what a chocolate chip cookie tasted like and most were now proficient with knives and forks. None of these things were a novelty.

Even more astonishing was a rumor being circulated that enrollment was down and the new administration was considering admitting boys to the student body next year! As universities scramble to meet their enrollment quotas and students clamor to enroll, educational bureaucrats have seen fit to lower the National Exam passing score. In the 1990s, about 40% of the students who took the test passed and were allowed to continue their education in some way. By 2013, 77% passed. Lowered standards meant more kids qualified for universities, leaving a smaller student pool drawn from students with even lower scores for the vocational colleges. Restricting the enrollees to girls was considered a luxury Hwa Nan could no longer afford.

Miss Lydia Trimble would be turning over in her grave! What would these modern women, the granddaughters of the generation to whom she devoted her life, make of this? Would they retain their independence and motivation on a campus shared with males? Boys traditionally are granted more attention and less discipline in Chinese classrooms. Would this be true at Hwa Nan? In a world of dwindling resources and increased competition for jobs and space, would Hwa Nan College and her daughters be able to compete? And would she lose her uniqueness by becoming the *alma mater* of sons?

Chapter 18: Looking Ahead – Views into the Lives of My Friends' Children

"Do not dwell in the past, do not dwell in the future, concentrate the mind on the present moment."
The Buddha

The younger generation is doing just fine, thanks—for the time being. Parenting their lovely, lively daughters in a changing China has presented very different challenges to the women we met in previous chapters as students or friends: Laura, Jane and Meiling. Each provides us a different perspective on what it's like to raise kids in 21st century China. Linda, who was mentioned only briefly in Chapter 7, created her own unique challenge by marrying an American and is now raising her Chinese-born children as citizens of the United States. Each of these women adores their offspring and have the same universal desires for them as moms around the world--that they'll be healthy and strong, that they will be able to fulfill their potential, and that they will lead a happy life.

Each child's basic temperament is further informed by a combination of cultural and environmental factors, as well as the family advantages with which they have been nurtured. As the 21st century unfolds, the underpinnings of Chinese family traditions and values are shifting beneath the heavy influence of a consumer society. Each of these women's offspring will bring their own unique personal characteristics to that equation. Let's peek back into the lives of Laura, Jane, Meiling, and Linda, now mothers of school-aged children, and see how their families are evolving and nurturing the next generation.

Laura, whose country village we visited on the occasion of the puppet show for the gods, continued her relationship with a young man she admired as a boy in her countryside school. She knew him to be kind and responsible, with an indisputable background, free from the taint of aristocracy. He attended university after high school and then began his professional life in a nearby hospital. Friendship and admiration bloomed into love and by 2003, the couple had married and were expecting a baby. Laura eventually accepted a job back at Hwa Nan College and was now living in a suite of apartments adjacent to the foreign teachers' dorm.

Their child was born in the spring of 2004. She was a fretful, colicky baby and nightly wails issued forth from the apartment in the foreign teachers' compound where the couple lived until they could afford an apartment of their own. Faithful to tradition, Laura was doing her month-in-bed with the new baby who was swaddled in layers and layers of fleece and wool. Whenever I got a glimpse of little Minqiao, she was covered with a red, prickly rash and obviously not happy to be here. Furthermore, she was a reluctant nurser. She cried the kind of desperate, gasping cry that makes the listener feel she will never be able to take in enough air to make that sound again, but she does.

The wails continued for months, much to my extreme distress as well as hers. A distraught Laura and her husband went without sleep as often as the baby did, and concern for the new little family seeped out of their apartment and engulfed us all. Instead of Laura's mother, her kindhearted father came to Fuzhou from his hometown to give support to the exhausted parents. Laura's mother, a woman of strong will and conviction, harbored resentments from her daughter's childhood and still maintained an emotional distance. Laura was so glad to have the calming presence of her father in the kitchen, preparing the vegetables for the mid-day meal, washing up, and holding the baby on his lap.

Then one day, three or four months after her birth, it seemed like Minqiao became resigned, even serene. It was as though she realized there was no going back to the comfort of the womb and she might just as well accept the fact of her tenure here on earth. The wails quieted, the rash disappeared and smiles emerged from all concerned. Minqiao changed slowly from a noisily miserable infant to an alert and curious toddler, examining everything thoughtfully, her black eyes intense with interest. As she began to babble, then talk and make friends, she became the darling of the dorm residents.

Her parents were conscientious in their intention to raise her with love and encouragement, but occasionally her toddler's defiance emerged, and she would be spanked. I often heard a child's mischievous explorations and drive for independence described as 'naughty' by my students and young parents; if the 'naughtiness' continued, physical punishment was the accepted parental response for defiance. Minqiao had trouble winding down and going to sleep. If she didn't to go to sleep, eventually she would be spanked. Those times were hard for me to hear, as voices were raised and the small body was smacked. Many minutes of shrieking would result, but by then everyone would have discharged their emotions (except me), and the family would fall into a sound sleep. Laura confided that it was hard for her, too, but her husband was a traditionalist and his ways would be respected.

By 2011, Minqiao had become a caring and capable schoolgirl: outgoing, fun-loving, and charitable with her classmates. She was devoted to her mother and father and strove to please them. Her father continued his work at a government-run facility in Fuzhou. Laura continued her work at the college but in an expanded capacity. Knowing I was interested in history, Laura invited me to go with her when she videotaped an interview with a former professor at old Hwa Nan College, now in his 80s, who told vivid tales of life as an academic before Liberation and after. The man was a famous finger-writer, a style of artistic calligraphy executed with only an inky finger, not a brush. His apartment was filled with gracefully executed scrolls of poetry and books on various styles of calligraphy that spanned centuries. He produced a tin box full of *chops*, the carved *shoushon* stone seals with which traditional Chinese signed their documents, dipping the carved end into red paste and pressing it into the paper. After a morning of his storytelling, this grand old man took *us* out for a ten-dish meal, as if we had done him the favor.

Today, Minqiao's little family lives in a modest comfortable apartment downtown. Both parents commute by bus to their respective workplaces. Minqiao attends a good public school nearby which she accesses by public bus also, as do many elementary school children. She is a natural born teacher and loves to help others, both in class and at home. Like most Chinese children, she participates in no after school sports (there aren't any), no organizations like Girl Scouts or Campfire Girls (there aren't any), and no community service projects (there aren't any). She goes to school, does her homework, spends extra time on her lessons to maintain a good standing in class, and helps her parents at home or in their weekend pursuits. Laura is justifiably proud of her daughter, especially her desire to please and help others. In the eyes of her parents Minqiao embodies the fierce spirit of the revolution, as well as the gentle and nurturing ideal of Chinese womanhood.

My old friend and tutor, Jane, was so busy tending to her own precious daughter that I didn't see much of her during Hui's toddler years. She was a devoted mother and a working scholarly woman without much time for casual friendships. Eventually Hui became a capable schoolgirl also, but her circumstances were quite different. The family lived in a professionally decorated apartment in the center of town and a busy life of art and dancing lessons on the weekends. These were new activities pursued by affluent Chinese parents in order to enrich their children's lives. When Hui began preschool Jane returned to work part time at a major Fuzhou university teaching philosophy and commuting to her classes at the University Village in her own car, a dark mid-sized sedan. Hui's father had risen in the ranks of his company and been offered a position in Beijing. Although this would represent more money and status, the family decided not to move to the capital city for many reasons. Jane and her husband found Beijing overwhelming crowded and polluted and they chose not to raise their daughter there.

"The pollution is so bad in Beijing and the incidence of pulmonary illness is so high," Jane explained, "that a rating scale has been established. On amber-rated days factory production is shut down and construction activities halted. On red-rated days, schools are closed and only half the registered cars are allowed on the road each day. We don't want to be exposed to that stress or pollution."

She was referring to a controversial new approach to limiting the 7.5 million drivers estimated to be on Beijing roads where most people in the past rode bicycles and buses to work. Cars with even-numbered licenses can drive even numbered calendar days, odd numbers on odd numbered days. "People rich enough for two cars often pay double the value of the cars to obtain complementary license numbers, and that is where the controversy arises," Jane explained.

There are many ways to circumvent the law if one has the yuan. The "little guy" takes the biggest hit, a story as old as China itself, perhaps as old as human history.

Hui misses her father when he travels, although they talk everyday on the phone and Skype frequently. It is not uncommon for modern Chinese families to be separated for long periods of time due to opportunities of employment; many of my students had fathers living in different provinces, even countries, and had for years, even before the more recent economic boom. But now the primary wage earners in families may be scattered all over China, wherever a new factory springs up or new professional positions develop. As compensation for a frequently absent father, Hui lives a life of comfort and privilege, attending the best schools, engaging in enrichment activities deemed appropriate for girls on the weekends, going on international vacations during her summer holidays. On Hui's birthday in 2011, Carol and I had the family over to the foreign teacher's dorm to make chocolate chip cookies, a new experience for this ten-year-old who has been given many more lavish treats. In family pictures taken that day, Hui can be seen leaning into the comfort of her father, who is proudly holding up the new pink-encased iPhone he recently purchased for Jane.

Having a completely different experience in parenting was Meiling, the woman who had yearned for a girl even though she had one much-coveted boy child already. In spite of the fines and loss of employment that resulted from her defiance of the one-child policy, Meiling was now raising two children and dealing with the synergistic dynamic of siblings. Even when she was the mother of one boy, Meiling felt often overwhelmed by his energy and his demands. He was a boisterous child, unmindful of cautions and with a high need for novelty. When the boy was about five years old, the couple had considered sending him to one of the new boarding schools for preschoolers that had sprung up lately to teach the boys, in a controlled atmosphere, the basic behavioral standards of the Chinese family: obedience, respect, sharing.

"Our son has been doted on by two sets of grandparents since birth, his needs met on an instant, and with all the toys in the house under his ownership. How could he possibly learn about sharing with without a sibling or a companion?" Meiling asked. This is a question echoed by many parents and educators in China and has implications for the larger society.

When little sister Hope (Qiwang) was born as the second child after so much subterfuge, her brother had a big adjustment to make. And he made it grudgingly. Because of being fined and losing their jobs when her daughter's birth was discovered, the family lived in a dingy apartment on loan from an "overseas Chinese" member of the Little Flower Church congregation. Sharing with a sibling was required, and the children's obedience became even more important. In cramped quarters, it also became more difficult. Outings with the children were trying events, as the exhausted parents, both of whom had now found other jobs, spent most of their time negotiating compromises and trying to keep the peace.

But Meiling never regretted her non-compliance with the one child policy. She holds firmly to the guidance and support of her Christian faith and tries hard to instill these beliefs in the children. Her son struggled with the confines of school, was as attached to his video games as any 12-year-old boy, and as restless in the confines of adult society.

"What can he do," I asked, "when he needs to kick or hit something? Does he play soccer? Baseball?"

Alas, these are not options in the daily life of the average Chinese youngster. One afternoon, I dropped by the apartment to return some books and found him sitting in the darkened apartment, kept company by the glow of the computer, admitting me guiltily because he knew he should be studying. Hope and her mother were out shopping, currently the number one Chinese recreation. I recently received pictures of these two children, the boy looking tall and handsome, surrounded by friends, Hope smiling and happy at her task. Strong-minded Meiling has made her dream come true.

Linda's dream was similar to Meiling's but with a different twist. Linda had been a student at Hwa Nan and stayed on to take some teaching assignments, even though she had not attained a four-year degree. In order to qualify as a fully vested teacher, she needed to earn a graduate diploma, but this seemed an insurmountable hurdle, both academically and financially. Linda was particularly fond of the foreign teachers. She befriended several of us, one being

292

a distinctive newcomer from the eastern United States named Howard. This unique man was a devotee of Chinese culture and could be seen roaming the streets of Fuzhou with his carved wooden staff and hair in a topknot on the crown of his head, taking an active interest in all he saw. He played the guitar when alone in his room and did not fraternize with the other teachers, preferring to remain aloof. His often baffled his students who reported being mystified by some of his lofty lessons but he found Linda's positive, intelligent and non-judgmental company irresistible.

With a little nudge from Mother Nature, the friendship grew into love. They married quickly when they discovered a child was on the way, and the college allowed them both to go on teaching. The baby was born during the summer months. Adorable and outgoing from birth, Zhan Si Min was another foreign teacher favorite, running up our dorm stairs with something to show, and trying to plunk out tunes on the old reception room piano. She wanted to be present for all our birthday parties and seemed to love the company of adults. Eventually, the couple moved off campus to their own apartment in which Linda's adopted brother, sister-in-law and her parents could also be accommodated, and the grandparents took on their traditional role as caregivers. The foreign teachers urged Linda and Zhan Si Min to visit us frequently back at the dorm. We all wanted to be aunties and uncles.

Our teacher grapevine eventually carried the news of Howard and Linda's plan to relocate to the United States. Linda was ecstatic; she wanted her child to have the advantages that growing up in America would give her. She thought only of her dream of a brighter future; she knew nothing of the unexpected challenges, even the possible disadvantages. A few years passed. Howard had ceased baffling students and was now spending the bulk of his time in America. Bureaucratic wheels turn slowly, he explained, and the documents necessary for his wife and daughter to join him there were unusually difficult to obtain. Linda, her brother and his family, and the grandparents had set up a happy living arrangement in an apartment in town where Howard came and went as an infrequent but regular visitor.

During one of these visits Linda became pregnant with their second child. Howard then returned to the States to resume dealing with immigration paperwork, to prepare an ancient family dwelling for their occupancy, and perhaps even to seek employment. No one anticipated a problem with the second pregnancy, as both children had an American father to whom the mother was legally married. But unanticipated problems often result in the greatest upheavals because they catch us unawares.

The Population and Family Planning Commission functions at national, provincial, and local levels but the one-child policy is enforced irregularly, depending on the zeal of the local Commission members. Their effectiveness is judged on the basis of quotas imposed from the higher levels; reward for their successes or censure for their failures is meted out according to how successfully these quotas are filled. Perhaps the local office had failed to meet its quota or the commissioners were feeling especially zealous that month. In any case, when murmurs of Linda's second pregnancy reached their ears, the Commission became determined to wage a campaign for her to abort. Remember this woman's childhood experience described in Chapter 7 of witnessing the abortion van pulling into the family compound to terminate her mother's third pregnancy? These images from her past played vividly in Linda's mind. The memory of her mother's struggles and her powerlessness haunted her. She had no intention of letting this happen to her and her unborn child.

Representatives of the Population and Family Planning Commission visited the college. They spoke sternly with Linda and also with college administrators in charge of faculty, reminding them of the fines and punishments imposed on those who were non-compliant. When Linda refused their 'invitation' to abort, they became more aggressive. Members of the Commission staged unannounced visits to her classroom. They harangued her about the illegality of having a second child on Chinese soil in defiance of the law. They indicated they were able and willing to take aggressive physical action if necessary. She was terrified and took shelter in the foreign teachers' dorm after class, afraid to go to her own home unprotected. She reasoned that American teachers, used to opposing government policies when they butted up against private convictions, could face the commissioners down; a Chinese person wouldn't dare do so. It was a nightmare for Linda, a recurring dream left over from her mother's life, and to be faced without the physical presence of her American husband.

Finally, a scheme was proposed by the resourceful Betts: what if they were to obtain immediate U.S. citizenship for Zhan Si Min, the first child, through the American Consulate in Guangzhou? A call was placed to the Consulate. They explained the dire circumstances and established that the father of both children, one live and one *in utero,* was an American. Betts and Linda were assured that, if the proper documents could be furnished, the process of granting citizenship to Zhan Si Min could be speedy and the ruling official. Then the unborn child would be considered the first *Chinese* child born to the couple and abortion demands would be unnecessary. A quick flight to metropolitan Guangzhou was arranged for the pregnant mother, her daughter and Betts. The deed was accomplished, the Population and Planning Commission's collective face was now saved, fines and termination of the pregnancy were avoided, and harmony restored. The second child, a boy, would now safely become the first Chinese child of the thoroughly stressed and frazzled Linda.

Soon after the birth of their son, Howard obtained the necessary documentation for Linda and their two children to join him in his family home in his small Midwest hometown. The house was an ancient structure without most modern conveniences, even a shower. But the family was happy to be reunited, and a few of Howard's relatives living nearby helped Linda become used to American ways of shopping, keeping house, and raising kids. Money was very tight due to Howard's unemployment but they made do. Linda learned to drive as a step towards completing her education and making a living. She wanted her daughter to have dance lessons, and she wanted both to learn to play piano.

People who knew her took an interest in Linda. They recognized her as intelligent, kind and optimistic. Her earnestness, her ambitions for her children and her willingness to work hard gained her supportive friends.

Plugging away at school, she managed to complete her B.A., then accumulated enough credits for one M.A., then another.

All this was not easy while juggling the care of two young children and a rather detached husband. Geoffrey, the toddler, was showing a talent for throwing two-year-old tantrums and demonstrating his resistance to authority. He wanted to make friends but struggled with social skills. Little Zhan Si Min (now called by the English translation of her name, Jasmine) had blossomed into an accomplished student who also enjoyed the company of peers. Linda felt like a one-legged stool. In China, the whole family raises children, and she sorely missed the presence of her parents and siblings as she strove toward getting a better grasp on the ways children's developmental behaviors were viewed in American culture. She struggled with driving in the snow that fell abundantly in the winter and with unfamiliar social influences on her children, who were now making friends outside of the family and coming home with new attitudes and demands.

The longer Howard remained unemployed, the more essential it seemed for Linda to go to work. She was fortunate to find employment in a small liberal arts college in which she could draw on her Chinese background. She was learning fast about the challenges of commuting and about politics in the workplace. She was happy to convert to the parenting style of praising children for good behavior rather than scolding or hitting them for objectionable behavior, but it was more difficult to accommodate the influence of their American pals around issues of food, bedtimes, and TV watching.

"It is very difficult to be a Chinese and an American mother!" she declared in frustration. Her fantasy about raising children in the West frequently collided with the realities of being a working mother of two children who were becoming strongly sculpted by their new country's culture. In the time she has been in the U. S. Linda herself had accomplished miracles of educational achievement and had established herself as a valuable employee but would the future of her kids be brighter for having been raised in America?

In fact, what kind of future are any of these children walking towards? Will Linda's kids eventually yearn for their roots and want to return to China? Will Minqiao, Hui or Qiwang try their best to emigrate to the U. S. when they approach adulthood, as many affluent Chinese do, especially by qualifying for an American university education? Or will they become a new generation of environmental crusaders, among them a Chinese Jessica Mitford or a Jane Goodall? Or even a Chinese Lydia Trimble, determined to improve the lives of women and spread word of the Confucian "Golden Rule". Miss Trimble may be justifiably uneasy in her eternal rest, but not for reasons Lydia could have anticipated in the 1900s.

All the families in these stories are openly proud of their country's modern cities, and the amazing economic achievements by which they were built. And they should be. The development and embellishment of large urban centers I witnessed during little more than a decade were astonishing. But it's a complicated and sometimes herky-jerky progress.

For instance, I watched as the lingering disappointment over losing their bid for the 2000 Summer Olympics to Sydney changed to elation when Beijing was chosen to host the 2008 Olympic Games. Determination to dazzle the world led to razing huge blocks of family residences in the city, shutting down air-polluting factories for days before the event, seeding clouds to encourage cleansing rain, instructing the citizens to form lines instead of pushing and shoving, and to refrain from public spitting. And dazzle the world they did! But Lui Xiang, the hurdler who suffered an ankle injury and dropped out of the 2008 race, went to America for his reconstructive surgery because of conditions in Chinese hospitals.

Participation in the Games is not a playful enterprise to China. To increase their chances of winning in more and more Olympic events, children who show early talent in a sport are recruited from all over the country and sent to specialized training centers where they live and worked at their sport, 24/7 for years, in order to "Go for the gold." There are now reputed to be about 250,000 young people in these training centers that focus on physical education in their specialty sport at the expense of other aspects of their education. No playtime for these kids. They are recruits in the serious business of public international competition, fully backed by the government from their recruitment to their retirement. After their winning potential peaks, they are cut loose to find their way in society as best they can.

Adults born in the 70s may vaguely remember that China was then one of the poorest countries in the world. The speed of its ascent from a feudal state to a major player in world affairs has been breathtaking. Economic advancement moved slowly under Mao who was fixated on purging capitalist elements from his reign, but after his death China shifted from a planned Communist economy to a market economy and the modernization of a wide range of industries began. Since then the government has reported that the value of all goods and services produced and sold in a year (GDP or gross domestic product) has increased 8% to 10% a year (although continuing controversy surrounds those claims and that number has recently been reduced).

Figures from the International Monetary Fund indicate China is now the world largest economy, surpassing U. S. output, but that figure does not necessarily translate into data that shows the majority of its huge population living well. Although over a million Chinese attained millionaire status by 2014, some sources report that almost an equal amount of people still live below the official poverty line, a line that is incredibly low--about $400 a year. Meiling, Jane and Laura's families are all living at a higher economic level than their parents or grandparents did, but are also spending more to satisfy basic needs. Has all this wealth and economic growth and global attention given these families a greater sense of confidence and well-being?

Laura and Meiling are deeply committed to the values of their countryside roots, their Christian faith, and the Chinese Communist Party ideal of a harmonious and stable society (in spite of the fact that the CCP's official spiritual position is atheism). They strive to do the best they can for their children's future on a day-to-day basis. They hope they will do well in school, go on to college, and succeed in their profession. But on a day-to-day basis, they struggle with uncertainties. And Linda wrestles with the conflicts of raising kids in a foreign culture, one with different advantages and pitfalls than she experienced as a child. Affluent but anxious, Jane worries about the food she buys in the market, particularly after the scandal about melamine being added to baby formula a few years ago. "We don't feel safe, even about the food we eat," she told me regretfully.

The melamine contamination exposure was followed by reports of tainted drugs and later pork. Expired beef and chicken found in meat packaged by a Chinese corporation for use in American fast-food chains in China has been reported in the international press. Jane admits that her family has toyed with the idea of immigrating to America or Australia but they have decided that the loss of economic status and resulting change of lifestyle would be too great a sacrifice. Linda, now firmly rooted in the U.S., has taken her kids back to China for visits during which they enjoyed the hospitality of a big rural family, but no plans are being made to return to China for good. A recent survey reported in the Wall Street Journal indicated that over 60% of well-to-do Chinese citizens are either in the process of emigrating or are planning to emigrate. Their three main motivating forces: to escape corruption, political oppression, and pollution.

I wonder where in the world they think corruption does not exist. New President Xi Jinping has intrigued China-watchers with an aggressive anti-corruption campaign that targets businessmen and politicians alike. Still, corruption, cheating, over-charging, and quality-fading are fine-honed economic arts, practiced by wily street marketers, idealistic students, millionaire corporate magnates and factory managers alike. In fact, "bamboozling", a new Chinese slang word meaning to trick or mislead someone into doing something in the bamboozler's interest, is a respected skill, openly acknowledged and widely boasted about when it's successful.

My students used to beg me not to go to the street markets alone. "They will cheat you!" they warned. "Pickpockets will steal your money."

"But I am a neighbor," I would counter, "a potentially returning customer, and a fierce bargainer myself. I'll be okay." In fact, my pitifully inadequate precautionary attitudes were no protection at all against the skill of the enterprising merchants and pickpockets. Although most Chinese I encountered were honest and kind to me, in the marketplace or on the bus I needed to keep a firmer hand on my purse than I did at home. And as for haggling skills, I soon learned that mine were pathetic compared to the energy and persistence of my students' bargaining abilities.

On a larger scale, companies who move their manufacturing centers to China find they must hire a robust staff of quality control overseers. One year I tagged along after a Relocation Counselor for a new automotive plant being established near Fuzhou, thinking I might try my hand at the job. The company's executives came from Germany, Argentina and the U.S. and brought with them a great deal of experience in quality oversight. However, they found that in China they also needed to preserve the "face" of the Chinese managers who are engaging in the deception. No one could be fingered, everything was negotiable and, if they wanted to have workers, their continuing relationship with the managers depended on a sort of Alice-in-Wonderland understanding and shifting identities.

My own feelings about China have changed as China has changed before my eyes. The college's glossy modern campus in the concrete neighborhood of University Village, with its population largely of 18-to-25-somethings is wonderfully impressive, but interests me far less than the old neighborhood with its winding alleys and fascinating intergenerational street life. The new college grounds with its functional dorms and improved facilities can provide more comfortable accommodation and a more viable education to its registrants, but as time marched on, the outdated quirkiness that I loved has been left behind. The students are now as preoccupied with their cell phones and their wardrobes as any Western college coeds and the Old Ladies are all home recovering from surgeries and nursing other ailments of the very elderly. Central Fuzhou has become ablaze with neon and clogged with cars.

I do not intend to minimize or disrespect the improvements that have made the lives of the residents of Fuzhou and the students of Hwa Nan more livable. My bemoaning the loss of the old ways could be viewed as a shallow understanding of the perilous and uncomfortable nature of living in China in the years before and after Liberation. There are good, big-hearted people I met during my time there who will never change no matter how rich or modern their country becomes. I miss the warmth of their friendship and enjoyed piggy-backing on their energetic anticipation of bright futures for a decade.

I began this book to answer the question "How was China?" more thoughtfully. I am still faced with trying to find an appropriate and thoughtful response to the <u>second</u> most frequent question that friends and family ask: "Will you go back to China?" If you are curious enough to want more than a simple yes or no, then the Epilogue is for you.

303

Epilogue

"If you try to change it, you will ruin it.
Try to hold it and you will lose it."
Lao Tzu

I can't go back. No, I'm not on China's Least Wanted list. Yes, it would be possible to get a tourist visa, buy a plane ticket, and connect the dots of San Francisco and Shanghai or Taipei and then fly on to Fuzhou. But I would not find myself in the same place, and even if I did, I'd be viewing it through different eyes.

When I left America in 2000, I was carrying baggage that wasn't included in my checked luggage. The heaviest invisible bag was full of concern for my young grandchildren who were living a more precarious existence than I wished for them. I'd been hovering around the edges of their lives since they were born, scooping them up as often as possible out of the sequence of the fluid and often stressed environments in which they lived. I could buy them tricycles, enroll them in summer programs, take them on camping trips, but I was fretful about the circumstances to which they returned. From my perspective as a psychologist, I began to view their lives through darker glasses than perhaps necessary, underestimating the resiliency of these bright and likeable kids.

By the time they were nine years old, we all needed to take a break. What I saw as trying to support an unstable situation was being resented as judgmental interference. Their family had an opportunity to move out-of-state (and out from under my critical eye), and I had an opportunity to leave the country. I figured at their age, the kids could call 911 or other family members if they needed intervention. I would turn my vigilance over to those entities for a year.

My other invisible bag was stuffed with nostalgia for a past life. I missed the diminishing rushes of adrenalin that powder snow and frothing rapids used to provide. Somewhere during my late fifties, the warmth of high energy that river rafting or snow skiing used to provide slipped into chills of anxiety. I used to love to take the Thursday night red-eye to NYC and emerge out of the bowels of Penn Station Friday morning for a 3-day weekend, but the last time I went, it was with trepidation and a sigh.

Was this change the results of maturing good sense? Hormonal changes? Creeping cronehood? All I knew was that my previous belief that any of life's cobwebs could be swept away by the joyous rigor of an outdoor ordeal or an urban adventure no longer held true. The loss was physical, emotional, and social as it compromised my self-image and thinned out friendships built around those pursuits. My last romantic interest was with a former CIA operative who turned out to have more layers of intrigue in his life than I was willing to tolerate. Even amorous adventures were becoming exhausting.

Like Victoria, I was afraid I had "lost my passionate." I needed to walk a different path as I entered my 6th decade. Plunging into a completely new culture, and taking on a role I had never experienced or even trained for, was the sort of "Read it and run it!" boating style that I admired in my river-running mentors. Maybe it would work for me in other pursuits.

And it did! Teaching English as a Foreign Language at Hwa Nan College was a tonic for my deflating self-esteem and lost sense of direction. Even though I was far from home in more ways than geographic, I was fortunate to join the faculty of a school with a deep commitment to friendship, inclusion, and community. The challenge was more appropriately intellectual than physical, plus I had the freedom to teach with creativity. The neighborhood was endlessly fascinating and the tender-hearted young women I taught were thrilled to have an older foreign teacher. "You are so wise," they would declare. "We are so lucky to have an old teacher!" Can you imagine this reaction from a class of American teenagers who think anyone over 30 knows nothing? Appreciation was laid out for us like the ubiquitous banquets arranged by the Foreign Affairs Office. This kind of bounty was almost as energizing as a running a rapid well.

Fifteen years have gone by since the kind man at the airport check-in line gave me 50 yuan. I'm better at "gracefully surrendering" and redefining myself in accord with this stage in life. I know that wistful yearning after 'the old days' is a pointless pastime pursued by many travelers who bemoan the way their favorite places used to be. I get it that the sound of the wrecking ball and the pile driver provide the accompaniment to growth. "Stop sighing about what has been lost," I chide myself. "Celebrate what has been gained." But I am hopelessly sentimental, and miss the bicycles and morning markets and vibrant street life of my early years in Fuzhou, even if those "old days" were only a decade ago.

The shifts in my inner landscape are minor adjustments compared to the seismic changes in Fuzhou's outer landscape. The new University Village does not offer the same innocence and intrigue as the old neighborhood on Nan

Ti Island did. As you have read in earlier chapters, ramshackle mazes of tipsy wooden houses that I loved to explore have been replaced by concrete apartment high rises with small, managed "green spaces" between them. Neon outlines the tall, modern business centers across the river, casting colored streamers along the murky current. Neighborhood lanes, previously full of flower and fruit vendors, wandering street artists, and wobbly bicycles, are now crowded by cars and trucks spewing exhaust, driven by their poorly-trained owners.

Chinese drivers now number roughly 300 million—almost the entire population of the United States—and that's another reason not to return. For a population new to the concept of riding in anything but a bus or the bed of a truck, getting behind the wheel of a private auto is a heady experience. Chinese friends of mine who purchased a car were always eager to share their new possession and skill, but I became increasing wary of taking road trips with them. Some were taught to drive by training schools with high tuitions but low standards. Licenses could be bought. Some skipped these stages entirely. After all, what was to learn? One pedal makes the machine go, the other makes it stop.

While on a road trip with a prominent member of the Fuzhou police department and his gynecologist wife, I nervously watched the speedometer needle on his tiny car climb from 80 to 100, then 130 kilometers per hour (about 80 mph) as we sped along the freeway. I decided to risk loss of face rather than loss of life by suggested that driving a light car at high speeds reduced its contact with the road and put all of us in danger. "Don't worry," he assured me. "It is completely safe. Look. The speedometer goes up to 200 kph. My car is made to go that fast."

"Walking Street," a pedestrian mall crammed with cheap stylish clothing, had been a sensational shopping destination in 2000. We foreign teachers walked to it frequently, down the long, stone stairway winding through mud-brick courtyards and across Liberation Bridge, to enjoy an afternoon of people watching and a McDonald's ice cream cone. Now it is a tacky, neglected area, totally out-classed by slick multi-storied shopping centers on the outskirts of town patterned after the Mall of America. Who wants to spend a day poking through smelly corridors of local pet and plant merchants at the Bird and Flower Market when you can drive to a glass-and-marble mall filled with designer clothing and Prada bags for some upscale window-shopping? After that, instead of a massage in a roomful of chattering blind people, why not repair to the new Hot Springs Park, where guests are wrapped in butter-colored terrycloth robes and sent into a 24-acre maze of warm pools in which jets, spays, and spouts erupt at set intervals? Tanks of tiny fish will nibble the dead skin off your legs and feet; there are small pools full of milk and wine.

Hopefully old neighborhoods and colorful street life continue to thrive in rural villages. But much of ancient China has become the domain of a tourist trade that flocks to shiny new "old" neighborhoods with fake facades and imitation antique trinkets (much like American 'Olde Towns,' where mercantile stores of the past sell silly hats and jelly beans). Being awarded World Heritage Site status or being featured in a popular travel book brings irresistible economic opportunities that can result in a Disneyland-style preservation. The beautiful Yangtze River side canyons I floated in 2001 have been filled to capacity by the Three Gorges Dam. In their place, is a narrow lake nearly 400 miles long. The 600-foot-high dam retains almost 32,000,000 acre-feet of stored water. The project required relocating 1.2 million disgruntled citizens who had lived and farmed in the fertile canyon lowlands for generations. Self-centered tourist talk? After all, people need electricity and flood control.

It's true. They do. And a booming industrial America dammed, destroyed, and drove over nature with a vengeance whenever it got the chance. Our Tennessee Valley Authority built a series of dams that linked the waters of the Tennessee River, and its tributaries, into a 600-mile-long navigational channel. The Glen Canyon dam in Arizona flooded one of the most beautiful canyons on earth. The Cuyahoga River became so polluted with industrial waste in the late 1960s that it caught fire, and added its own fuel to the environmental movement. Many times it took a disaster for people to finally wake up and realize that following *only* the lure of economic gains leads to stupendous losses.

Is it because I live in a country that has already built its dams and malls that I selfishly want the Chinese countryside undisturbed and the street craftsmen to be able to ply their trade? Or is it that I am involved with environmental movements that protested further damming of wild rivers? Did supporting organizations seeking to regulate polluters and protect habitats for creatures that live there make me anti-development for countries not my own? I don't know. But witnessing how fast natural and cultural landscapes can be destroyed to clear the way for massive growth in China

309

stirred in me feelings more of sorrow than celebration. I hesitate to hear or breathe or witness much more.

Apparently, I'm not the only one. China has now surpassed Mexico as the largest provider of new immigrants to the United States. In 2014, Chinese millionaires maxed out the quota for U.S. visas granted under the Immigrant Investor Program. As well as deeply entrenched corruption, oft-cited reasons for this exodus revolve around health-related issues. I wonder if these *nouveaux riches* understand that heart disease and cancer are currently competing for recognition as the leading cause of death in the U. S. as well as China? Perhaps they do. Although the rise of diet and lifestyle diseases is often linked to the new affluence in China, successful business people hope to escape the environmental degradation they have created, and are now yearning for regulations governing the food they eat and the air they breathe. They also seek better educational opportunities for their kids. In fact, that is one of the more popular gateways through which a Chinese family may slip out of the home country. Chinese students' applications for admission to U.S. colleges and universities account for more than 60% of applications from all other students from all foreign countries. Graduates then stay on to secure employment; in due time, their families follow.

So where does that leave Laura and Meiling and all the other women I met and taught and became close to and traveled with? Do they want to immigrate or to stay in their country and try to make things better for their children and grandchildren? How will they define "better?" Their lives have certainly been materially enriched compared to those of previous generations, and even their own early years. Will

310

their children, born into a world of plenty, finally get enough and begin to demand clean air, clear streams, and a quality of life that includes protecting the natural and cultural environments so precious to this unique nation? Will they encourage China's global importance in helping protect the planet?

In a recent article in the New York Times, author Peter Hessler, a long-time observer of contemporary Chinese life, described his young white-collar Chinese readers as a generation of individualists with their own ideas and thoughts. I trust his perspective and hope it is true. What I more often encountered, granted in primarily urban settings, were new consumers receiving lessons in sophistication from movies, the advertising industry, and the World Wide Web, not their elders or schoolteachers, or the ideals of Confucius, as in previous generations. The old ways of life seem to be jettisoned just as fast as the landscape is transformed from rural to urban. Confucius expounded the dignity of human life, consideration for the feelings of others, and self-respect, arising from orderly family relationships. Most modern trendsetters trumpet messages of conspicuous consumption, getting rich, and the cult of personality.

There are some who relish the speedy modernization and development of China because it offers investment opportunities and empire-building potential. They are dazzled by the new all-electronic stock exchange in Shanghai and the high-speed rail system between Beijing and Guangzhou. They stand in awe of the acres of skyscrapers, the miles of super-highways, the factory towns—even the efficient combination of one-party government and private influence that avoids the messy procedures of a democratic system. All are undeniably awesome and envied by many.

Alas, not by me. In a growth-fueled economy, 'enough' rapidly becomes 'too much.' I have lived to see similar trends in my own country towards bigger houses, more possessions, and faster roads. These, so celebrated at first, lead to unintended consequences: fiercer competition, more stress, spiraling ambition. Joni Mitchell sang: "You don't know what you got 'til it's gone." Often what's gone is gone for good, and the substitutions are shoddy.

My first year at Hwa Nan, I learned it was traditional for one of the foreign teachers to don a Santa costume and show up at the English Corner close to Christmas, dispensing hearty ho-ho-hos and candy treats from a sack. The students were shy and a little frightened of this big-bellied figure in a red suit and long beard, and approached cautiously for their treats. In my last year at the old campus, "Santa" was physically mobbed by the much less bashful students who now anticipated his appearance and wanted to see who was behind the beard as well as to get a plentiful share of the goodies. Saint Nick became overwhelmed, dropped his sack and fled. It was not a tradition continued at the new campus.

In the decade I taught in Fuzhou, I watched the new economy provide refrigeration and plumbing to ordinary people. I often saw new refrigerators occupying pride of place in apartment living rooms, public proof of affluence and modernization. The Chinese Communist Party, with a unique mix of socialism and capitalism, eventually liberated millions from grinding poverty, but the historical gap between rich and poor continues and intensifies. Nurturing this new standard of living requires expanding its appetite for resources to Southeast Asia and Africa, and altering the landscape and cultures on other continents as well (yes, much as the economies of the United States and Europe did decades before). China is rightly proud of a rich cultural history and of ancient philosophers who preached harmony and concern for others. Can they carry the Tang dynasty poet's love of nature, the wisdom of Confucius, and the ideals of the Tao with them into the future? Can behaviors that exhibit respect for the earth, that support a social order beneficial to all, and strive for virtue and harmony be of value in the world of corporate competition and bear markets?

In the midst of all these changes, the valiant institution of Hwa Nan Women's College continues to offer educational opportunities to high school girls, and now boys, who did not qualify for university, but have the drive and capability to excel in a broad range of businesses. They are more difficult to enchant in the classroom, more enthralled by the apps on their own handheld electronics than any teacher's presentation, but are as ambitious and hopeful as young people anywhere.

My own grandchildren are well into their 20s, working, going to school and having adventures of their own. The circumstances of their childhood have changed; in fact, my entire adult family seems to be steering a generally steady course toward personal fulfillment and economic stability. The riches I acquired from being in China cannot be measured in dollars or yuan, but in some currency much more valuable. I am grateful for the experience of being there at such a time of potent change, grateful for making the acquaintance of generous, warmhearted friends and their

313

endearing families, and equally grateful to be home again among my own.

So, no, I'm not planning to go back to teach again any time soon. But you never know. My goodbyes have proven to be unreliable in the past and I still have a perfectly good mind to change if I want to. How about you, reader? Go west! If my complaints in the Epilogue sound too gloomy, remember— these are my views, my perspectives. Go and look with new eyes. You may see a different China, and collect your own fresh stories and impressions. There are so many answers to the question "How was China?" I hope you will seek out your own.

Acknowledgements

Boundless gratitude goes to the staff, my students and colleagues at Hwa Nan College for Women. Without them, there would be no stories, no book. The Old Ladies gave deeper meaning to concepts of valor and dedication. The young faculty was wonderful to behold as they matured from post-graduate novices to the resolute and creative managers they are now.

I suspect I was often unknowingly rude, thankless, or stingy according the Chinese code of gracious behavior extended to honored guests. In spite of these breaches, the women of Hwa Nan were unfailingly polite, kind and generous. Both students and staff included me in their lives, bade me fond farewell when I said goodbye forever and warmly welcomed me back when I returned a few years later.

I am particularly indebted to Xu Daofeng for loaning me books, sharing her morning exercise routine and sharing stories. In response to thanks, Xu Daofeng would always reply, "It is my duty and my pleasure." Jessica, in the Foreign Affairs office, has a special place in my heart for tracking down loose ends of information for me when she was busy with many other demands of her office. Amy, Rose, Xiuping and Nell were also helpfully responsive to my questions and attempts at communication. As always, my requests were in English and these people answered in English, taking the heaviest end of the burden. The gorgeous paper cutting used on the cover was executed by talented scissor artist Zhuo Yan, a faculty member of new Hwa Nan College for Women. Ellen Baxter added her classy artistic input to the cover design.

Permission to reprint the old pictures of Hwa Nan and its founders was given by the United Board for Christian Higher Education in China, an organization that has been faithfully supportive to the college. The pictures are stored in the Archives of the United Board for Christian Higher Education in Asia, Record Group No. 11, Special Collections, Yale Divinity School Library. The iconic picture on p. 17 of the man under the old banyan tree was taken by Elizabeth Ann Stewart and used by permission.

Because this book was patched together from historical references, letters to friends and family while I was in China, and my imperfect memory, I owe a great debt to those who helped me sort out the important from the trivial, uncover repetitions and get my sequences in order. Eric Tomb, "China hand" and bookseller, was abundantly helpful in ferreting out passive voice, and incorrect historical references. Ralph Hitchcock read each chapter with intelligence and a gimlet eye, challenging my punctuation and deploring my use of semicolons and ellipses....thanks, Ralph! Carol Nimick, my traveling companion in 2011, read and reread the fledgling stories and has been an enthusiastic cheerleader. Joyce Wilson gave thoughtful feedback regarding the Epilogue. Adam Verhasselt was the teenage tech wizard, helping with cover design and setting up contact resources.

Deep appreciation to Susan Gabrielle who read every word many times, suggested changes with delicacy, and tried to keep track of my progress as I sent her random chapters from Oaxaca, Seattle, Morro Bay. Will Dane, of Dane Creative Ways, deftly shepherded the book through final editing and key technical aspects of the evolution from screen to page.

Postscript

Late in October of 2015, Chinese leaders surprised even its citizens by announcing that all couples will now be allowed to have two children. Enforcement of the One Child Policy had been softening since 2013, but the timing of this announcement added urgency to the change.

Reasons cited for lifting of the ban were the need to replenish the aging workforce and to encourage consumer spending in the face of a slowing economy. China's economic growth had been reported as a whopping 10% in the last few decades (although those figures had been viewed as 'tainted' by some). In 2015, that figure fell to around 6.8%.

The challenges of an older population that increases simultaneously with a decrease in the birth rate may have influenced this change of policy, too. Before the One Child Policy, the population pyramid had a wide bottom, narrowing through the working adult years of 16 to 59, and becoming pointy on the top when the average person could expect to live to their mid-60s. The shape of the data has now become a column, reflecting as many elderly as young or middle-aged adults. More young people are needed to support the elderly.

Also, older people have lived through hard times; they are savers, not spenders. China now needs spenders to buy the consumer goods that have saturated overseas markets. But even though stock prices of companies producing disposable diapers and formula rose after the announcement was made, young couples are assessing the realities of parenthood in terms of money and energy. Rising home prices and new standards of success may limit the number of children parents choose to have as effectively as policy.

About the Author

Dodie Johnston is a Licensed Educational Psychologist who worked in public elementary schools prior to teaching in China. She has written articles for local newspapers and magazines wherever she has lived, as well as endless psychoeducational reports. She lives in the Sierra Nevada foothills of northern California where she is a member of Sierra Writers. She is available for readings and presentations. Please contact her at howwaschina@hotmail.com or via her Facebook page *How Was China*?

Made in the USA
San Bernardino, CA
20 June 2017